BLACK RELIGIOUS LEADERS

Photo courtesy of the Library of Congress

BLACK RELIGIOUS LEADERS

Conflict in Unity

PETER J. PARIS

Westminster/John Knox Press
Louisville, Kentucky

Acknowledgment of copyrighted material may be found on page 325.

Book design by Gene Harris

Second edition

Published by Westminster/John Knox Press
Louisville, Kentucky

PRINTED IN THE UNITED STATES OF AMERICA

9   8   7   6   5   4   3   2   1

Library of Congress Cataloging-in-Publication Data

Paris, Peter J., 1933–
   Black religious leaders : conflict in unity / Peter J. Paris.
      p.   cm.
   Rev. ed. of : Black leaders in conflict. c1978.
   Includes bibliographical references.
   ISBN 0-664-25145-5

   1. Afro-American leadership.   2. Afro-American clergy—Political activity.   3. Afro-Americans—Civil rights.   4. Afro-Americans—Religion.   5. Jackson, J. H. (Joseph Harrison), 1900–   .   6. King, Martin Luther, Jr., 1929–1968.   7. X, Malcolm, 1925–1965.   8. Powell, A. Clayton (Adam Clayton), 1908–1972.   I. Paris, Peter J., 1933–   Black leaders in conflict.   II. Title.
   E185.615.P335   1991
   323′.092′2—dc20   91-4518

For my children

Valerie Lynn Tokunbo

and

Peter Brett

Contents

Acknowledgments

Numerous colleagues, clergy, students and friends have often expressed their hopes to me that one day a second edition of this book might be published. Those sentiments eventually motivated me to seek the opinion of Dr. Davis Perkins, the editorial director of Westminster/John Knox Press. From our initial telephone conversation about the matter up to the present time, his warm encouragement and helpful advice have been greatly appreciated. I am also most grateful to the copy editor, Katy J. Monk, whose excellent suggestions for clarity and precision saved me from many errors.

Assuredly, my family has been single-mindedly convinced about this book's enduring value, and none more so than my spouse, Shirley McMillen Paris. I am most grateful for their faithful support.

Introduction

While it is generally assumed that Black religious leaders disagree with one another on many matters, it is a fact that they rarely do so publicly. Although their views are often shared with close associates, they seldom reach a wider audience. Contrary to popular opinion, high priority has always been given to the maintenance and promotion of harmonious relationships among themselves. A laissez-faire attitude toward one another's leadership helps to minimize possible disputes. The dearth of publications written by them (apart from devotional materials) contributes also to the lack of controversy. Their interrelationships tend to enhance fellowship both personally and institutionally while precluding discussion and debate on controversial issues. Hence, their experience in forming alliances for cooperative social action is limited.

The early '60s witnessed a novel occurrence. Several Black religious leaders publicly disagreed with one another on various matters pertaining to civil rights. At first their opinions were confined to their respective constituencies, but as these leaders increased in national prominence, so did their views on public issues; their speeches and sermons became important source material for the news media. They were also effica-

cious in shaping the style of associational life within
and between their respective institutions. In varying
ways they guided the response of the nation as a whole
to its paramount domestic problem—racism.

Among those engaged in the controversy were Joseph H. Jackson, Martin Luther King, Jr., Malcolm X,
and Adam Clayton Powell, Jr. In this book I have
done a comparative analysis of their thought, because
they represented the main alternative positions in that
dispute. As religious men and race leaders they were
strongly opposed to racism; their writings, speeches,
and actions evidence that fact. However, they were
also opposed to one another, and that constituted a
major political problem. Although they all agreed that
racism should be opposed, they vigorously disagreed
on the form(s) that opposition should take. The nature
of their disagreements constitutes the subject matter of
this analysis.

This study focuses on a practical problem that has
plagued the Black community for many decades,
namely, the lack of cooperation on the part of Black
religious leaders in opposing racism. Unfortunately,
most of the scholarship on this subject has helped to
perpetuate the problem. Much of the literature of the
present century has been dominated by modifications
of a basic classification scheme which, upon close analysis, reveals two basic political styles that are polarized around the problem of racism. These styles have
been variously named: right-wing and left-wing, accommodative and protest, moderate and militant,
conservative and liberal, and so on. Such categories
are inadequate, because they fail to describe the diversity among such leaders as the four I have selected to
study, and thus they contribute nothing to the resolution of the conflict that has characterized the leaders'
relationships. Inadvertently, that type of scholarship
has provided theoretical justification for dividing the
universe of Black religious leaders into two irreconcilable groups.

This study reveals a distinct correlation between the

political and religious understandings of each of the four leaders. In doing so it discloses the coherent nature of their respective views. Even though each of them considered racism to be the primary political problem in the social order, each also regarded it as a fundamental threat to the nation's highest religious and moral principles. Each believed that effective opposition to racism would be important for moral, political, and religious reasons.

Many contend that much of the divisiveness among these four men centered on the way in which each justified his particular method of opposing racism. It appears that they themselves believed that their respective forms of action were rooted in contradictory convictions. I argue that their theological propositions and political principles, when abstracted from the problem of racism, provide little ground for cooperative action. Consequently, a new beginning in the argument occurs when careful attention is given to their respective understandings of racism.

The final phase of this argument focuses on the different understandings of racism held by the four leaders in order to demonstrate that these beliefs are not contradictory but, rather, complementary. My analysis reveals that they are all adequate within certain limits. In other words, each is limited by the others, but all are necessary for any comprehensive understanding of racism. Further, I argue that the respective conceptions of racism imply forms of action that are also complementary. As a result, this work lays the foundation for a loosely constructed coalition composed of those who have various understandings of racism and who advocate various forms of action on the basis of those understandings.

Black religious leaders can now achieve cooperative action in their common fight against racism without losing their specific identities in the process. Up to this time, a call for cooperative action in the Black community had implied that various leaders and/or groups were expected to sacrifice their diversity to some type of uniform thought and action. Such a strategy is neither desirable nor practical.

I conclude that effective opposition to racism requires pluralistic appreciation of the problem and pluralistic forms of action, as advocated by these four leaders. How these leaders could have been more effective while maintaining their diversity is the main subject of this inquiry.

The argument is developed in seven chapters. Chapter 1 shows that actual contention and disagreement have characterized the relationships between these four personalities, and further, that those conflicts are not personal and private but involve matters of political judgment, ethical argument, and religious commitment. Chapters 2–5 offer a careful internal analysis of the theological and political thought of each of the leaders, respectively, so that the leaders' specific views of the problems and issues raised in chapter 1 may be better understood. Chapter 6 describes the differences and similarities among the four figures and concludes that the argument must have a new beginning in order to establish grounds for cooperative action. In chapter 7, I examine the several understandings of racism embodied by each leader and demonstrate how the leaders' political understandings are derived from their respective conceptions of racism. Further, I argue that these concepts and their implied policies complement one another and that that fact provides the grounds for cooperative action in the form of a federation as well as other types of coalition.

Introduction to the Second Edition:
A Methodological Essay

In this book, I advance the bold claim that any contemporary Black American religious leader will discover his or her leadership style analyzed in a critical and sympathetic way. In other words, I am convinced that I have constructed a leadership typology that is adequate for describing the logic of all Black religious leadership, both past and present. This does not imply, however, that every leader will find himself or herself strictly locked into one particular style. As will become apparent below, my typology, like all ideal types, is a logical construct. Thus, many will rightly discover that they tend to move in and out of different leadership styles depending on various circumstances. Yet I claim nevertheless that careful analysis of any one person's ministry will reveal that one of the four styles of leadership is dominant and, hence, rightly descriptive of that person's leadership style.

In the thought and action of Martin Luther King, Jr., Adam Clayton Powell, Jr., Joseph H. Jackson, and Malcolm X, we discover the four predominant paradigms of Black religious leadership relative to the quest for racial justice in America. Although two of the four leaders were assassinated within a three-year period (Malcolm X in February 1965, and Martin Luther King, Jr., in April 1968), and although Adam

Clayton Powell, Jr., was stripped of his congressional seniority in 1968, and although Joseph H. Jackson was voted out of office in 1982, each of the four reached the zenith of his leadership during the first half of the 1960s.[1] As will be shown below, their leadership styles form a continuum ranging from conservative to radical modes of thought and action with respect to social change.

Conceptually, I find it helpful to view these leadership styles as historical instances of certain "ideal types,"[2] thus making it possible to analyze the logic of each unencumbered by the many and varied ambiguities that attend his particular context. It is important to keep in mind, however, that "ideal types" are formal conceptual constructs employed for analytical and descriptive purposes only and that no historical representation of them is ever likely to be completely unambiguous. That is to say, particular persons in any period may well exhibit characteristics pertaining to more than one of the ideal typifications, yet, in the main, the style of each particular leader will tend toward one of the types, even though from time to time each may exhibit some amalgam of the styles.

By introducing the conceptual tool of "ideal type" I am now willing to make claims about the universe of Black American religious leadership that I was not ready to make when this study was first published thirteen years ago. Careful study and observation of the subject matter over the years has helped me see that the leadership styles of these four men were not peculiar to them alone but, rather, that each was nurtured in an ecclesial tradition that produced in him a certain disposition toward adopting one style over the others. Interestingly, that ecclesial tradition—namely, that of local congregations within the National Baptist Convention, U.S.A., Inc.—was the same for all four of the leaders. Thus, one can readily discern that church's capacity for including a vast amount of diversity within its institutional framework, diversity which, I might add, has not been the sole preserve of the National Baptists but, rather, has been characteristic of other Black denominations as well.

Because the Black American religious tradition predated its institutionalization in the nascent independent Black church movement of the late eighteenth century,[3] so did its leadership. Further, since Black churches constituted the primary agency for the development of social cohesion and social organization in the Black community during the post-slavery era, they nurtured, trained, and launched virtually every credible Black leader in religion, business, politics, music, education, and civil rights. From the earliest times up to the present, Black religious leaders have been models for all Black leadership. This has been evidenced in the form and substance of Black leaders' rhetoric, their definition of social issues, their strategies for social change, and the locus of their appeal for both financial and moral support.

The four ideal typifications of Black religious leadership are *priestly, prophetic, political,* and *nationalist.* Each has been opposed to racism and desirous of a racially just society. The societal vision and political strategy of each is a correlate of its theology. The political strategy of each presupposes a definition of the social problem somewhere within the range of the continuum between conservative and radical. Relative to racism, I claim that neither their definitions nor their implied political resolutions are totally wrong. Rather, each alone is limited and inadequate and all of them together are needed for a comprehensive understanding of the problem and its resolution. Without entering into the substantial difference between the four leaders, let me describe the logic of each type.

The priestly type. The role and function of priests is to serve the temple (that is, the house of God). Their ministry is to represent God to the people and to intercede on behalf of the people before God, and/or to instruct the people firmly and authoritatively about the nature of their religious responsibilities and obligations. Their self-image, together with the people's perception of them, is that they primarily interpret the symbols of the faith, administer the rituals required by the faith, exorcise demons, and motivate the people to religious conviction via reason, passion, performance, and example. Their ordination involves a commitment to the truths of their religion and fidelity to those truths in thought, speech, and deed. Through the act of ordination the priests choose to inherit and commit themselves to preserve the religious customs and conventions of their religious institutions and vow to promote their expansion. Changes that the priests might advocate publicly are justified by demonstrating their constructive contribution to the religion, its survival, and its enrichment.

Religious institutions always exist in a societal context that acts as a limiting condition on their pursuits. If those limits are broadly drawn, priests will normally feel that neither their religion nor their office is threatened and, consequently, they will likely assume a stance of celebration of and thanksgiving for the basic societal structures. Hence, the relationship between the religious institution and the state becomes one of mutuality, which enables the respective leadership elites to have direct access to each other for mutual support and friendly advice.

The priest aims at no significant societal change. Rather, the basic structures of the society are perceived as fundamentally good and worthy of God's favor being sought through prayer and supplication. In brief, the societal structures are thought to be grounded in the ideals of God and, for the most part, are viewed as already actualized. Any problems within the system are considered not to be inherent in the basic structures or values of the society as such but, rather, are seen as instances of "wrongdoing" on the part of the few. Most important, the priestly type considers all such wrongdoing as readily correctable by the due processes of law. Social deviants must be arrested lest they infect the body politic as an unchecked cancer threatens the well-being of a healthy body. The aims of social policy are basically viewed as punishment and rehabilitation for wrongdoing, and education and moral development. Power to effect any desired social change is thought of as influence on and access to those elites who are decision-makers. A basic assumption underlying this mode of action is that all elites are similar to the priestly elite in that they are made up of persons of goodwill who are disposed toward responding justly to their colleagues in similar positions of institutional leadership. In other words, goodwill is a *sine qua non* for all rational conversation and constructive negotiations among leaders.

Thus, the priestly model is a consensual one. It abhors conflict, viewing it as the cause of bitterness, which, it believes, leads to hate. In all situations polarized by hate, priests believe that those with the power to act have only two options: (a) to refuse to act constructively; or (b) to decide to use their power to enhance the repression. This latter possibility constitutes their greatest fear and motivates them to minimize conflict.

Historically, this priestly style of leadership is the oldest in Black America, having roots in Africa prior to the trans-Atlantic slave trade. W. E. B. Du Bois contended that the natural leaders among the slaves were those who would have been the priests and medicine men in traditional African culture. Their role was to comfort the sorrowful and instill hope in those standing on the brink of despair. Their awareness of the sociopolitical impotence of Blacks caused them to focus their attention on the eschatological vision of heaven, which implicitly served as a principle of criticism of historical realities. In nurturing the virtues of humility, patience, and goodwill, the priestly function has tended to accommodate itself to the conditions of racism without affirming these conditions. In other words, priests have helped the people to endure those things they could not readily change and to make constructive use of every possible opportunity for self-development under the conditions of bondage.

The prophetic type. Unlike the priestly type, the prophetic style is characterized by the principle of criticism. Prophets are reformers. They never accommodate to the status quo and often are viewed as social misfits. They tend to make people uncomfortable, even the ones with whom they are closely associated. They emerge out of the same tradition in which priests are nurtured. The principal difference between the two is that prophets are purists in terms of both theological doctrine and political principle. They flatly reject any compromise relative to either. They are oriented to an ideal past and see vividly the estrangement of present thought and practice from their roots. They boldly expose that estrangement in courageous forms of action and in speech that is both shocking and perceptive.

The prophets view God as the source of social justice and are absolutely certain that God is on their side in the quest for social reform. Their strategy aims at condemning the evil that is visible and revealing the evil that is concealed. Their judgments are not made in accordance with their own sensitivities and values but in accordance with what they discern to be the will of God. They do not seek to overthrow the societal system per se but to reform it so that it conforms once again with the fundamental principles in which it is grounded. That is to say, they view the fundamental structures and values of the societal system as potentially good but dangerously threatened by actual societal practices. Hence, they work zealously for the actualization of the society's ideals as mandated by God and affirmed by its founders. They employ every possible method to convince the society that the threat is real and that, if allowed to persist, the society will be destroyed from within.

Since the prophetic end sought is a moral one, the prophet must also be moral. Since the nature of prophetic power is moral force, prophets must embody the morality they seek or they have no efficacy. In fact, only those with moral sensibilities, utilizing moral means, can effect the kind of moral redemption the prophet demands. One major assumption underlying this method of action, however, is that the society has a conscience formed by its basic ideals, though its conventional practices have caused that conscience to become estranged from itself. The prophet believes that the collective conscience can be reawakened by the prophetic message and moved to correct its wayward conduct. Militant prophets summon the society to bring its habits of thought and practice into accord with its fundamental principles and beliefs. The prophetic struggle is one between truth and falsehood, good and evil. Constructive social change is the desired goal.

Clearly, the prophetic model is conflictual in its strategy while assuming a basic societal consensus concerning the society's fundamental values and ideals. The prophetic aim is to bring the society's practices into conformity with its fundamental values.

Historically, the prophetic style of leadership in the Black religious tradition is rooted in the antebellum opposition to slavery that predates the official abolitionist organizations. Soon after the birth of the independent Black churches in the late eighteenth century, Blacks began to advocate the abolition of slavery via the art of moral suasion. This prophetic style is the locus of some of the finest rhetoric in American history and the source of some of the most persuasive arguments against slavery and other forms of racial injustice.

The political type. The political type of religious leadership is closely related to the prophetic type, the chief difference being its tendency to focus less on the relationship between politics and religion and more on problem-solving techniques. The political type readily assumes a theological grounding of politics but is not inclined toward giving theological justification for every political thought or act. In other words, although it admits a positive relationship between religion and politics, it does not confuse the two and never attempts to reduce the one to the other. Rather, it views the points of contact between them as necessarily tenuous, since it holds that the imperfect nature of humans prevents anyone from fully embracing the truths of religion, the locus of which lies in the perfect will of God. This type upholds the belief that since all human action is necessarily tinged with imperfection, it need not adhere rigorously to any absolute principle of action. Hence, there is freedom for pragmatic decision-making and, consequently, this type of leadership engages in a minimum of philosophizing and theologizing and expends immense energy calculating effective means to limited, concrete goals.

In large part, this type of leadership assumes the reality of natural law wherein good historical reasoning is thought to be commensurate with supernatural reason. That is to say, the just laws within a state are considered compatible with the law of God and, hence, strategies to promote their emergence are justified by the end they serve. Thus, this type of leadership is goal-oriented and unafraid of compromise. It prefers to obtain a portion of its goals rather than none and is thus the most pragmatic of all our ideal types. As with the other types, this type enjoys a high degree of confidence relative to the virtue of its thought and action and believes implicitly that God is on its side, guaranteeing ultimate victory.

This type of Black religious leadership was born during the Reconstruction period in America and is, therefore, the most recent of all the leadership types. Both the brevity of the period and the subsequent disfranchisement of Blacks seriously limited its development. The civil rights bills of the 1960s provided the necessary conditions for its rapid growth during the past two decades.

The nationalist type. The nationalist type of leadership aims at a fundamental reordering of the structures and values of the society. Its goal is a new social order with little or no continuity with the old. Consequently, it appeals to no historical precedents apart from references to similar imperatives for radical social change in other times and places. Unlike the prophetic style, this type is convinced that the society lacks the capacity for repentance since it is viewed as morally decadent to the core. Evil is thought to be endemic, pervading every dimension of the society's life from the beginning to the present. Hence, this type calls on its followers to disassociate themselves completely from the society and to set themselves to constructing a new society that bears no trace of the old.

Though the priestly and political styles view the societal history as embodying the necessary elements for a just society and the prophetic style views the society as having strayed from the moral vision of its founders, the nationalist type proceeds with no historical basis whatsoever. Rather, it aims at pure novelty. The power of the nationalist type is that of the idea or ideology and its ability to take root in the consciousness and being of its followers. A collective consciousness of suffering and injustice, together with an explicit awareness of who the enemy is, provides the fertile and necessary ground for the desired psychic change. Whether or not the ideology takes root and grows to maturity is directly dependent on a multiplicity of social, political, economic, and psychological factors.

The basic strategy of the nationalist model is that of polarizing the situation in a struggle between cosmic forces of good and evil. Clearly, it is not a conflict between the good and the prodigal but between the divine good and its radical opposite. Within the ranks of the enemy there are none good either potentially or actually. This type may or may not choose violence as a strategy. Its primary goal is that of liberating its followers from the evil that controls all dimensions of their lives. Short of waging warfare, this type may advocate self-imposed separation from its enemies.

Historically, this type of leadership had its beginnings among Black Americans in the African colonization movement prior to the Civil War. Its most characteristic feature was the feeling of cynicism and disillusionment caused by its judgment that America was incapable of ever treating Blacks justly. These advocates have considered racial injustice inevitable as long as Blacks are controlled by whites, and, consequently, they have advocated some form of racial separation in order for the race to gain the necessary control over its own destiny. Many of its prominent representatives have called for the founding of a Black nation (either in Africa, America, or some other place), believing that the principle of national sovereignty is a necessary condition for racial justice. Prominent exponents of this leadership type have been Bishop Henry McNeal Turner, Alexander Crummell, Marcus Garvey, and, in our present period, Albert Cleage.

Clearly, the priestly and prophetic types are in conflict with each other by definition since the latter seeks the reform of the former while appealing to a common source of legitimation. Further, the priestly and prophetic roles orient themselves differently toward the societal powers. Priests tend to seek the support of those powers in the pursuit of their objectives while prophets are skeptical of all established powers, seeing them as potential and/or actual sources of social injustice. Although priests and prophets often exhibit strong agreement on theological issues, they disagree just as strongly on the implications of those theological positions for social change.

In a country such as the United States, the priestly and prophetic styles have an uneasy relation to legitimate political leaders, because the source of the leaders' power and authority is secured by the supreme law of the land rather than by ecclesiastical law and tradition. This difference gives the legislator a broader range of independence, and when he or she is also a clergyperson, power and influence is multiplied considerably. Under the conditions of church-state separation, the priest's function in the church is similar in some respects to that of the legislator in the govern-

ment. Both have their respective sources of legitimation and realms of power and influence. Similarly,
each has a range of duties and responsibilities to constituents. In many ecclesial contexts, however, the
priest may be bound by fewer democratic processes in
decision-making than the legislator in a democratic
congress. Clearly, neither the priest nor the legislator
can be coerced by the other. They can relate to each
other in ways of support, opposition, or indifference.

As will be shown below, Adam Clayton Powell, Jr.,
moved back and forth among the priestly, prophetic,
and political leadership types, taking care not to confuse them. As pastor of Abyssinian Baptist Church, in
New York, he comforted the sorrowful and proclaimed hope to the troubled through regular rituals of
worship and pastoral ministry. From the same pulpit,
as well as from other public platforms, he issued
countless prophetic utterances relative to racial injustice and summoned the nation to change. He even
found a way to give visibility to his prophetic orientation within Congress via his "Powell Amendment,"
which would deny government funding to any institution practicing segregation. His political style, however, gave him greater freedom than any of the other
leadership types to form alliances with all the others
without having to affirm the totality of their respective
understandings and/or programs.

Clearly, the priestly type continues to characterize
the vast majority of Black religious leaders. These
leaders provide a potential reservoir of support for
those in the Black community desirous of entering the
arena of electoral politics, and this fact has been demonstrated time and again, whenever Blacks have run
for political office. Always the churches have been involved in a variety of ways—by lending their buildings
for rallies, registering voters, collecting contributions,
serving as poll watchers, campaigning, and the like.

Numerous studies have shown that among Black
leaders the prophetic type often becomes a political
type. A brief glance at the Black congressional caucus

reveals four Black religious leaders who were at one
time unequivocally viewed as prophetic types, namely,
representatives William H. Gray III, Walter E. Faunt-
roy, John Lewis, and Floyd Flake. Former congressman Andrew Young should also be mentioned in this
category, as well as Jesse L. Jackson, who is presently
the shadow senator for the District of Columbia.
Many more such leaders exist across the country in
municipal and state offices. Once the political office
has been secured, it is not surprising to discern a corresponding change in leadership style. If the person is a
clergyperson, one will see a diminution of prophetic
utterances while observing various attempts on the
part of the official to place the prophetic substance on
the political agenda. The nature of political office,
however, requires a movement from the left of center
to the right of center, thus making it very difficult to be
both prophetic and political within the same arena.
Adam Clayton Powell, Jr., may well be unique in that
respect. Jesse Jackson, nationally known as a representative of the prophetic type of leadership, seems reluc-
tant to forsake that style in spite of his two campaigns
as a presidential candidate. His apparent interest in
combining the two types of leadership may well lessen
his prospects for a victory in the political arena since
success there depends so much on cooperative action
among diverse peoples and interests as well as on
structures of accountability both to the party and to
constituents.

During the past two decades the self-understanding
of Black Americans and every dimension of their cultural life has been profoundly affected by the phenom-
enal attraction of the nationalist leadership tradition.
The most enduring expression of this change is the
demise of the word "Negro" in favor of the nomenclature "Black American" and/or "Afro-American" and,
more recently, the widespread use of the term "African-American." Undoubtedly, the Black Power movement of the late '60s played a major role in this
cultural renaissance. It, in turn, was heavily influenced

by the principles underlying Malcolm X's Organization of Afro-American Unity. The theological justification for that organization was provided by the nascent Black Theology movement, which is often dated with reference to the 1969 publication of James H. Cone's book, *Black Theology and Black Power.* In the following year this movement became institutionalized in an academic association, the Society for the Study of Black Religion.[4] As the theological arm of the Black Power movement, the impact of the Black Theology movement was felt throughout the ecclesiastical and academic communities both within the nation and abroad.

Almost overnight, Black caucuses emerged within predominantly white denominations and in various academic and professional societies. All were motivated by and advocates of similar values of racial self-respect and self-determination. The rapid rise of Afro-American Studies programs in many institutions of higher learning further indicated the import of this cultural change and the desire of many to make the African-American experience subject matter for academic study and research. The widespread academic debate relative to the rise of Black Theology served to legitimate the Black religious experience as a subject matter for academic study, and many institutions felt the need to hire Black professors. In both the churches and academe, however, the influence of the nationalist leadership tradition did not result in advocacy for any complete separation of Blacks from whites. Rather, in the main, Blacks formed racially separate caucuses and integrated study programs within predominantly white institutions. These constituted prophetic challenges for institutional reform based on the demand that the historical experience and moral concerns of Blacks be given significant institutional visibility and importance in those institutions' respective programs, including their recruitment, promotional and retention policies.

Finally, the practical side of my methodology issues

in a proposed resolution for the problem that is produced by the conflicting styles of Black religious leadership. My call for a federation representing the various leadership types is in accord with the formation of various Black ecumenical associations, the most notable of which are the Interdenominational Theological Center in Atlanta, Ga., and the Congress of National Black Churches, Washington, D.C., as well as various interdenominational associations of Black churches and/or clergy in most of the major cities around the nation. All of these have chosen forms of cooperation appropriate for maximizing their capacity for achieving their respective goals. Full-scale studies of these associations are needed in order to demonstrate both the importance and effectiveness of such cooperative activity in the pursuit of constructive social change.

PART ONE

Diversity in Conflict

1

Diversity in Conflict: Pluralistic Proposals for Political Action

It is important to set forth certain facts at the beginning of this inquiry in order to demonstrate that the Black religious leaders selected for this study held many conflicting understandings about important matters relating to the struggle against racism. In spite of the fact that they were in full accord on some subjects, their strong disagreements about others dominated their specific proposals for action and thus severely limited the possibility for any collaborative public action. A clarification of the nature of these disparate understandings and the concomitant disagreements is necessary in order for any desired cooperative activity to become a real possibility. The discovery of the latter is the end this inquiry seeks.

A presupposition operating throughout this study is that an inquiry in social ethics should begin with some actual, concrete problems arising among human beings in their public actions. That is to say, such an investigation should begin with some conflicting views about the good that humans can and should do. These conflicting views are problematic for human action in that they can limit and threaten the possibility for creativity. The result of such an investigation should be some resolution of the problem or a restatement of the problem in order to liberate the agents and their activ-

ities and to establish thereby the conditions for more
creative enterprise. In short, the subject matter of our
inquiry is human action, and the goal of that inquiry is
the enhancement of human action.

There are other presuppositions underlying this
study that, when clarified, will help to illumine the
perspective of my approach. First of all, an inquiry
such as this is and always has been difficult and complex, because Black religious leaders frequently have
occupied an uncomfortable space between the Black
masses and the white institutions of power. Black leaders inevitably are dangerously circumscribed; Black
constituents demand courage, forthrightness, and effective action, while white opponents devise many and
varied techniques to hinder and/or destroy their effectiveness. Some Black leaders have allied themselves
too closely with certain white benefactors and patrons,
thus running the risk of being subjected to epithetical
designations that question their loyalty to Black people in the task of opposing racism. Others have identified themselves with the anger of the Black masses and
have communicated that anger in their rhetoric and in
their action. By their white opponents they have been
considered, at worst, enemies of the state and, at best,
dangerous racists and ignoble citizens. And so the
pressures on Black religious leaders have always been
great. They come from within and from without the
race. They come in varying forms of malicious rhetoric, questionable compromise, personal deals, and de-
vious cunning. The moral integrity of Black leaders is
constantly threatened.

Further, there has always been considerable diversity among Black religious leaders and very little cooperative unity. The latter has been problematic for
many reasons, some of which will become clear as this
study unfolds. But every Black religious leader has had
a constituency of support within the Black community
and frequently has had some cooperation from certain
elements of the white community. The problem of sustained cooperative action among Black religious lead-

ers has been a persistent one. My specific and selected focus is an attempt to determine whether there are forms of understanding among the selected figures that hinder cooperative activity and whether there is in the leaders' respective thought some basis for cooperative activity.

Moreover, I assume that in America all Black people have shared, at least since the Civil War, the common experience of being second-class citizens. One important fact of such an experience is that among Blacks, none has affirmed such a status. Rather, all have desired and many have actively sought (some more self-consciously than others) the goal of first-class citizenship. Therefore, all public leaders who have dared to oppose racism as the fundamental cause of second-class citizenship status have been giving expression to the basic desires and convictions of the people. Thus, no Black leader is ever required to undertake the task of proving to other Blacks that racism in any form is an evil or that it should be opposed. When desires and convictions are embedded in the fabric of a culture, members of that culture would be considered insane if they thought it necessary to show evidence, via rational proofs, of the evils that threaten those desires and convictions. Black leaders need offer no such rational proofs as a prerequisite for action aimed at the actualization of those desires and convictions. George Barratt, of *The New York Times Magazine*, grasped this fact when he quoted, in 1957, the statement made by a Black girl after a prayer meeting, which he felt gained the support of all present. "Our white families say to us it's such a terrible thing that a man like that Reverend King comes here and gets the colored people all stirred up, and we say, 'No, ma'am, the Reverend, he didn't stir us up, we've been stirred up a mighty long time.' "[1]

Similarly, the eminent historian John Hope Franklin concludes his masterful volume with a statement that I have taken as an assumption for this book. "Looking back on their 350 years of residence in the Western world, Negroes could correctly visualize themselves, from the beginning, as an integral part of the struggle for freedom."[2]

In this study I am focusing on the thought of four leaders: Joseph H. Jackson, Martin Luther King, Jr., Malcolm X, and Adam Clayton Powell, Jr. Many feel that the great differences in their styles overshadow many similarities. Each was brought up in a Black Baptist church. The fathers of all except Jackson were ordained Baptist preachers; however, Jackson's father was an elder and often preached. Each possessed great skill in oratory, which has contributed in no small way to the measure of success he achieved. Each was a leader at an early age. Each had a strong sense of having been summoned to national leadership and sought, with relative success, a national constituency. Each had strong charismatic qualities, evidenced in the ability to move mass audiences to a feverish pitch of excitement and commitment, together with a personal magnetism that could attract and maintain a large body of loyal followers. Each discovered ways of dramatizing the national dimensions of racism. Each exerted great energy in developing an organizational base of power and support. Each had impressive overseas experiences that helped to shape his political ideology, to solidify certain convictions, to justify certain priorities, and to give breadth to the problem of racism and the principles employed in opposing it. Each attained the height of his public career in the early '60s.

Perhaps what is most important for our purposes is that they were contemporaries fighting courageously against a common enemy: racism. However, they did not agree with one another on many things and often spoke disparagingly about one another in harsh words and in strident innuendos. Yet they knew that each in his own way was aspiring toward that awesome goal of leading his people into full and equal citizenship rights. The rightness and goodness of lofty principles such as freedom, justice, equality, and human dignity were taken for granted and were never disputed by them, and they longed for the actualization of those principles in the lives of their people. Each fought racism with astounding diligence and amazing consistency. But they fought in different ways, and that is the heart of this descriptive analysis. Further, they could not ignore one another, because the influential impact of each was constantly a part of their operational context. That is to say, many followers of any one of these men were sympathetic to the thoughts and advocations of one or more of the other leaders. Each leader, therefore, expended much energy necessarily in nurturing his followers in the supremacy (moral and otherwise) of his own thought and action while, directly or indirectly, refuting alternative methods. Charles V. Hamilton discussed this kind of delicately ambiguous operation in his analysis of the impact on Black parishioners of differences of opinion among their religious leaders concerning social activism: "There has developed over several centuries a very close, almost familial tie between the black preacher and his people. They have come to rely heavily on each other, and they have come to know the strengths and weaknesses of each other."[3] In this context Hamilton is able to account for many occasions when members of a congregation disagree with the preacher's thought on social issues, but because of the preacher's other strengths no issue is made of the area of disagreement. Further, a leader knows the limits beyond which one should not go in criticizing other leaders publicly.

Two of the leaders who are discussed in this book were born and reared in northern states: Malcolm X and Adam Clayton Powell, Jr. Their careers were sparked and lived out in northern cities, and their point of departure in thought and action was the plight of Blacks in those cities, which they considered illustrative of the national problem.

King and Jackson, on the other hand, were born and reared in the South. King worked primarily out of that context, giving the weight of national significance to it. Though Jackson spent half his life pastoring a large, historic congregation in Chicago, his national importance was due to his leadership in a convention that is largely southern in its basic support, facilities, leaders, concerns, and objectives. This is not intended to indicate that the problems of Blacks in the North were radically different from those in the South, but it is important to clarify the experiential starting points of the four men. Their respective backgrounds may, to some degree, account for the open brashness and hostile militancy of Malcolm X and Adam C. Powell in juxtaposition to the gentility, the carefully calculated action, and the moderate speech that characterized King and Jackson.

The specific problem examined in this study emerges out of actual contention and disagreement among these personalities. Because they all were contemporary public figures who opposed racism, they were concerned about some of the same events and issues and, in some cases, were among the principal interpreters of those events and issues.

No Black leader, including those discussed in this study, ever opposed any court decision or law that was intended to confer upon or expand citizenship rights to Black Americans. In 1954 the Supreme Court declared segregation in public schools unconstitutional. It is not surprising, therefore, that all Blacks hailed that event as a notable landmark along the road to full citizenship rights. It is possible that that decision marked a turning point in American race relations. Indeed, among others, Pulitzer prize winner Anthony Lewis thought so. "But revolutions require a spark, a catalyst. For the revolution in American race relations this was the School Segregation case, decided by the Supreme Court on May 17, 1954."[4]

J. H. Jackson referred to that decision as "a new epoch in the struggle for freedom."[5] From that day to this, May 17 has been celebrated throughout the churches of the National Baptist Convention, U.S.A., Inc., as a special day of thanksgiving, and several attempts have been made by Jackson and others to cause it to be designated a national holiday.

Martin Luther King, Jr., in one of many references to the 1954 Supreme Court decision, wrote: "For all men of good will May 17, 1954, marked a joyous end to the long night of enforced segregation."[6]

Louis Lomax quotes Adam Clayton Powell, Jr., as expressing the sentiments of many: "This is a great day for the Negro. This is democracy's finest hour. This is Communism's greatest defeat."[7]

With characteristically practical concerns, Adam Clayton Powell described his anxiety with respect to such an important decision. "I wondered what could be done to make the 1954 Supreme Court decision more effective."[8]

In speeches delivered at the Leverett House Forum at Harvard University, Malcolm X did not attack the Supreme Court decision per se but concluded that it would never be fully implemented. That was his criticism of it and of all similar attempts to integrate public schools. He knew that Blacks wanted equal education, and he felt its availability would lead to the demand for equal rights, which he strongly believed would not be granted. "Equal education will increase their spirit of equality and make them feel that they should have everything that you have, and their increasing demands will become a perpetual headache for you and continue to cause you international embarrassment."[9]

Jackson, King, and Powell saw the Supreme Court decision as providing the first legal base in a half century for the eventual death of racial discrimination and segregation. Thenceforth they would apply themselves to cause its actual fulfillment and to draw out from that legal precedent as many opportunities for other dimensions of life as possible. Malcolm X, however, could not believe there would be any effective implementation of the decision because of his own evaluation of the character of white America vis-à-vis the question of racism; therefore, his response to it could only be one of suspicion regarding the actualization of its implications. As a formal decree he could

not deny its value. But he was completely skeptical of
its being an act that would effect significant social
change. Because of this skepticism he continued to
criticize all efforts of other Black leaders that were
aimed at legislative change but did not condemn the
formal aspects of civil rights laws themselves.

The positions taken by these four Black leaders on
the 1954 Supreme Court decision are comparable to
their positions on other civil rights legislation that
eventually was signed into law. But it appears that
Jackson became increasingly uncomfortable with protest activities that were aimed at formal legislative
change rather than "productive change."

There were great differences of opinion about other
important matters, also. Some of these matters are
worthy of note, because they reveal political positions
and religious perspectives that form the subject matter
for this inquiry. Further, these matters become the occasion for us to see the concretization of the thought of
these men and to discover that each one's thought has
its own internal consistency and coherence.

The Rev. Joseph H. Jackson, pastor of historic Oli-
vet Baptist Church on Chicago's South Side, one of the
largest churches in the country, became president of
the National Baptist Convention, U.S.A., Inc., in 1953
and remained in office until 1982. Thousands of people, white and Black, have typified him as being a conservative on all matters pertaining to the struggle
against racism. Frequently, this classification is bestowed from an ideological point of view that denies
any genuine integrity to his thought. In the early 1960s
Jackson became widely known among Black church
people as an outspoken critic of the tactics of civil
disobedience being utilized by Martin Luther King, Jr.
His disapproval of King's strategy gave rise to considerable opposition. In June 1963 his opponents made
their greatest public display by heckling him while he
tried to speak at a youth rally, organized by the National Association for the Advancement of Colored
People, in Chicago's Grant Park. His appearance on a

platform shared by Chicago's Mayor Daley seemed to heighten rather than minimize the emotions of the audience. Subsequently, this embarrassment provided him one reason for making an extensive and clear statement regarding his position on civil rights, which was presented as part of his presidential address at the meetings of the National Baptist Convention, U.S.A., Inc., in September 1963. Clearly, the context for that address must have been shaped also by King's historic March on Washington, which had taken place one week prior to the convention's opening. Jackson did not support the march and, for the most part, tried to ignore it, although he did affirm the policy of lobbying for civil rights legislation. The form such lobbying should take became a matter of serious dispute between him and King.

Jackson had not always been in disagreement with King, however. He had been a strong supporter of the Montgomery bus boycott, and according to the annual minutes, he raised enough money in his church and in the convention in 1956 to contribute toward the purchase of two station wagons for the Montgomery Improvement Association. In later years, however, Jackson minimized the importance of the Montgomery bus boycott by linking it to what he believed to be its model, namely, a boycott organized three years earlier in Baton Rouge, Louisiana.[10]

The Baton Rouge boycott had been organized by clergy who, in later years, would remain loyal to the National Baptist Convention, U.S.A., Inc. That fact had no small significance in Jackson's thought, for it places his former support of the Montgomery bus boycott in a different context. Henceforth, he would take care to emphasize that the bus boycott model had originated within the convention and had not come from the Montgomery Improvement Association.

King's father, Martin Luther King, Sr., had been a close associate of Jackson for many years and had been an important member of the board of directors of the National Baptist Convention, U.S.A., Inc. Until

the late '50s Martin Luther King, Jr., had been a loyal
member of the convention as well and had sought to
win the convention's official support for his civil rights
activities. He desired and worked diligently to form a
working coalition with the convention, the NAACP,
and other organizations. But time would demonstrate
that he would be more successful with the NAACP
and similar associations than he would be with his
own convention.

Jackson presented King to the 1956 annual meeting
of the convention. The official minutes of that convention record the following statement:

> After fitting words of gratitude to the convention with
> special mention of Dr. Jackson for support to the boy-
> cott effort, Dr. King announced as his subject "Paul's
> Letter to American Christians." The content was fresh
> and dynamic and the speaker was poised and masterful
> in his delivery.[11]

Following King's address the minutes report the
passing of a resolution that committed the conven-
tion's support to certain efforts opposing racism. "Dr.
L.K. Jackson, Indiana, read a resolution calling for the
support of boycotts and other efforts to emancipate
Negroes in America, the condemnation of the White
Citizen's Councils, and the signers of the Southern
Manifesto."[12]

Further, the official historian of the convention reported the following:

> It was significant that in March of this year, during the
> early days of the Passive Resistance Movement in
> Montgomery, Alabama, a movement that is led by a
> fellow member of our National Baptist Convention and
> supported by other members of our Baptist family, that
> our President from his vacation quarters, called upon
> every leader of our denominational work across the na-
> tion to support this movement to the full extent of their
> ability, and from across the nation came the amazing
> response.[13]

In 1957 Jackson prepared for wide circulation a special paper on white citizens' councils, which became one of the convention's many official policy statements regarding particular social problems. In the same year his support of the Little Rock, Arkansas, desegregation procedures was evidenced by his presentation to the convention of one of the instructors of Central High School and one of the Little Rock Nine children, who had been prevented by Arkansas Governor Orval Faubus's National Guard from enrolling in the all-white Central High.[14]

But 1957 was also the year when any careful observer at the convention would have been able to notice the development of a split between the "King forces" and the "Jackson forces." Perhaps the first obvious demonstration of that cleavage was seen when King was nominated for vice president of the Sunday School and Baptist Training Union Congress, an important organ of the convention. Some viewed this as a step in the direction of King eventually becoming president of the convention. He was soundly defeated. That was also the year when the famous question of tenure, with respect to the president of the convention, was debated; once again the Jackson forces emerged victorious. However, that action generated a major battle that was destined to last for four years. Edward Peeks describes the bitterness that characterized the convention of 1958, when the so-called Jackson forces blocked the sale of King's first book, which told the story of the Montgomery bus boycott.[15]

The cleavage between King and Jackson was irrevocably established at the 1960 convention, in Philadelphia, when the King forces, bent on unseating Jackson, organized support for the Rev. Gardner Taylor, their candidate for the office of president. Taylor, the distinguished pastor of Concord Baptist Church in Brooklyn, had served as president of the Protestant Church Council of New York City, was the only Black member of the New York City Board of Education, and was active in many civil rights organizations. The 1960 convention ended in pandemonium, with each side going away thinking it had elected its candidate to the presidency.

During the next two years the issue of the presidency and questions of due process and constitutional legality were fought in the courts, with Jackson eventually emerging victorious. By 1961 the King forces indeed had become dissenters. They split off from the convention and formed the National Progressive Baptist Convention. The term *progressive* had been used by the group in reference to itself in previous years. It represented a specific ideological position with respect to how church people should oppose racism. The split hardly affected the ongoing stability of the parent body, although many hypothesize (with no small amount of evidence) that it drained off from that body many of its younger, better educated, and more progressive civil rights leaders. Arguments concerning the cause of the split continue to be heard. Some hold tenaciously to the view that Jackson's tenure of office was the sole issue, while others believe that it was Jackson's moderation in committing the convention and himself to what was then called an active and militant stance regarding civil rights and how racism should be opposed. And there are some who reduce the whole issue to matters of petty jealousies, personal egotism, and other personality traits of the two leaders. Still others contend that it was caused by a combination of all these issues. Nevertheless, the split was a political event of no small consequence, and its institutionalization in two conventions gives substance to the reputation that each has gained over the years, each reflecting the political understandings of the two men in question, J. H. Jackson and Martin Luther King, Jr. And further, the extent to which these political understandings are related to the respective religious understandings of the two leaders gives the split religious significance as well.

It is not surprising that the two men would continue to oppose each other. William Robert Miller writes that in 1962, at the height of the desegregation campaign in Albany, Georgia, Jackson had nothing but condemnation for that crusade, and Miller quotes Jackson as saying that "it is hypocrisy for a delegation to leave Chicago and go to Albany to fight segregation."[16]

Jackson contended that his philosophy of preparation was more adequate for solving the race problem than was that of protest. However, while Jackson was making his comments opposing the tactics being used in Albany, the National Progressive Baptist Convention was meeting in Philadelphia. As might have been expected, this convention went on record as reaffirming its support of Martin Luther King and his tactics.

When King brought his movement to Chicago in 1966, Jackson issued a statement separating himself from any connection with the Southern Christian Leadership Conference's movement in that city. Miller writes: "On July 6, Dr. Joseph H. Jackson of the National Baptist Convention issued a public statement disassociating himself from the event and peppering its unnamed instigator with politely worded abuse."[17]

Another biographer of King writes about the same event in the following way: "*The Chicago Tribune* had given exaggerated coverage to the denunciation of Martin's rally by his consistent adversary, Dr. J. H. Jackson, president of the National Baptist Convention."[18]

Jackson dedicated a full chapter in one of his books to setting forth a critique of the Chicago campaign of 1966 and concluded by praising its failure.[19] In Jackson's opinion, that outcome evidenced the need for civil rights organizations to wage the battle where and how it ought to be fought—in the law courts and by manifesting a spirit of goodwill.

It is clear from all public statements Jackson made regarding SCLC and its affiliates that he granted no value to their tactics of nonviolent direct confrontation. He argued that the techniques of nonviolence and especially any form of civil disobedience breed lawlessness, violence, riots, bitterness, and the polarization of the races. Further, he stated that such methods, together with their inevitable consequences, threaten the efficacy of both the Christian gospel and genuine patriotism. His opposition to such techniques was both adamant and consistent.

Jackson followed the practice of not naming the people with whom he radically disagreed. It appears as if he thought the naming in itself might contribute some measure of legitimacy to them. In spite of the fact that the annual sessions of the National Baptist Convention were held one week after King's massive March on Washington—a march that captured the news media for several days—no official mention of King or the march is recorded anywhere in the record of those meetings, notwithstanding the fact that Jackson delivered one of his longest and most carefully constructed position papers at that convention. Further, Jackson's book *Unholy Shadows and Freedom's Holy Light* is one that mainly describes his understanding of racism and the struggle for civil rights. Yet in that book there is only one obscure direct reference to Martin Luther King, Jr., a sentence stating that he and his father were members of the National Baptist Convention, U.S.A., Inc. But even though he rarely referred to King by name, the severity of Jackson's criticism of him was always unmistakably clear.

King made few attacks on Jackson in public. Indeed, his criticism of Black church leaders usually took the form of generalized statements. For purposes of expediency such a tactic was probably necessary, since King relied so much on Black church people for support of his movement. Gayraud Wilmore is correct in writing

> King was too loyal a churchman to voice a public complaint about the failure of the Black church to support him, but he did on occasion point out that "too many Negro churches . . . are so absorbed in a future good 'over yonder' that they condition their members to adjust to the present evils 'over here.' "[20]

Although King and Jackson were foes in the civil

rights struggle, they did have some things in common. Chief among these was their mutual support of the historic National Association for the Advancement of Colored People and the National Urban League. From Montgomery to Memphis, King worked hard to maintain a working coalition (tenuous at times) among the Southern Christian Leadership Conference, the NAACP, and the Urban League—a coalition frequently referred to as the King-Wilkins-Young coalition (after the respective heads of the organizations: King, Roy Wilkins, and Whitney Young). Jackson often extolled the virtues of the NAACP and considered it the most appropriate model for action aimed at correcting racial injustice. Also, he held Wilkins in high esteem.

King, in contrast, was deliberately moderate in his praise of the NAACP. Frequent tensions between him and the NAACP, which threatened the continuing viability of their coalition, usually were resolved through various kinds of compromises. Yet, strange as it might seem, Jackson never attacked the NAACP for its support of King. Perhaps a closer study of that coalition would reveal that the NAACP official support came only in those situations where the action was undoubtedly commensurate with its own methods, for example, consultation and litigation through the courts.

By 1964 in a number of northern cities a series of public school boycotts had already taken place for the purpose of pressuring school systems to redistribute pupils in order to accomplish racial integration. At the time, this was the most notable and newest form of civil rights protest. Public school boycotts were indeed a form of civil disobedience. They violated the laws that make attendance at school mandatory for schoolchildren. In February of 1964 the Rev. Milton A. Galamison, chair of the Citywide Committee for Integrated Schools in New York, led an effective school boycott in that city. In the same month Chicago and Boston each organized its second school boycott. This form of protest soon became very controversial, and

leaders such as Galamison became increasingly isolated from major civil rights leaders. Malcolm X gave
his support to Galamison's plans for a second school
boycott in New York, while the NAACP, the Urban
League, the Congress of Racial Equality, and other
groups that were formerly supportive withdrew their
support. Adam Clayton Powell, Jr., gave his full support and condemned by name certain civil rights leaders who had withdrawn from the battle. Powell
denounced "ivory tower" Black leaders and charged
James Farmer (CORE), Roy Wilkins (NAACP), and
others with having "sold us out."[21]

The condemnation of school boycotts by J. H. Jackson came as no surprise, since he had consistently denounced all forms of civil disobedience. Benjamin
Muse reports that the executive board of the National
Baptist Convention, at a meeting in January 1964,
condemned all such boycotts and called for a more
moderate approach.

> At a meeting in January, attended by 600 members, its
> executive board overwhelmingly adopted a resolution
> calling for moderation and "goodwill," and condemn-
> ing school boycotts. Its president, Dr. J. H. Jackson,
> said: "we must keep the struggle within the framework
> of law and order. . . . The atmosphere has to change, or
> anarchy awaits us."[22]

Jackson himself had presented a motion to the board
in 1963.

> If occasions arise when adults must object to unfair ed-
> ucational policies, and if the conditions require them to
> react through the pressure of protest, we must encour-
> age our children to remain in school and use to the best
> of their abilities the available educational resources for
> their growth and development. The youth of our land
> are the potential soldiers for tomorrow, and tomorrow
> belongs to the best trained mentally, morally, and spiri-
> tually among us. However important a picket line may
> be, the most important place for growing minds is in an

institution of learning until their talents and capacities have been fully developed.[23]

Adam Clayton Powell, with his pragmatic interests, gave credibility to the possible practical effects that might emerge out of any nonviolent demonstration or boycott that had clearly defined objectives. King, on the other hand, was usually apprehensive about such events, especially those wherein the marchers were not indisputably committed to nonviolence in the face of possible violence that might be perpetrated upon them. He always wanted to keep the marches within controllable bounds. Therefore, he was not able to give solid support to the school boycotts in the North and, specifically, to those boycotts or demonstrations that did not rely primarily on his leadership. This is not to imply that King was unconcerned about the problem of de facto segregation in northern schools. Indeed, that was part of the agenda during his conference with Lyndon Johnson on that day in 1965 when the latter signed into law new voter rights legislation.

Both Jackson and King publicly opposed Black Power. King's book *Where Do We Go from Here: Chaos or Community?* is his clearest and most reasoned statement in opposition to what appeared to be a creeping nationalism that advocated a radical departure from the nonviolent technique for effecting social change. Jackson wrote an essay in response to the Black Power phenomenon in which he attempted to equate it with a reversed racism reminiscent of the Ku Klux Klan and, above all, in which he condemned it as unchristian. The NAACP went on record as strongly opposing Black Power. This was predictable, since Black Power advocates took no pains in sparing the NAACP condemnation for its style of reformist activity via judicial and legislative processes. There is evidence that strongly supports Wilmore's thesis that as time went on King gradually altered his position on Black Power in the light of mass Black opinion in the northern cities, which he encountered while organizing the Poor Peoples' Campaign.[24] If mass Black opinion was not the primary determining factor for King's change in perspective, perhaps the strong advocacy of Black Power by some of his closest staff associates was.

Certainly, in the early days of the national fury (generated by both Blacks and whites) over Black Power, King and Jackson tried to stay aloof from it by ignoring it. But as time went on it would have appeared to any observer of national events that, quite surprisingly, perhaps, the symbol found an astounding affirmation among millions of Black Americans. Its impact was such that many interpreted it as the dawn of a cultural revolution. Obviously, important leaders such as King and Jackson could not ignore it for long. They were drawn necessarily into public discourse concerning it and were forced to respond to it in a manner that was commensurate with their political and religious philosophies and that was constructive vis-à-vis their respective constituencies.

Adam Clayton Powell, Jr., a leader respected by King though rather influential in forcing King to drop Bayard Rustin from his executive committee,* was an ardent advocate of Black Power. In 1956 J. H. Jackson's high regard for Adam C. Powell was seen when Jackson and his executive board worked with Powell. Their aim was to have Powell introduce in Congress a

---

*In his Pulitzer prize-winning book, *Bearing the Cross: Martin Luther King, Jr., and the Southern Christian Leadership Conference* (New York: William Morrow & Co., 1986), pp. 138–140, David J. Garrow claims that in an attempt to prevent King from allying with A. Philip Randolph (President of the Brotherhood of Sleeping Car Porters and a close associate of Rustin) in calling for massive demonstrations at the 1960 national conventions of the Democratic and Republican parties, Powell let it be leaked into the public arena that if the march were not called off, he would reveal shocking information about Rustin and King. Although Powell never revealed the exact nature of that information, the veiled threat seemingly had considerable effect on both King and Rustin. The latter soon submitted his resignation, which King reluctantly accepted—an act that some said revealed a lack of courage on King's part. Interestingly, however, the march went on in spite of Rustin's absence.

resolution to make May 17 a national holiday in commemoration of the racial progress accomplished by the Supreme Court's ruling on public school desegregation. Jackson, together with the official historian of the convention and the displays at the J.H. Jackson Library, attested to that alliance with no small amount of pride. This pride was not attached to any specific outcome, since the resolution was never debated in Congress, but was in the fact that for the first time Blacks had introduced a motion advocating a national holiday for an event aimed specifically at guaranteeing them an important measure of civil rights.

It was Powell who called the first National Black Power Conference in Newark, New Jersey, in 1967, even while smoke from the riot-scarred city continued to fill the air with its own peculiar stench. Neither King nor Wilkins nor Jackson was present. This was significant, for it marked the beginning of a new movement, with new actors embodying a new rhetoric. These newcomers sought a public space to demonstrate this distinctiveness and to set themselves apart from the thought and action of Black leaders past and present. Wilmore is acutely perceptive:

> It was becoming increasingly clear that the N.A.A.C.P.-Christian, non-violent hegemony over the Black revolution had entered upon and was out of phase with a development in the revolution that was primarily northern-based, cultural as well as political, self-righteously secular and radically alienated from American values and the traditional quest for Negro civil rights.[25]

In the same year Jackson presided over a meeting of one hundred clergy in Chicago, which issued a manifesto categorically repudiating Black Power. Thus, on the issue of Black Power, Jackson and Powell were diametrically opposed, and the possibility of any future cooperation was seriously jeopardized. This, I contend, is true, notwithstanding the fact that Jackson seemingly supported Powell's effort to retain his position as chair of the Congressional Committee on Education and Labor and Powell's later moves to retain his congressional seat.[26]

At one time King and Powell had what might be considered a good relationship. They were friends. They traveled together to Ghana's Independence Day celebrations in 1957, and on several occasions King had been Powell's vacation guest on the island of Bimini. But their friendship declined considerably after the Rustin episode and the subsequent March on Washington, when Powell was given no significant position either in the planning stages or on the occasion of the march itself. Their differences of opinion regarding Black Power did not improve that relationship. Many have suggested, even as Wilmore does, that Powell's affirmation of Black Power was at one and the same time a public stand against the NAACP, King, the SCLC, and others. Some have tried to reduce Powell's position to certain peculiar personality traits and needs that caused him always to endorse the latest thing. Others view this stand on the part of Powell as consistent with the enigmatic, independent, left-wing, mass-based politics that characterized his entire public career. But regardless of the measure of truth or error contained in any of the views, one thing is clear: Powell publicly identified himself with a political ideology that implied forms of action that were to the far left of King or Jackson. His baccalaureate sermon at Harvard University in May 1966 and his subsequent sponsorship of the first National Black Power Conference made his position abundantly clear.

Powell's position on Black Power came as no surprise to most Black people, since he had been in association with Black Power's patron saint, Malcolm X, since at least 1963. On many occasions he referred to Malcolm X and to Martin Luther King as his friends. He seemed to have no difficulty in being publicly associated with both. But, like Malcolm, he could not justify whites in positions of leadership in civil rights organizations. By 1967 he felt that the day had come when the white person had no role to play in the policy decisions of Black organizations. Further, he criticized civil rights organizations that drew their major financial revenue from white sources, because he was convinced that such dependency necessarily limits freedom of action. In other words, the one who pays the piper calls the tune. Similarly, this became a main theme in Malcolm X's repudiation of the NAACP and similar organizations. Powell, for different reasons than those of Malcolm, concluded likewise. Strangely enough, however, Powell continued to retain his life membership in the NAACP, as did King and Jackson. Powell had the peculiar genius of being able to criticize organizations and their leaders for wrong or antiquated thinking while not disassociating himself completely from such centers of action. Powell's thought and action on public matters were always integrally practical. This was demonstrated by his ability to attend to both short-range and long-range goals at one and the same time. Gertrude Samuels describes an occasion when Powell and Malcolm shared the same podium and reports that the congressman spoke these words:

> I tell you again and again, we are not going to get anything more in this life except that which we fight for and fight for with all our power. Unless we can seize completely the administration of our national Negro organizations, then we must say there is no hope there for us. This may sound like black nationalism. If it is, then what is wrong with it?[27]

However, Powell emphasized time and again that he did not agree with Malcolm X on a number of things, chief of which was the latter's doctrine of the separation of the races. Nevertheless, he had great admiration for many of Malcolm's perceptive insights. Powell believed in what he frequently called "collective social action," which referred, in part, to the importance of Blacks uniting in various coalitions in order to maximize their power to oppose racism and its injustices. In an interview with Robert Penn Warren he spoke of

the advice he had given the leaders of the nascent organization ACT, a coalition of Black organizations
aimed at bridging the gap between civil rights organizations and Black nationalist groups. That advice
could be viewed as the guiding principle that shaped
his political thought and action: "And I said, 'What
you should try to do is to make your umbrella big
enough to include everyone.' "[28]

In relation to Malcolm X, Powell set himself to the
task of discovering how an integrationist like himself
could collaborate with a separatist. He resolved that
practical dilemma not by focusing on integration, a
view they did not hold in common, but by concentrating on segregation, a problem they both opposed. Powell placed the desegregation task in the controlling
hands of Blacks, and this was the real point of harmony
between him and Malcolm X. From Powell's point of
view, after achieving desegregation the people could decide which way they wanted to go in terms of philosophical preference. "Desegregation now, then let each
one indulge whatever philosophical view they have."[29]

Unlike King or Jackson, Powell had had considerable experience in relating to Black nationalist groups,
although he did not give his support to their entire
philosophy. He never advocated any kind of colonization scheme for Black Americans, whether voluntary
or imposed. However, that did not prevent him from
admiring Marcus Garvey for other things with which
he could agree. He had learned this truth from his father, who had preached next door to Garvey's Black
Freedom Hall for two years and whose admiration of
Garvey was great. Garvey has been honored by the
Black Muslims as an important predecessor whose
work the Nation of Islam understands itself to be continuing. Powell has written appreciatively of Garvey
and his leadership: "Marcus Garvey was one of the
greatest mass leaders of all time. He was misunderstood and maligned, but he brought to the Negro people for the first time a sense of pride in being black."[30]

The ability to appreciate America's foremost Black

nationalist and his contribution to Black Americans is simply one example of Powell's breadth of political thought. Over the years he had managed to gain endorsements from many religiopolitical nationalists in Harlem. Consequently, Powell was prepared to deal constructively with Malcolm X when he emerged with considerable power in the congressman's district and certainly could not be ignored by the congressman. In short, Powell had a knack for working out operational coalitions and alliances with radically different types of organizations and associations—especially those that displayed some measure of real power. For King and Jackson, Black Power and Malcolm X posed major philosophical and theological problems. For Powell, they posed practical problems, and although the practical and the theoretical may be related, they are not the same thing. For Powell, a practical coalition for specific purposes did not necessitate any major philosophical commitments or compromise.

Another area in which these selected leaders had diverse understandings was their respective views of America. Jackson had almost a sacred view of the nation and spoke about his religion and his patriotism as if to imply an interdependent relationship between the two. In his perspective the American way of life is the paramount standard for all struggles aimed at the correction of social injustices. In his annual address at the 1964 session of the National Baptist Convention he said,

> In our struggle for civil rights we must remain always in the main stream of American democracy. Our cause must never be divorced from the American cause, and our struggle must not be separated from the American struggle. We must stick to law and order, for as I have said in the past I say now, there are no problems in American life that cannot be solved through commitment to the highest laws of our land and in obedience to the American philosophy and way of life. In spite of criticisms and not-withstanding threats and open at-

tacks, I have not retreated from this position and never will as long as America is the America of the Federal Constitution and a land of due process of law. We cannot win our battle through force and unreasonable intimidation. As a minority group we cannot win outside of the protection and power of the just laws of this land.[31]

Similar sentiments are contained in his 1966 presidential address:

We are in harmony with and support those methods of procedure in the quest for first-class citizenship that are sanctioned, supported, and directed by the supreme court of the land, the courts, and the enlightened concern for the rights of others as well as our own. No group of citizens should seek their rights in such a way that goodwill shall be impaired and the life of the nation jeopardized and imperiled.[32]

Jackson's perspective was optimistic with respect to the progress America was making in race relations, and although more could and must be done, he was not impatient and sounded no clarion call of urgency. An overview of his speeches and writings leads one to conclude that his dominant interest in civil rights activities was to save America from the possible abuse, bitterness, and alienation that could be inflicted by certain militant unlawful activists. He took a dim view of any situation that might have the consequence of polarizing the races. Affability rather than conflict was, in his view, a preferable condition for political results. Jackson expended minimum energy in being critical of America. Rather, he produced an abundance of writings and oratory appealing to the good conscience and to the moral and religious integrity that, he believed, resides in the country's top leadership.

Martin Luther King had a profound love for the Constitution and an abhorrence for the American practice of racism that would segregate and dehumanize 10 percent of its citizenry. His position is comparable, in many respects, to that set forth by Gunnar Myrdal in his classic work, *An American Dilemma,* a comprehensive analysis of the American race problem.[33] Both believe in the American Dilemma: the contradiction between a constitutional ideal, around which there is a consensus, and the actual conduct of everyday life. Martin Luther King saw his task as being that of illuminating the moral dimensions of that conflict by bringing racial hatred into the public view. Unlike Jackson, he wished to create tension and conflict through nonviolent means. Out of that ensuing conflict he hoped the desired resolution would emerge. He believed that such tension in an environment controlled by the practice of nonviolence would be creative and redemptive. Like Jackson, he believed that America had a conscience that would not tolerate the continuation of gross injustices once they had been revealed. King spent considerable energy and employed much imaginative oratory in depicting the actual condition of Blacks and what the nation could become if it so desired. The latter formed the substance of his dream, which he equated with America's dream. In his famous "Letter from a Birmingham Jail" he sets forth that attitude very clearly.

> Actually, we who engage in nonviolent direct action are not the creators of tension. We merely bring to the surface the hidden tension that is already alive. We bring it out in the open, where it can be seen and dealt with. Like a boil that can never be cured so long as it is covered up but must be opened with all its ugliness to the natural medicines of air and light, injustice must be exposed, with all the tension its exposure creates, to the light of human conscience and the air of national opinion before it can be cured.[34]

In the same letter King takes issue with those who have a complacent attitude toward America and with those who have lost faith in America (referring to the Black Muslims). Between these two he takes a middle road.[35]

Malcolm X condemned America for being racist in its essence and incapable of constructive social change vis-à-vis Black people and their rights as citizens. He opposed all attempts to appeal to a national conscience, because he did not believe that one existed. Similarly, he criticized all efforts aimed at integrating Black people into the so-called mainstream. He advocated the separation of the races in order to foster racial pride and self-respect. His doctrine of separation, though greatly misunderstood by most of his contemporaries, is distinguished from segregation. He advocated separation in order that Black people might be able to control their own institutions, communities, and destinies. He opposed segregation. "A segregated district or community is a community in which people live, but outsiders control the politics and the economy of that community. . . . When you're under someone else's control, you're segregated."[36]

Yet, surprising as it may be, Malcolm was able to work with many who opposed segregation even though his ultimate goal was often different from theirs, especially when the effort of the latter was directed toward some form of integration.

Malcolm's statement that he was not an American certainly radicalizes his view of America and his relationship to the other figures in this study.

> No, I'm not an American. I'm one of the 22 million black people who are the victims of Americanism. One of the 22 million black people who are the victims of democracy, nothing but disguised hypocrisy. So, I'm not standing here speaking to you as an American, or a patriot, or a flag-saluter, or a flag-waver—no, not I. I'm speaking as a victim of this American system. And I see America through the eyes of the victim. I don't see any American dream; I see an American nightmare.[37]

In contrast, although Powell viewed America as profoundly racist in its habits, customs, and law, he believed that it was capable of change if the agents of such change could master the courage and power and diligence to fight continuously with all appropriate means. Malcolm had an absolute pessimism about America's capacity to treat Black people justly. Adam Clayton Powell had a relative pessimism; he believed that white America could change if confronted with its own techniques set to use in favor of Black people. Powell and Malcolm addressed themselves primarily to Blacks and only incidentally to whites. Both knew how to anger and how to cajole whites, a necessary tactic for building solidarity among Blacks in the face of their enemy. Both knew the psychological value of vicarious participation with them on the part of many angry Blacks. Powell also knew how to gain the kind of power that whites strive for and how to use it when it was at hand. The latter was not true of Malcolm. He was nation-building, while Powell was capitalizing on an old ethnic group power technique long utilized by European immigrants in this country. Like the immigrants (especially first generation), Powell had an ambiguous view of America.

In short, it might be said that in the main Jackson praised America while calling it to even greater heights of social justice; King pleaded for the conscience of America to be true to itself and to end the long dark night of contradiction in its moral life; Malcolm condemned America outright and called for the development of a separate nation within the geographical borders of America; Powell treated America circumspectly, never trusting it completely and always feeling the necessity to fight for racial justice. It was perhaps not mere contempt but the final scene in a long and uncertain pilgrimage that led Powell to respond on the day he was dismissed from the House and lost his position as chair of the Education and Labor Committee: "Today marks the end of the United States of America as the land of the free and the home of the brave."[38]

From the Montgomery bus boycott to King's assassination, the long, hard struggle of Blacks had come to be depicted by one term—civil rights. On that issue there was not complete agreement among the four

leaders. Not that there was radical disagreement
among them regarding the right of first-class citizenship for Blacks, but for various reasons they did not all
make that concern a major priority in their opposition
to racism. Jackson had contended for a long time (as
early as his 1957 annual address to the National Baptist Convention, U.S.A., Inc.) that Blacks should not
spend all their time seeking civil rights but instead
must take the initiative to invest in constructive efforts of production with whatever meager resources
they might have.[39] In keeping with this line of thought
Jackson launched several small projects on behalf of
the convention as symbols that Blacks can help to develop themselves economically. Chief among these
projects was the Freedom Farm, approximately five
hundred acres in Fayette County, Tennessee, which is
owned and managed by the convention. How this understanding of priorities shaped his major political
philosophy of production over and against King's primary thrust, namely, bringing pressure to bear on the
federal government for legislation that would establish
formally the context for freedom and equality in the
states, will be discussed later. Jackson did not oppose
such legislation, even though he did not consider it
a matter of high priority after the Civil Rights Act
of 1957.

Adam C. Powell supported all measures aimed at
the improvement of the condition of Blacks, including
those whose ends were formal and legislative and
those that advocated more immediate and tangible results. But his emphasis was always on the issue of enforcing the laws, and out of this concern emerged the
famous Powell Amendment, which he sought to attach
to all domestic bills. It was designed to force all agencies, institutions, and so on to comply with the federal
government's position on racial equality if they were
in any way receiving federal monies. For several years
Powell gave high priority to that form of action in his
political struggle against racism.

Malcolm X never criticized civil rights as a princi-

ple. However, his position was shaped by his estimation of its practicality. He caricatured civil rights as an
activity whereby those who did not have civil rights
requested those who denied them civil rights to change
their minds. He considered this to be futile. Rather, he
thought that Blacks should seek human rights instead
of civil rights. Then their opposition to racism could
appeal to a world forum of justice rather than to the
sovereign institutions of America alone. Consequently,
he pressed the issue of human rights and sought to persuade an African country to present the concern to the
United Nations. He believed that if twenty million people are seriously oppressed in this country, the United
Nations should take it upon itself to resolve the problem and give protection to those victims.

> The American black man is the world's most shameful
> case of minority oppression. What makes the black
> man think of himself as only an internal United States
> issue is just a catch-phrase, two words, "civil rights."
> How is the black man going to get "civil rights" before
> first he wins his *human* rights? If the American black
> man will start thinking about his *human* rights, and
> then start thinking of himself as part of one of the
> world's great peoples, he will see he has a case for the
> United Nations.[40]

On the question of poverty, each of the four figures
selected for this study demonstrated time and again
his concern for the plight of people (especially Black
people) entrapped in its grip. A close examination of
the way each addressed himself to that problem
reveals rather graphically the economic implications
of his respective political philosophies and priorities.

Jackson constantly admonished his followers to invest their resources in business activities and to demonstrate to the nation their resourcefulness, their
capacities, and their talents. In this admonition he
called upon the old principle of self-help. Following
the Civil Rights Act of 1964 and the Voting Rights Act
of 1965, King devoted considerable time and energy to

the task of highlighting the need for a federal program that would systematically and effectively eradicate poverty from the land and provide a sufficient number of adequate jobs. At the time of his assassination he was working on two projects: assisting the garbage workers in Memphis, Tennessee, who had organized themselves for union recognition, and planning a massive demonstration of the nation's poor (whites, Indians, Blacks, Chicanos, etc.) in the form of a live-in in Washington, D.C. As chair of the powerful congressional Education and Labor Committee, Powell effected the successful passage of scores of important bills that were aimed at ameliorating poverty and at enhancing the capacity of Blacks and others to participate more meaningfully in the nation's economic life. Malcolm X turned his attention to educating his followers about the necessity of Blacks controlling the economic and political resources of their communities. With respect to economic control he unceasingly advocated the necessity for Black-owned businesses, which would cause the money of Blacks to circulate in the Black community, rather than the traditional process of being spent in white establishments and thereby perpetuating the poverty cycle within the Black community.

Malcolm's economic arguments made a lot of sense, and the other three men did not criticize those arguments publicly. Obviously, none was in a position to attack the substantive legislation initiated and brought into the light of day by Powell and his committee. Powell supported King's proposed demonstration in Washington, D.C., and it appears that Malcolm might have done likewise had he lived. Jackson was lukewarm about it and made no public statements concerning it. Perhaps his familiar stance of silence was expedient, when one considers that several of his loyal clergy were involved in significant ways in King's program for the poor. It is possible that in this case his silence implied consent, rather than the usual opposition.

In this chapter I have demonstrated that the Black leaders being studied have held conflicting views on many matters related to the struggle against racism. It is true that there was greater divergence among them on some issues than on others, but I assume that all their views present certain problems to any who would seek a working coalition in which they might all participate. In at least one instance the political differences resulted in the birth of a new religious organization, the Progressive National Baptist Convention, which institutionalized the cleavage. In the case of Malcolm X we see a leader emerging in the public arena as a representative of an institution (the Nation of Islam) that considers itself a distinct alternative to Black churches, the SCLC, the NAACP, and all other traditional organizations and institutions that have enjoyed some measure of respect in the Black community. Adam Clayton Powell's leadership is most difficult to understand, because his public life manifests so many complexities and apparent contradictions. It is puzzling and important that he could maintain significant affiliations at the same time with left-wing nationalist groups and with right-wing integrationist groups.

Thus, I have stated but not yet analyzed the fact that these four leaders held divergent understandings and that they proposed conflicting forms of action on such crucial issues as civil disobedience, school boycotts, civil rights legislation, Black Power, and the goodness of the nation. Further, on the question of poverty we discovered that they all strongly supported action aimed at its eradication. Further still, there is little evidence that they disagreed with one another regarding programs and policies for combating poverty. Rather, they appear more united on that issue than on any other. No attempt has been made as yet to explain the various understandings; that will be the central task of chapters 2–6.

In pointing out the various positions, we are left with at least one conclusion. In relation to their respective positions on selected issues, these leaders can be grouped in varying combinations. However, we do not and must not suppose that a position held by two or more of the leaders on any issue implies commonality of understanding regarding that issue. In other words, two or more persons might either affirm or negate a policy on a particular issue for different reasons.

The following chart, which indicates the measure of divergence that existed, merely summarizes schematically the various positions of the leaders (not the understandings). There has been no attempt to explore the meanings of their various convergences or to draw any implications from them.

Schematic Summary of Positions on Selected Issues

Issue	*Strong Affirmation*	*Moderate Affirmation*	*Negation*
Supreme Court decision	Jackson King Powell	Malcolm X	
Civil disobedience	Malcolm X	King Powell	Jackson
School boycotts	Powell Malcolm X	King	Jackson
Civil rights legislation	Powell King	Jackson	Malcolm X
Black Power	Powell Malcolm X		King Jackson
The goodness of America	Jackson	King Powell	Malcolm X
Struggle against poverty	King Malcolm X Powell Jackson		

PART TWO

Theological and Political
Understandings

Photo courtesy of the National Baptist Convention,
U.S.A., Inc.

2

Joseph H. Jackson

In chapter 1, I have shown that the Black leaders selected for comparison held varying positions on several important issues pertaining to the struggle against racism. The chapters in this part constitute an inquiry into the reasons for those positions. No attempt will be made to employ categories of understanding other than the ones they themselves use. That is to say, the understanding of each leader will be described in terms of his own conceptual framework.

The basic thesis that I resolve to prove in these chapters is that each of the four figures justified his practical choices by an appeal to a relatively coherent set of theological concepts and political principles. The procedure I shall follow is to deal with each personality separately: first, to describe his theological thought while taking care to show its implications for his political thinking; second, to describe his political thought and show how it relates to the former[1]; third, to consider the issues raised in chapter 1 in order to show his justification for the particular stand he took on each of them. No attempt will be made in these chapters to relate those various understandings to one another; that will be the task of chapter 6.

The Theological Position of Joseph H. Jackson

Jackson considered himself a preacher and not a systematic theologian. In that respect he drew a distinction between the theoretical task of learned scholars and the practical task of professional preachers. He concluded that the latter function was not dependent upon the skills of the former. That is to say, one does not need the skills of the systematic theologian in order to lead ordinary people in the ways of God as proclaimed by Jesus Christ. Rather, the task of the preacher is dependent upon a simple but firm faith in Jesus Christ as the way of truth and eternal life. In his view the substance of the Christian faith is available to all, while the details of theological erudition are reserved for the few. The latter is important but not essential for the faithful proclamation of the gospel. However, Jackson contended that Christians ought to avail themselves constantly of new experiences in the diverse orders and disciplines of Christian communities so that their understanding might be enriched and that their appreciation of others might be broadened and deepened. In autobiographical reflection he is moved to apologize for the narrow sectarianism that characterized his life in his home church in Rudyard, Mississippi, while taking courage in the fact that the basic substance of the faith was communicated to him by ordinary farmer-preachers.

The narrow sectarianism of Rudyard became crystal clear at Vatican II, which (he said) he attended by personal invitation of Pope John XXIII. That experience also revealed to him with greater clarity than ever before that those farmer-preachers had proclaimed the gospel of Jesus Christ with as much faithfulness and meaning as the most learned theologians. The grace of God had enabled those semieducated preachers not only to grasp the essence of the gospel and its moral implications in an adequate way but to proclaim it with an untiring zeal.

Lest it be unclear, Jackson was no anti-intellectual.

Indeed, any such judgment of him would do the man a gross injustice. But he did believe that the substance of the Christian faith had not been given to the learned alone. His evaluation of the farmer-preachers in Rudyard implies a form of criticism toward any who would contend that formal education is a prerequisite for grasping or communicating the Christian faith. Rather, God's grace transcends all limits, and God is able to use even the unlearned to proclaim the message faithfully. Thus, Jackson saw no radical discontinuity between what he received at Rudyard and all his subsequent Christian experiences. The latter gave breadth and depth to the former without nullifying it.

Jackson's sentiments about the agents of the gospel's proclamation are shared by Baptists the world over. In that respect he was consistent with his broader heritage. But the sectarianism that often accompanies such sentiments was not shared by him, and insofar as it was present in the Rudyard experience, then in that respect alone, he admitted that he could never go back to Rudyard. His participation in the ecumenical movement at home and abroad evidenced that cleavage.

Jackson's understanding of his faith was tied integrally to the Bible. His explication of the faith was void of any attempt to introduce philosophical categories or, in any way, to establish the truth of the biblical message by an appeal to reason. His fundamental presupposition was that the biblical record of the story of Jesus as told in the Synoptic Gospels and as explained in the epistles of the New Testament is wholly true. Not only is the Bible the source and ground of truth, but it is also the basis for what is good and right. In his book *Many But One: The Ecumenics of Charity* he offers an argument for the divine inspiration of the scriptures by saying that since Jesus left no written record and since the preservation of his teachings was dependent on the memories of those who heard them, the Holy Spirit functioned as an effective guard over those memories, shielding them against all evil notions bent on distorting the truth.[2]

In 1971 Jackson wrote a brief statement on the basic theological position of the National Baptist Convention, U.S.A., Inc., which was adopted by the convention as representing its official position.[3] It is also one of the clearest statements of his personal theological understanding. Interspersed throughout the paper are selected quotations from scripture, demonstrating the source of his understanding and his criteria for truth. In that statement he gives a special place of importance to the Sermon on the Mount, in which the personality of Jesus and the principles of the kingdom of God are set forth.

> Our acceptance of Jesus Christ as our personal Savior is based on His message from the Sermon On The Mount, His personality and life force that He sheds in the gospel writings and through the revelation of truth that comes to us in all of the epistles of the New Testament.
>
> We are drawn to Him by His divine character and by His redemptive love and mercy, and the goodness and justice through which and by which His kingdom is built—and by His sacrificial life, death, and resurrection, all sinners are invited and made welcome into His eternal kingdom.[4]

It is significant that in such a brief but important document, considerable attention is given to a careful analysis of race and racism and to how they are related to the gospel. Appealing to Paul's letter to the Romans, he concludes that there are no superior nations or races in the world, but that all people are sinners, incapable of saving themselves and dependent on the grace of God for any complete salvation. Similar and frequent appeals to scripture characterize his claim that all humankind is loved by God and is equally in need of salvation from sin. The oppression of one race by another cannot be justified, because it violates the principle of the kinship of all humankind, a principle derived from the belief that God is the parent of us all.[5]

Since the statement of theological belief was intended to be a preamble to his rejection of James

Cone's *Black Theology and Black Power,* Jackson includes in it a clause depicting the kind of theology he abhors, namely, racist theology.

> Racial discrimination and any form of racial segregation cannot be supported in the light of the principles of redemption as stated above. There is no revealed truth that teaches us that God is white or black. God is a spirit. National Baptists was founded and organized by Negro Christian leaders, and they themselves refused to restrict their message to their own race and their own nationality. They have not written a creed of exclusiveness against other races or nationalities. What we say against white segregationists by the gospel of Christ we must also say against members of our own race who insist on interpreting the gospel of Christ on a strictly anti-white and pro-black foundation.[6]

Indeed, Jackson's view of the Christian faith underlay all his public speeches and actions. Further, it controlled his judgments about right and wrong, good and bad. "Our faith encourages us and our theological position allows us to feel a sense of obligation to help break the chains of all those who are oppressed."[7]

As early as 1961 he wrote:

> As Christians we are committed to freedom, and as Christians we give priority to the Kingdom of God and its righteousness in all that we seek and in all that we do. Hence all methods employed for the realization of first-class citizenship and the human dignity of man must be judged in the light of that social order that Jesus called the Kingdom of God, and whatever we seek to achieve whether it be a solution to a domestic problem or the problem of world peace, as Christians, we must accept and employ those methods that are just, seasoned with love, and based on the brotherhood of all mankind and the fatherhood of God. . . . But every method must be tried and tested by the spirit and ethics of Jesus, and the church must align itself with those

procedures that can be sanctioned and validated by the spirit and teachings of Jesus Christ.[8]

In Jackson's thought, Jesus is the example par excellence of how life ought to be lived. The biblical affirmation that God is love implies that God's son is love also. Love, therefore, must be the supreme principle by which all human action is to be judged. The manifestation of that principle was the spiritual power Jesus uniquely contributed to the world.[9]

It must be stated at this point that Jackson's understanding of Jesus as the divine embodiment of sacrificial love had many implications for his understanding of the struggles in which humanity engages. That is to say, the suffering of Jesus becomes normative for the suffering of humanity. Any action, therefore, that implies revenge, hatred, bitterness, malice must be condemned outright, for such cannot be compatible with the life of Jesus. Similarly, neither war nor any kind of conflict is justifiable. The central historical symbol of that sacrificial love is the cross, and beneath the cross is the rightful place of all who dare to call themselves Christian. That is the place where mercy, forgiveness, and goodwill are dominant.[10]

Jackson viewed the church as the potential exemplar of the norm of Christian kinship. In the ecumenical movement he argued for a kind of denominational unity that does not imply organic unity. He contended that the essential substance of the Christian message concerns the unity of spirit and does not imply the union of structures. His view of unity did not involve any dissolution of organizational form, but on the contrary, he emphasized the kind of unity that was capable of affirming denominational plurality. To that end he sought genuine harmony among diverse groups without destroying the diversity. But the purpose of the unity would be the proclamation of the gospel for the salvation of souls, and the form of the unity would be the fellowship produced by those working for a common goal. He argued that the church ought to demonstrate such a unity to the world and in so doing be an agent of social change. Thus, the church would manifest its spiritual aim to the world by exemplifying the meaning of unity. The world would then be so impressed that it would eventually pattern its own life after that of the church.

Throughout Jackson's writings about the Christian faith there is an unmistakable implication that those who are faithful to Christ's ministry do, in fact, participate in the building of the kingdom of God. Since they must strive for the realization of that ideal in their historical period, it follows that the task of Christians in any society is to make that society the beloved community of God.

Jackson's understanding of the importance of humanity was based on a fundamental presupposition that humankind "is the primary object of salvation."[11] That is to say, God's grace is aimed primarily at the human race. Humankind's need of that grace is rooted in its sinfulness. The sinfulness springs out of the freedom to make choices. Human beings have the potential to make good choices but are prone to make wrong ones and in so doing to destroy their basic values. Jackson understood the message implied by the Garden of Eden story as one that clarified such an anthropology. Humans misuse their precious assets; the divine image in them is marred—not completely destroyed, but partially lost.

In much of his writing Jackson implies that the source of sin lies in the emotions. In spite of the fact that he repeatedly allied himself with Reinhold Niebuhr's understanding that a person is a unity of body and soul, nature and spirit, and does not sin merely in the one or the other dimension but, rather, in the center of his or her being, Jackson's underlying understanding was that humans are led to sin by their emotions. Elsewhere he spoke of humans as creatures who know their weaknesses and who desire to overcome them in their own way. But he believed that they were fully understood only in the gospel of Christ, which recognized their whole nature and addressed them as both sinner and *imago Dei*. He contended, however, that humans tend to sacrifice the latter to the emotions that control their center, namely, the will. Consequently, they are captured inevitably by deceit, which is not only vain but also vicious.

On the question of authority, Jackson believed in the separation of church and state, with each exercising control over its own rightful domain. His opposition to the state exercising control over the church was dramatically evidenced in 1968, when he rejected all attempts on the part of the federal government to make the Social Security Act compulsory for the clergy, regardless of its proposed benefits. His argument was based on the principle that the authority of the state should never be exercised over the life and thought of the church.[12]

Two other implications of Christ's gospel for society pertain to matters of leadership and suffering. Jackson contended that moral persons must work for morality and oppose the wrong with all their energy. But they should not focus on wrongdoing in their protest, for that is the negative side of protest. Rather, the positive side is that the right ought to be done. In its most excellent form, protest is embodied by the extraordinary religious person, whom Jackson calls "some gifted apostle of Truth."[13] Such a person is a religious prophet who acts for and under a higher law in order to realize ends that are more virtuous than the mundane ends of human politics. And the prophet's task is undertaken without breaking the law. Rather, the prophet, as viewed by Jackson, is one who corrects social wrongs by injecting new spiritual and moral substance into the social order. This person is not a political reformer who tries to bring about justice through conflict and agitation but is a religious seer whose personality demonstrates a higher order to which the social order should be conformed. Hence, the source of good social action is extraordinary personal, spiritual, and moral refinement.[14]

Jackson spoke time and again of the lower and the higher levels of a person's being. Though not systematically developed, these refer, on the one hand, to the mundane world of affairs and, on the other hand, to the moral and spiritual realms. The religious prophet is bent on bringing in the kingdom of God by using methods that are appropriate to the kingdom of God, rather than using those pertaining to the condition that would be changed. That is to say, this prophet, who is no lawbreaker, has values that are higher than those the law can embody and acts out of a conscience that has been touched by the eternal truths of God. The model clearly is Jesus Christ, who did not throw himself against the Roman Empire, led no boycotts, joined no picket lines, and participated in no mass demonstrations. Such acts were not in accordance with a higher conscience and loftier ideals. Such an understanding of the relationship of the religious prophet to the world of mundane affairs implies action of a certain kind, which, alone, Jackson would justify as appropriate for social change.

On the subject of suffering, Jackson returned to the sacrificial love of Jesus, which is symbolized for all Christians by the cross. He viewed that central symbol as one that reveals the courage and the love of Jesus, who was prepared to endure the evils of the world in order to make way, in God's way, for the implantation of new spiritual and moral substance in the world. Jesus' task was to lift people up from the low way of life to the heights of God's redemptive life. Jesus aimed at bringing in the kingdom of God, and for that end he endured humanity's insults, hatred and persecution, unjust laws, and merit system. Consequently, Jackson called Black people and white people of deep sensitivity and religious vision to endure in the world not for the sake of endurance but for the sake of changing the world by introducing new spiritual and moral substance into it. This was not a plea for political passivity; rather, it was a call to use the values implied by the ethic of God's kingdom as the means for effecting the

kind of social change that would be based on the purposes and ways of God and not on political expediency.

Jackson's Political Thought

While it is difficult to make a sharp distinction between Jackson's religious thought and his political
thought, each had certain distinctive characteristics.
Although he considered the two to be closely related,
he did not suggest that religion and politics were the
same thing or that the one could be reduced to the
other. That is to say, he deemed the Constitution of
the United States and the Christian gospel to be mutually compatible but not synonymous. His ultimate
principle of criticism was Jesus Christ and what
Christ's life, death, and resurrection imply for humankind and society. He examined the American way of
life in the light of that principle and concluded that, in
terms of full actualization, the American way of life
was incomplete but that in terms of potentiality it was
sufficient. Thus, in Jackson's view, politics is firmly
rooted in religion. Moreover, he viewed the fundamental principles of American nationhood as
grounded in biblical truth. In his reasoning, the nation
and the Christian church are under the sacred umbrella, since both appeal to the same sources for their
respective justifications and both aim at similar ends.
In his annual address to the convention in 1966[15] he
expressed praise for the American form of government, its philosophy of freedom, and its just laws,
while clearly linking the Constitution of the United
States with Judeo-Christian precepts. In arguing that
the Constitution is the embodiment of the sacred law,
he implied that it is vested with sacred truth.

Jackson maintained that the difference between
American democracy and totalitarianism was comparable to the difference between Christianity and other
religions. That divergence rests on the respective understandings of the nature of humankind. In his view,
the doctrine of humanity as expressed in the Declara-

tion of Independence is close to that proclaimed by the Christian church, the latter being the custodian of God's eternal truth. Jackson regarded human individuality as the primary object of Christian salvation and the preeminent center of a democratic creed. In this respect he concluded that Christianity and democracy shared a common view of humanity.

Moreover, Jackson believed that basic human rights could neither be fully taken away from humans nor be established by them. Rather, he contended that they are indelibly etched on the fabric of humanity and are in no way determined by external conditions.[16] Hence, he argued that when the founding fathers made the assertion in the Declaration of Independence, "We hold these Truths to be self-evident, that all Men are created equal, that they are endowed by their Creator with certain unalienable Rights, that among these are Life, Liberty, and the Pursuit of Happiness . . . ," they were implicitly acknowledging the moral authority of the Creator and the sacred nature of all persons. From Jackson's perspective this was virtually an affirmation of the Christian view of humanity.[17]

Further, Jackson pointed out that the laws of the American nation do not impinge upon matters of conscience. Rather, the Constitution orders the relationship of citizens to citizens and the relationship of citizens to the government. It is silent, however, on matters pertaining to the private sphere of conscience in which religion has its locus. Consequently, since the law does not impinge on matters of conscience, citizens ought not to attack the government or a law from a position that is based on conscience. In other words, citizens would be justified in disobeying the law only if it trespassed on the domain of conscience.[18]

Throughout his public career Jackson proclaimed a doctrine of loyalty and respect for law and order and took pride in love of country. This was a love that was profoundly influenced by his views of the nation's past glories and victories in liberating its citizenry from various kinds of oppression. But it is important to note that he did not subsume all important activities in the body politic under the rubric of law and order. On the contrary, he was aware of the limits of law when it is viewed as an agency for changing the moral character of human beings. In his understanding, law cannot make one person love or even respect another; very little actual moral improvement can be accomplished by law.

Although the law is not an agency for moral reform, Jackson contended that the just laws of the land must always determine the context in which civil rights struggles are to be waged. In this respect the law must always be obeyed. Winning people by faith rather than fear implies a respectful stance toward constitutional law, and those who work for the rights of citizenship ought to manifest such an attitude in all their actions.

More specifically, Jackson argued that the evolutionary development of constitutional law in the United States accounted for the problematic time lag in the realization of full citizenship rights for Blacks. Fortunately, the supreme law of the land, appropriately amended by due process, holds out a promise to Blacks that gradually has been honored and that will be more completely fulfilled in due time. That supreme law of the land prescribes the rights and privileges of all its citizens. In the event that any state or group withholds those rights and privileges, the citizens have recourse to the supreme law through the courts. And that mode of action was strongly advocated by Jackson, since, as he saw it, the only alternative was that of individuals or groups "taking the law in their own hands" and thus setting the stage for anarchy and/or mob rule. Such a state of affairs, he contended, characterized the racial segregationists in the South and elsewhere. In other words, those who denied full citizenship rights to Blacks during much of this nation's history were in violation of the just laws of the land and in such disobedience had constructed their own law.[19] Jackson expended considerable energy during the '60s in admonishing civil rights workers not to employ similar methods. Rather, he preached that every citizen should have faith in the legal machinery of the nation and in the justice set forth so prominently in the federal Constitution. Any and all infringements of constitutional law are matters best handled by the federal government, whose rightful duty it is. Citizens must not be encouraged to fight their own battles. Rather, they must obey the law and follow procedures set forth by the Constitution for effecting changes.

It is evident, even to a casual observer, that Jackson's understandings of the Constitution, the American society, and the nature of humankind were characterized by optimism. In spite of his rather frequent quotations from Reinhold Niebuhr about the nature of sin, he did not dwell on a person's propensity to err but rather emphasized the potentiality for good. This fact, in part, accounts for Jackson's reluctance to apply his descriptive abilities to portray the unfortunate aspects of the plight of Blacks in this country. He often expressed his abhorrence of any preoccupation with the negative, which he considered to be a threat to national unity. Frequently, he engaged in long descriptive analyses of the evils that are inherent in totalitarian states. He justified those arguments by an appeal to the principle of national defense. He believed that in the American context, attacks should be leveled against individual perpetrators of evil and not against the nation as such. To do otherwise must necessarily threaten the nation's internal unity. All who engage in such activity must, by definition, be enemies of the state. Those who persist in describing the manifold brutalities and hatreds visited upon Black people do, in his opinion, become hindrances to the loftier aspirations of national unity and belonging, goodwill, and cooperation. In fact, they themselves are morally infected, since they tend to develop a character that is bitter and cynical, and all their actions are thereby directed toward polarizing the nation into two hostile camps. Therefore, it is not surprising that Jackson would set forth the following basic principles for national survival: faith in the American system and loyalty to it; mutual trust in one another as persons and as groups; and a spirit of cooperation and goodwill.[20]

Jackson's views on slavery are instructive at this point. How did he correlate his views of the slavery system with his principles of faith and loyalty to the American system? His argument proceeds in the following manner. Slavery was a cruel institution that negated the vision of freedom and the spirit of idealism held by the nation's founders. It was created and maintained by the evil purposes of self-serving persons who were successful in gaining some measure of ascendancy. (Curiously, he never seemed to attend to the fact that these founders themselves were slaveholders.) He praised the Emancipation Proclamation for having promised freedom to the slaves, thus rekindling hope in their lives. But, once again, the promise of freedom was thwarted by the wicked designs of selfish people who have always been this nation's agents of evil.

It is important to note that Jackson believed the racist duality of citizenship, one for whites and the other for Blacks, was inimical to those who established this nation and to the constitution that they formed. He viewed the perpetrators of racism as disloyal, tyrannical anti-Americans bent on promoting a system of racial segregation and discrimination as a new form of oppression, similar to slavery and destined to rob Black people of the nation's promise of freedom—a promise that had inspired the fundamental hopes of the diverse peoples who first caused this nation to come into being.

Jackson did not hesitate to say that throughout their history Black Americans had struggled to reconcile the theory of freedom, that is, the ideals of the Constitution, with the nation's actual practice. He recognized that some were overwhelmed by the burden of oppression and ceased to struggle, while others kept alive the hope of freedom promised by the nation's ideals, by protesting vigorously and in various other ways. Their valid objections, however, were always in accordance with the laws of the land, for they could justify no other form of protest. And that fact is the key to an understanding of their complaint, since only in legal protest could they manifest their love for America and their faith in its promises.

Jackson concluded that positive protest is legal protest and that the right of legal protest is implied by a view of humankind's essential being as freedom. In this regard he viewed the Christian gospel and the Constitution of the United States as compatible in their understandings of human freedom. Freedom is the essence of the gospel; sin is a distortion of that freedom. God created persons as free agents, but they have chosen bondage by preferring their own self-destructive ways. Their sin, however, does not completely destroy their desire for freedom; it resides in them as a natural urge. Consequently, when human beings are in bondage they will inevitably protest that captivity because they can do no other, not because some law says that they may. And that natural urge reflects the freedom intended by their creator.

Thus, Jackson perceived the law of the land, in its admission of positive (legal) protest, as complying with and deferring to the Christian understanding of humanity as essentially free and as having that understanding stamped on its nature. He rejoiced in the fact that the right to protest on behalf of freedom is rightfully circumscribed by the Constitution. Once again the dangers of anarchy and of mob rule would become acute were that right not controlled in the manner in which it is. It is right and praiseworthy that the Constitution affirms and protects the freedom that people have been endowed with by their creator and that is evidenced by their natural urges.

In Jackson's understanding, the intrinsic justice of the Constitution is that it grants its citizenry the right to criticize its government by legitimate procedures. Legal means are provided for citizens to check their government when it is considered to be acting contrary to the ideals and principles of the Constitution. Further, citizens have a duty to assist the government in uncovering the loci of injustice in the body politic and in describing its nature. However, citizens do not have the right to take the law into their own hands and to pronounce guilt or to prescribe punishment. Grievances must be redressed by the legitimate authority. Lawful petition to make grievances known and to seek their just resolution is the form that protest should take under the laws of this nation.[21]

Jackson understood American constitutional law as being an evolutionary process that will actualize itself in the body politic one day, so long as hindrances to that process do not slow it down unduly. All impediments are inimical to the spirit of the nation. Those who would halt the natural growth of the nation are anti-American. Public officials and their assistants, together with an aroused citizenry, must constantly be on the alert to weaken any and all enemies of the principles on which this nation's moral character depends. Jackson contended that the primary form of protest was the ballot.[22]

Jackson distinguished between lawful objection and unlawful objection. The former is good; the latter is always evil. In other words, he distinguished between the kind of protest he believed to be aimed at assisting America to fulfill its dreams and promises and that kind which is bent on the destruction of the nation. In his view, legal dissent never takes the form of condemning any particular group of Americans but only those individuals whose actions threaten the well-being of the nation. In its best form, legal protest is initiated by a group that manifests racial diversity in its composition. That is one reason why Jackson held the NAACP in such high esteem. Its organizational structure from the beginning implied a tribute to those whites who had always protested with Blacks for citizenship rights.[23]

Jackson declared the supreme law of the land to be the norm for evaluating civil rights organizations.

That is to say, he evaluated the latter by the manner in which they related themselves to that law. Obedience is their obligation, and all who would engage in any form of civil disobedience must be viewed as destructive agents of social change.

In this connection he strongly condemned Black leaders who, in their opposition to racism, devised strategies and techniques that failed to honor humanity's higher nature and higher aspirations, which are determined by its spiritual being. Demonstrations of the masses tramping through the streets were viewed as forms of action that underrate the higher gifts and capacities Black people possess. In Jackson's view, many civil rights activities operate on the assumption that the structure of white-Black relations will always be the same: namely, whites in control of the political and economic institutions and Blacks fighting perpetually for enhanced justice in that relationship. Rather, he believed that Blacks should and could rid themselves of such slave mentality and could aspire to the end of constructing a creative and productive Black community. That notion of a productive Black community had great importance for his political views regarding the priorities Blacks should have. Further, the concept of production was used operationally as a principle of criticism of protest activities. The principle of production is extremely significant, since it formed the basis for Jackson's philosophy of ethnicity and its implications in the struggle against racial prejudice. This philosophy of ethnicity was Jackson's sociological justification for the affirmation of racial preference, which must not be confused with racial prejudice. In this context Jackson advocated certain Black self-development programs as a major priority once the law was sufficient to legitimate the civil rights of Blacks. Further, his view of racial preference was set forth as a natural grounding for all racial groups. That fact becomes the basis for such further operational doctrines as racial pride, racial self-respect, and racial self-development, doctrines that he believed should be the guidelines for all programs that aim at constructive social change among Blacks and between Blacks and whites. But let us now attend more carefully to the distinction he made between racial preference and racial prejudice.

In Jackson's thinking, racial preference does not necessarily imply a negative valuation of other racial groups. He considered it natural for a nationality, a race, or some other group to prefer its own people. Not only is that not a sin, but, up to a point, it is a virtue. He was of the opinion that many whites had not seen this characteristic among Black people but, rather, had viewed Blacks as simply wanting to break into the white race and to share the benefits without having exerted the effort. In part, such a view reinforces prejudices against Blacks. He condemned Black leaders who strongly advocated integration for not identifying themselves with the Black race and for not exerting effort toward helping Blacks utilize their resources (however meager) in refurbishing their communities. He accused them of wanting to lead crusades against white people for the liberation of Blacks although they did not attend to those things that Blacks desired and that they themselves could do to liberate themselves from bad housing, poor education, economic deprivation, vice, and so on. He also condemned those leaders who, he believed, merely preyed upon the frustrations and hatreds of the Black masses and sought to mobilize them for rebellious purposes in order to inflame the white community. Neither group of leaders is working for constructive social change. Rather, he judged that both were exploiting the masses for private and selfish ends.

Jackson believed that an affirmation of racial preference as a virtue could be one resource for destroying racial prejudice. Since the latter, in large part, is rooted in a false knowledge that Blacks prefer whites to themselves, such an affirmation could destroy that misconception.[24]

Jackson's perspective implies that the problem of

racial prejudice is caused largely by a mistaken understanding of how Blacks relate to what is, in truth, a
matter of nature, namely, that members of a racial
group prefer one another to outsiders. That fact, according to Jackson, has been misunderstood not only
by whites but also by many Black leaders. Or, if those
leaders have known it, they have lacked the courage to
make it known lest they be considered in league with
the segregationists and thereby be misunderstood in
yet another way.

Jackson's doctrine of racial preference involves such
positive values as racial pride, racial respect, self-
criticism, and self-development. He argued that the
Black race must take on a positive view of itself and
must cease to judge itself by the standards of segregationists. Further, as a result of being controlled by the
segregationists' view of them, Blacks spend all their
time focusing on the evils that have been perpetrated
upon them rather than concentrating on the possibilities of creativity they could effect. Frequently, Jackson
admonished Blacks to become more self-respecting as
a race and to cease measuring their worth in terms of
white criteria.[25]

One of Jackson's basic presuppositions was that
Black people had the ability to do much more than
they were doing on every level of life. He proposed
that Blacks build and rebuild their communities with
such excellence that whites might envy them and desire to move in. He did not support separatism as an
ideology, because racial preference does not imply being antiwhite or anti any other group. Should it ever
become such it would become anti-America, anti-
democracy, and, in the final analysis, anti-Black and
therefore would be self-defeating.

Jackson was keenly aware of the possibility of racial
preference leading to racial prejudice and thereby becoming degenerate. Racial prejudice leads to racial
discrimination and segregation. He described racial
prejudice as a prejudgment of the worth of others
based on one's own specific preferences and the con-

comitant denial of their rightful place in the community and/or nation.[26]

Jackson considered racial preference to be a private matter, and as such it is not in opposition with the federal Constitution, which admits no jurisdiction over that domain. Similarly, poetry, religion, and home life occupy the private realm and in their rightful function do not threaten the well-being of the state. He also argued that racial prejudice was a private matter, since it was a degenerate form of racial preference. But the problem for the nation (hence, a political problem) arises when that private realm seeks domination over society as a whole. Curiously, Jackson did not condemn racial prejudice so long as it remained in the private domain. When it threatens the lives of other people, however, then it transgresses the supreme law of the land by attempting to set up its private ethic as normative for the whole. Any such transgression is a threat to democracy and to all its institutions. Discrimination is that overt act whereby racial prejudice enters the public domain.[27]

Therefore, Jackson concluded, civil rights groups ought not to lead drives against legitimate, wholesome preferences but against the overt acts of prejudice. In other words, civil rights leaders should not attempt to get whites to break up their preferences and to begin preferring Blacks or even attempt to make Blacks co-equal in some white private domain.

Jackson recognized the fact, however, that the solution to the racial prejudice problem rests in the citizenry broadening its circle of preference in the interest of national unity. He admitted that there is a tension between private preferences, which might become racial prejudice, and the public solidarity of nationhood. Building a secure nation is a common interest of whites and Blacks and could serve as a unifier, since it engages the minds and emotions of both groups.[28] In the final analysis it appears that Jackson would desire the nation to display the character of one gigantic private family wherein national and public aims would coincide with private preferences.

It is important to note that his thinking about private preference was linked with his view of Jesus, who Jackson said did not discredit family ties but placed them in a broader context, namely, the will of God, which enables a more inclusive kinship. In the interest of a more inclusive kinship, the lesser circle of privacy is made secondary in order to receive its true fulfillment. From that scriptural perspective Jackson argued by analogy for the relationship of private preference to national preference.

Further, he was convinced that prejudice is a serious sickness of the mind and of the emotions. People blindly make it a major principle for shaping and guiding their ways of life. It grows like a cancer until it consumes the character and action of humans in every dimension of their lives. Its advocates themselves become victims, unable to escape from its grip. It is possible that the one who is in chains may be freer than the one responsible for the chains. One can prevent prejudice from getting a foothold by maintaining a mind free from hate and an attitude guided by love.

Jackson considered laws necessary to establish the rights of the victims of prejudice and to structure the relationships of all citizens, but once again we discover that he believed the laws to be incapable of destroying racial prejudice completely and of delivering its agents from their peculiar bondage. Prejudice is a disease that can be cured, but the cure cannot be swift. Various kinds of interracial exposures for the purpose of sensitizing and educating are needed and should be encouraged. More important, Jackson felt, some cause great enough to gain the support of whites and of Blacks could be discovered that would effect the desired end. He viewed as his mission in life the liberation of whites and of Blacks, since both are victims of prejudice in different ways.

Closely associated with his devotion to such a desirable cause was his adamant opposition to racial bitterness, especially bitterness that he thought was often generated by Blacks in their opposition to racism. In addition to principles of law and order for effecting racial justice in the American society, he advocated the attitude of goodwill as a necessary ingredient in the struggle. In addition, he called for a militant patriotism as the means of completing the endeavor.[29]

Those who do not speak and act in a spirit of goodwill toward others and especially toward the nation, Jackson would regard as dangerous enemies of the state. In dealing with these enemies, he advocated firm action that does not necessarily exclude even capital punishment, which he contended could be justified by an appeal to holy scripture.

Significantly, the 1968 minutes of the National Baptist Convention, U.S.A., Inc., contain a statement likening Jackson's presidential address at the convention in Atlanta to Booker T. Washington's Atlanta Exposition address in 1895. Indeed, the statement is entitled "A Second Great Atlanta Speech."[30] Characteristically, Jackson spoke about the proper relationship that should exist between citizens and the nation, calling for cooperation among all groups in the nation rather than competition, for goodwill and mutual respect rather than bitterness and strife. He argued impressively that the nation's problems could be solved by the moral force of the Constitution, the just laws of the land, the American philosophy of freedom, and the goodwill of the citizenry. He expressed faith in the legislators and spoke against various kinds of mass pressures and techniques aimed at informing the legislators of their patriotic duty. He emphasized that all groups ought to put the national interest first and ought to use their own resources, however meager, to develop not only themselves but the entire nation into a strong, defensive force against those who are bent on its destruction.

Nowhere does Jackson appear more ambiguous than in the tension that exists between his thinking about patriotism and his thoughts concerning racial preference. On the one hand, he advocated an unquestionable loyalty to the national interest, expressed in the unity and cooperation all should manifest at all times. On the other hand, while not losing sight of the national interest, which by itself should inspire all, he affirmed racial preference and racial togetherness and admonished Blacks to embody a spirit of self-development in all dimensions of their lives. Obviously, he took pride whenever Black persons were elected to office, because he saw such events as signs that the substance of American ideals was being realized. Similarly, he was gratified by every Black person who achieved some measure of success, for example, economically, socially, educationally. Jackson emphasized what Blacks should do for themselves in order to solve the American race problem and de-emphasized what America should do for Blacks. What, then, was his evaluation of the civil rights movement? Simply stated, he viewed that movement as progress toward first-class citizenship for Blacks. But he hastened to point out that, in itself, it was not enough. The next step must be made by Blacks themselves. And he believed that the time was then ripe for that second step. In the second stage, success would depend on what Blacks were able to do for themselves and not on what they could force others to give or to do for them. For many years Jackson advocated a program called "From Protest to Production" as a model for this second stage. In his view, protest is aimed at changing the minds of segregationists or at least their actions; it dwells on the wrongs they do and on their self-destructiveness. That form of action was considered by him to be passé and no longer appropriate to the present. Blacks must now assume responsibility for production. One of Jackson's clearest descriptions of production is found in his presidential address of 1962,[31] in which he affirms such principles as racial self-production, racial self-development, racial uplift (moral and spiritual), racial self-respect, racial self-reliance, racial independence. Many programs advocated by him and adopted by the convention as attempts to actualize the above principles have been undertaken.[32] He argued further that individual and group initiative as well as commitment to and participation in the life of the nation are basic requirements of all Blacks who have been formally granted the rights of citizenship by the Constitution. That expresses the spirit of integration, which was never intended to degrade or lessen the process of racial group development. In light of that understanding, Jackson opposed any attempt at racial mixing as an end in itself. Rather, he insisted that Blacks submit themselves to the merit system that is applicable to the situation.

I have said that Jackson opposed denominational organic union on the grounds that he did not consider it implied by the Christian message. That position has implications for his reluctance to affirm integration if it should mean institutional mergers. He vigorously supported unity (fellowship) among all people and all groups, but that does not include organic union. In spite of the fact that during the late '60s·several Black denominations opened talks with white denominations about possible mergers, Jackson refused to enter into those discussions. He believed that white liberals were willing to entertain such mergers because of their past sins of racism and as a palliative for their guilt. But Blacks do not share that guilt and would weaken their institutional strength as well as their moral character by assenting to such mergers.[33]

Jackson strongly felt that if Blacks were to merge with whites, they would eventually begin to develop Black caucuses aimed not at the spiritual and moral refinement of the group but at presenting lists of demands to the respective church boards and at protesting to the white majority for certain things the Black minority felt it should have. Once again, the Blacks would be forced into a situation in which they would be making demands of whites rather than progressing along the lines of self-development and racial independence. Jackson used strong language to condemn an appeal made by several Black Baptist leaders to the

Chicago Baptist Association, in which they called for that association and the American Baptist Convention to help Blacks develop in terms of racial identity and cultural heritage. Since most of those leaders had once been members of Jackson's National Baptist Convention, he criticized them for not having continued in a Black institution that had a history of nearly one hundred years of independence and that was able to give them all that they were asking of the white Baptists. Then he raised the most threatening of questions, namely, do Blacks think they are incapable of achieving any good short of being led or assisted by white leaders and/or white organizations?[34]

The concept of Black self-development and Black independence was a consistent one throughout Jackson's public life. Its substance is identical with the thinking of many Black nationalists, but its form is different. For him, racial self-development requires the rights of first-class citizenship and a vigorous patriotism. A nation composed of many diverse parts can only become strong and independent by each part making itself strong and independent. The aggregate of strong and independent parts, exemplifying a spirit of goodwill and mutual respect, constitutes the strength and independence and peace of the whole.

Civil Disobedience

Jackson rarely discussed Martin Luther King, Jr., in public, although it was usually clear that King was the one he had in mind when he criticized the techniques of civil disobedience. King's understanding of civil disobedience was greatly influenced by the thoughts of Henry David Thoreau and of Mahatma Gandhi. Jackson chose to attack King indirectly by critically examining the nature of civil disobedience as it was advocated by Thoreau and Gandhi in order to demonstrate that neither approach is appropriate for the contemporary American situation. He sought to malign Thoreau's credibility by depicting him as a bachelor

who had neither a family life nor a church life and as a
poet and recluse who had no appreciation for the importance of political organization. Further, he pointed
out that Thoreau was basically antigovernment and
viewed it as less powerful and as possessing less vitality
than an individual. Even though Jackson considered
Thoreau's abhorrence of slavery to be praiseworthy, he
hastens to remind us that Thoreau spoke and wrote
about that subject prior to the issuance of the Emancipation Proclamation.[35] Jackson concluded his analysis
by saying that Thoreau advocated civil disobedience
without acknowledging the achieved values and potentialities of the American nation and without making
provision for their preservation and maintenance. That
is to say, Thoreau made no attempt to set forth measures for the construction of an orderly democratic
society wherein harmony, peace, goodwill, and cooperation might be manifested.

Jackson understood Thoreau's civil disobedience as
a form of protest with no other substantive goal than
protest itself and, therefore, bent on the overthrow of
the government rather than on its improvement. But,
more important, Jackson understood all forms of civil
disobedience similarly. They are techniques for destruction. As a corrective he proposed his concept of
production as a substantive strategy that goes beyond
protest.

Jackson held the view that in Gandhi's situation
there were certain conditions present that made his
method justifiable. The British were foreigners and
were a minority that did not have the confidence of the
majority of the population. In a similar way and via a
similar method the American War of Independence
was waged and justified. But, in spite of Gandhi's great
success with the method of nonviolent civil disobedience in India, Jackson contended that this system did
not make him a success as a political leader. He was
against the partition of India. The people opposed him
on that question and later betrayed all his teachings of
nonviolence. Jackson concluded that Gandhi's great-

ness was more a result of his saintliness than of his nonviolent civil disobedience.

Jackson reasoned that the Gandhian method was inappropriate in America, because the latter made available all the necessary avenues for altering social practices of injustice. Further, he argued that the tactic of nonviolent civil disobedience relies on coercion and fear and aims at negative ends that fail to serve the positive goal of substantial development.[36]

Jackson constantly returned to the judgment that those who practice civil disobedience are anti-American, enemies of the state, because they do not believe in the lofty principles on which this nation is built. Further, they help to create the belief that civil disobedience is better than civil obedience and civic responsibility. Without denying the limited benefits derived via such methods, he was adamant in his contention that this technique was not good in the American situation.

In short, he considered civil disobedience to be close to high treason in that it is encouraged by and based on lawlessness and criminal acts of major proportion against the state and in that it implies a repudiation of the federal Constitution, the evolutionary processes of political growth, litigation via the judiciary, amendments and revisions to the Constitution, and the substance of the American way of life. Those who advocate civil disobedience focus all their attention on the evils of the society, past and present. They give their followers no hope except in the destruction of the system. They were regarded by Jackson as agents of despair in that they expend their energies sowing seeds of bitterness, hatred, conflict, and even violence. He contended that one cause of the urban riots during the mid-'60s was the civil disobedience of the civil rights movement, which nourished an atmosphere of lawlessness in the land.

As stated earlier, Jackson considered religion to be a matter of conscience. As such, he believed that the federal Constitution does not interfere with it, since all private matters of conscience are outside the realm of constitutional authority. Further, he maintained that civic virtue is a matter of obeying the law, rather than of disobeying it, especially since the supreme law of this land is just and respects religion. All citizens, therefore, ought to work constructively for the law's full realization.

Jackson was of the opinion that nonviolent civil disobedience inevitably leads to violence. This, in his judgment, was the case when, on the eve of independence, Gandhi wept because the country was at war with itself and had not embodied the virtues of nonviolence. He claimed that similar evidence was manifested during the 1961 split in the National Baptist Convention, U.S.A., Inc., when the anti-Jackson forces (of whom Martin Luther King, Jr., was a prominent member) staged a march-in at the convention. In the confusion caused by a mass rush to the platform, an elderly clergyman fell from the platform, broke his neck, and died the same night. And the violence that spread over the cities of America in the mid-'60s provided more evidence for Jackson that nonviolent civil disobedience leads to violence, whether intended or not. Accordingly, he argued that such a technique, which he also called a "destructive ideology," is self-destructive at worst and counterproductive at best. Even though the advocates of nonviolence do not condone the use of weapons against their opponents, he indicated that they thrive on mental torture, intimidation, community disruption, lawbreaking, and various other forms of social and private abuse. Therefore, they are enemies of such ethical standards as community well-being, respect for others, goodwill, and cooperation. Further, he declared that these advocates acted against the higher aspirations and values of Black people, since nonviolence as an ideology is based on a slave morality characterized by mental intimidation, deceit, and other forms of nonphysical coercion. In summary, Jackson argued that the civil rights struggle was a moral and spiritual struggle and not just a social and political one. While fighting for social and political rights, one must at the same time struggle for the full realization of the moral and spiritual dimensions of life. That can be done only by using moral and spiritual methods that are justified by the laws of the land and the Christian faith.

School Boycotts

In 1970 Jackson opposed forced school busing on these grounds: he reasoned that integration means equal opportunity to participate in the fruits of the society and cannot be represented by a numerical quotient. Further, integration must not be used as a tool for punishing others for past sins, which, he contended, had been an unfortunate element in its implementation vis-à-vis schools.

Jackson's severe criticism of school boycotts rested primarily on the understanding that schoolchildren should not be used as instruments in the hands of adults to punish others or to advance the mere numerical quota of integration.[37] Children should be encouraged to go to school and to respect their teachers. When they are used in a conflictual situation, it is natural for them to assume the attitudes of disrespect, bitterness, and hatred, which characterize those adults who manipulate them. The inculcation of such negative values could render a death blow to their entire educational careers; this would be a tragedy. The responsibility all adults have to children is to enable them to embody positive values toward their teachers, administrators, and education, rather than negative ones. Jackson's position on school busing was established on similar grounds.[38]

Black Power

It is clear that Jackson opposed any understanding of Black Power that would foster racial separation from the nation. Similarly, he opposed any understanding of racial appreciation that depreciates other races or groups. In his understanding, the advocates of Black Power propose a new form of racism. Their racial preferences have already degenerated into racial prejudice. In his view, this is evidenced by the fact that they wage battle with all white people and not simply the perpetrators of racism. They have no respect for the good that has been realized in American history and are bent on revolution. They are enemies of the state and will its complete destruction. Further, they have chosen to fight the evils of racism by employing the same methods the racists have used for so long. Racism, whether Black or white, thrives on hatred, bitterness, malice, and violence. Its agents become arrogant, rude, and, most of all, self-serving and deceitful. In short, racism breeds immorality; it can do none other.

Jackson opposed Black Theology on similar grounds.[39] He enumerated several weaknesses implied by such a theology: the reduction of Christian theology to the historic conflict between Blacks and whites; lack of appreciation for the universality of the Christian gospel of liberation; the reduction of Christ and of God to the level of Blackness; its potential for being a gospel of hate; its potential for violence; its potential for the polarization of the races with no future hope of reconciliation. Finally, Jackson concluded that if the Black church should accept the perspective and leadership of Black Theology, then Black people would become the outstanding proponents of racial segregation in the United States of America.

The Goodness of America

Jackson was a great patriot; his love for America and his belief in the goodness of its achievements were paramount in his thought. Much has been said about that fact, but it can be demonstrated more graphically by a brief look at some of the programs he advocated and certain important documents he penned. We have seen that, in his view, campaigns of nonviolent direct confrontation can easily be converted into episodes of violence and, therefore, are inappropriate methods for effecting constructive social change in these United States. He assumed that the agents of such campaigns necessarily disavowed the goodness of the nation and sought its defeat. In relation to that problem, he called untiringly for the embodiment of the spirit of patriotism by all good citizens.[40]

Jackson's commitment to law and order and the obligation of obedience on the part of all citizens is abundantly clear. But he did not see the law as the full solution to the problem of racism. Laws can force people to act in certain ways, but laws cannot make them moral beings. That is to say, insofar as racism is a moral and spiritual problem, one must not expect its solution by law alone. Rather, he insisted that a movement dedicated to changing the hearts and minds of racists was needed and argued that that higher task of changing hearts and minds was the function of churches and schools respectively. Education aims at constructive change in peoples' minds, while religion's function is to change their hearts. Therefore, schools and churches have important functions in the battle for first-class citizenship rights. More than this, he viewed the struggle as one that ought to be waged by the cooperative hands of the church in close alliance with the legal means afforded it by the Constitution. At this point gospel and patriotism are closely related in a common enterprise.

In his 1963 official statement on civil rights Jackson depicted a close relationship between the federal Constitution, the American way of life, and the Christian gospel and viewed each as contributing an important and binding principle to the struggle.

> Whether applying pressure by protest or pressure by production or whether in demonstrations, mass marches, or

quiet reasoning around the conference table, we urge
that the following three determining standards will always be recognized:

1. That the Federal Constitution will be the legal standard.
2. That the American philosophy of freedom will reg-
   ulate all efforts and actions.
3. That the Spirit of Christ will be accepted as the
   ultimate standard of moral and spiritual aspirations.[41]

In 1970 Jackson appealed to the young people of the
convention: "In brief we are asking young Americans
to join us and the nation in uniting the ideals of Christianity and patriotism to save the nation."[42]

In praising America for the legacy of freedom and
liberty bequeathed by its founders, Jackson asked in
1962 that the nation actualize what its soul is, namely,
undying devotion to freedom and truth. The virtues of
the nation are seen in its commitment to democracy
and to the Judeo-Christian God.

America, tell the world who you are. A land of the free
and home of the brave; a community of all races, nations, kindreds and tongues under a government of the
people, for the people and by the people and a Republic
where all citizens are free and all men are civil brothers
living under one flag, united by one central democratic
purpose and in appreciation of the blessings of nature
and in loyalty to the God of history and eternal father
and Lord of all mankind.[43]

Jackson wrote a statement in 1959 called "Reaffir-
mation of Our Faith in the Nation,"[44] which was
adopted by the convention as an official document. In
that statement he reaffirms the belief that the practice
of segregation and discrimination based upon race, nationality, or religion is inimical to the fundamental
laws of the nation and to God and, therefore, ought to

be struggled against in the interest of the nation and of God.

Another official document, "The National Baptist Convention Program on Christian Civic Responsibility," which Jackson wrote in 1965, calls for a commitment to Christian patriotism, among other things.

> . . . Let us begin from this session to take the steps to build up a large bloc of independent voters across the nation dedicated to Christian patriotism.
>
> . . . Let us combine love of Christ, love of country, and love of mankind in such a way that a dynamic and inclusive form of Christian patriotism will emerge.[45]

A good summary of much that has been written about in this chapter is contained in Jackson's "Call for National Unity," published in 1965.[46] It clearly sets out Jackson's understanding of the primary principles involved in assuming political and religious responsibility for curing the nation of the ills of racism.

Photo courtesy of the Library of Congress

3

Martin Luther King, Jr.

King's Theological
and Political Understanding

The public career of Martin Luther King, Jr., began in December 1955, when he was suddenly propelled into the leadership of the Montgomery bus boycott. At the time, none could have predicted that such an event taking place in the heart of the Old Confederacy would mark a significant new beginning in the history of protest for civil rights. It was during the yearlong boycott that King and his followers discovered a method for opposing racism that they considered to be politically effective and theologically sound. This method of non-violent direct resistance was institutionalized in the Montgomery Improvement Association. When it became apparent that the problems confronted in Montgomery were widespread throughout the South, and when it became clear that nonviolent resistance should be a model for effecting social change in the South, the Southern Christian Leadership Conference became the official institutional embodiment of the method. During the ensuing decade the national crisis in racial justice would be energized by King, who was destined to become internationally respected as the personification of the method and its institution.

Primarily, this section will deal with King's theological views and their relation to his understanding of the kinds of actions and deeds he deemed justifiable in the struggle against racism. It is well known that Martin Luther King, Sr., was the prestigious minister of Ebenezer Baptist Church in Atlanta, wherein his son had been nurtured all his life. At an early age, the younger King went across the city from that bastion of religious fervor and conviction to attend Morehouse College. Under the influence of President Benjamin Mays, Professor George Kelsey, and others, he decided in his second year to enter the ministry. Soon thereafter he preached his first sermon in his father's church and became the assistant minister for the remainder of his studies at Morehouse. Later, following the Montgomery event, he returned to that church as cominister with his father. In the meantime he had studied for the Bachelor of Divinity degree at Crozier Theological Seminary, one of the few remaining schools of theology in the country that could be classified as a bulwark of evangelical liberalism. From Crozier he went to the Boston School of Theology to study for the Ph.D. degree. At the time, the latter school was characterized by the personalist school of philosophy.

In all of King's thought, speeches, and writings no other theme is more pervasive than that of God. I contend that all other important concepts pervading his works—for example, nonviolence, love, justice, human dignity, reconciliation, freedom, morality—are either explicitly or implicitly related to his understanding of God. A book by Kenneth L. Smith and Ira G. Zepp[1] makes it abundantly clear that King's thought was heavily influenced at many crucial points by such schools of theology as evangelical liberalism, social gospel, and personalism; such theologians as Reinhold Niebuhr, Paul Tillich, and Walter Rauschenbusch; and such philosophers as Karl Marx, E. S. Brightman, G. W. F. Hegel and Mahatma Gandhi. Be that as it may, I contend that King cannot be classified easily as a disciple of any of these particular schools of theological or philosophical thought. Rather, he was influenced by many differing forms of thought without becoming a mere disciple of anyone. Yet he was able to arrive at coherence in his own thinking by a certain methodological dependence on the Hegelian dialectical method, which enabled him to combine alternative positions in a synthesizing conclusion.

In his dissertation "A Comparison of the Conceptions of God in the Thinking of Paul Tillich and Henry Nelson Wieman," the Hegelian dialectical method is employed heuristically. That method enabled him to discern the erroneous limitations of Tillich's and of Wieman's understandings of God and to posit a fuller understanding by synthesizing the two.

> To sum up, both Wieman's pluralism and Tillich's monism are inadequate as philosophical and religious world-views. Each overemphasizes one phase of reality while totally neglecting another important phase. Here again, the solution is not *either* monism *or* pluralism; it is *both* monism *and* pluralism. Tillich and Wieman fail to see that both positions can be meaningfully maintained. It is impossible to hold a quantitative pluralism while holding a qualitative monism. In this way both oneness and manyness are preserved. Neither swallows the other. Such a view defends, on the one hand, individuality against the impersonalism and all-engulfing universalism of any type of ultimate monism. On the other hand, it vindicates the idea of a basal monism against the attacks of any ultimate pluralism.[2]

A basic presupposition of the dialectical method is that truth is always a union of apparently contradictory elements. Since every affirmation implies a negation and vice versa, the synthesis is a product of the "yes" and the "no." That method is a great reconciler. Time and again King used the dialectical method to affirm the truth implied in seemingly contradictory positions without affirming the extremes of either position. It is important to note that the synthesis always introduces a third position and, therefore, a new reality.

It was extremely important to King that he develop throughout his studies a theological understanding that was intellectually sound. His careful analysis of the conceptions of God in the thinking of two of America's leading theologians is indicative of that fact. However, King did not become a disciple of Tillich or Wieman, though he often borrowed certain conceptual terms and notions from their thought in order to explicate his own. Nowhere is this seen more clearly than in the following: "At the center of the Christian faith is the affirmation that there is a God in the universe who is the ground and essence of all reality. A Being of infinite love and boundless power, God is the creator, sustainer, and conserver of values."[3] King learned much from Tillich about the power of God and from Wieman about God's goodness and creativity. But what impressed him most was the fact that for each of them God was an undeniable reality. King said of them, "They are so convinced of the reality of God that they would dismiss all arguments for his existence as futile and invalid."[4] However, one of his major criticisms of them was that their preoccupation with such a troublesome question as the existence of God culminated in each giving up too much in order to answer the question satisfactorily. Each, he believed, had given up certain essential elements of the traditional Christian view of God, chief among which was the notion of God as personality. In King's opinion, one of the foremost characteristics of the biblical view of God is personality. He admits, however, that he became more convinced of this fact during the agonizing experiences of the civil rights movement. In a moving passage he describes how his philosophical thought about God became living reality.

> More than ever before I am convinced of the reality of a personal God. True, I have always believed in the personality of God. But in the past the idea of a personal God was little more than a metaphysical category that I found theologically and philosophically satisfy-

ing. Now it is a living reality that has been validated in
the experiences of everyday life. God has been profoundly real to me in recent years. In the midst of outer
dangers I have felt an inner calm. In the midst of lonely
days and dreary nights I have heard an inner voice saying, "Lo, I will be with you." When the chains of fear
and the manacles of frustration have all but stymied my
efforts, I have felt the power of God transforming the
fatigue of despair into the buoyancy of hope. I am convinced that the universe is under the control of a loving
purpose, and that in the struggle for righteousness man
has cosmic companionship. Behind the harsh appear-
ances of the world there is a benign power. To say that
this God is personal is not to make him a finite object
besides other objects or attribute to him the limitations
of human personality; it is to take what is finest and
noblest in our consciousness and affirm its perfect existence in him. . . . So in the truest sense of the word,
God is a living God. In him there is feeling and will,
responsive to the deepest yearnings of the human heart;
this God both evokes and answers prayer.[5]

Throughout his public career, King believed intensely in a God whose character is personality and
who relates to persons in love and grace in the midst of
immediate experience. That is the understanding of
God that he had heard proclaimed since his childhood
and that he relied upon for inner strength and courage
during perilous times. No Tillich or Wieman ever
wrote about the kind of personal experience of God
that King described following a telephone threat on his
life. Neither Tillich's God nor Wieman's God exempli-
fies the personality characteristics that would motivate
the kind of personal communication contained in the
following:

It seemed that all of my fears had come down on me at
once. I had reached the saturation point. . . .
In this state of exhaustion, when my courage had almost gone, I determined to take my problem to God.
My head in my hands, I bowed over the kitchen table

and prayed aloud. The words I spoke to God that mid-
night are still vivid in my memory. "I am here taking a
stand for what I believe is right. But now I am afraid.
The people are looking to me for leadership, and if I
stand before them without strength and courage, they
too will falter. I am at the end of my powers. I have
nothing left. I've come to the point where I can't face it
alone."

At that moment I experienced the presence of the
Divine as I had never before experienced him. It
seemed as though I could hear the quiet assurance of an
inner voice, saying, "Stand up for righteousness, stand
up for truth. God will be at your side forever." My
uncertainty disappeared. I was ready to face anything.
The outer situation remained the same but God had
given me inner calm.[6]

King's theological position is deeply rooted in the
biblical tradition. He employed the insights of philosophy, social science, literature, and general historical
experience whenever their findings supported some
particular biblical understanding. This does not imply
that he adhered to any form of dogmatic fundamental-
ism. Rather, as a result of his study of theological liberalism, he continued to be impressed by the rational
quest for truth—a methodology that would provide a
firm ground for the knowledge of faith. His basic presupposition is that the biblical understanding of a God
of history, who is creator and savior, is true. "Christianity affirms that at the heart of reality is a Heart, a
loving Father who works through history for the salvation of his children."[7]

Knowledge of God, in King's understanding, is
gained only by knowing Jesus Christ in faith, which
implies a commitment to Christ. Mere scientific
knowledge is not sufficient; only the knowledge of faith
reveals the nature of God.

Where do we find God? In a test tube? No. Where else
except in Jesus Christ, the Lord of our lives? By knowing Him we know God. Christ is not only God-like, but

God is Christ-like. Christ is the word made flesh. He is the language of eternity translated in the words of time. If we are to know what God is like and understand his purposes for mankind, we must turn to Christ. By committing ourselves absolutely to Christ and his way, we will participate in that marvelous act of faith that will bring us to the true knowledge of God.[8]

King frequently drew upon the symbolism of the exodus to depict God's action in history and the inevitable self-destruction of evil. He believed that God is in control of history, guiding it to its true end, and further, that any apparent victories of evil over good are illusory. Rather, Christianity has always affirmed that in the long struggle between the forces of good and of evil, the former will be victorious, even if it be crushed to the ground. The forces of good in history are identified with God and, therefore, cannot be destroyed in any complete sense. "The death of the Egyptians upon the seashore is a vivid reminder that something in the very nature of the universe assists goodness in its perennial struggle with evil."[9] In King's understanding, every attempt to crush human exploitation and injustice is evidence of the continuation of the exodus event and of the activity of God in history.

> Above all, we must be reminded anew that God is at work in his universe. He is not outside the world looking on with a sort of cold indifference. Here on all the roads of life, he is striving in our striving. Like an ever-loving Father, he is working through history for the salvation of his children. As we struggle to defeat the forces of evil, the God of the universe struggles with us. Evil dies on the seashore, not merely because of man's struggle against it, but because of God's power to defeat it.[10]

Since King held the firm conviction that God was the creator of the universe, who protects and preserves it like a loving parent, it is not surprising that he would consider God the source and the ground for ethics. The God of Christianity is not characterized by indifference or caprice. God's will is perfect goodness; God's purpose is that all of creation might live in accordance with that will in peace, harmony, and freedom, which are the fruits of divine love. For King, theology and ethics are inseparable, since both originate from God. Even a cursory analysis of King's thought would reveal that his ethics are derived entirely from a reflection on Jesus and his prophets.

Ethical knowledge is rooted deeply in King's understanding of the nature of humanity. His argument proceeds in the following way. The question "What is man?" has been answered by materialists and by humanists. The former perceives humankind in extremely pessimistic terms, while the latter affirms an extreme optimism. After studying both positions carefully, King employed the dialectical method in order to arrive at a more realistic view of humanity, a view that would reconcile the truths implied by the materialists and by the humanists in a synthesis that would avoid the extremes of either. He considered the Christian conception of humankind to be that more realistic view. In explicating that understanding, King borrowed heavily from the thought of Reinhold Niebuhr. Christian realism recognizes the fact that a person is a unity of body and soul, of nature and spirit. The fact that God created humans with bodies implies, for King, that Christians cannot ignore bodily needs, since the condition of the soul is largely dependent on the condition of the body. He also argues that the Christian church cannot ignore social problems.

> In any realistic doctrine of man we must be forever concerned about his physical and material well-being. When Jesus said that man cannot live by bread alone, he did not imply that men can live without bread. As Christians we must think not only about "mansions in the sky," but also about the slums and ghettos that cripple the human soul, not merely about streets in heaven "flowing with milk and honey," but also about the millions of people in this world who go to bed hungry at

night. Any religion that professes concern regarding the souls of men and fails to be concerned by social conditions that corrupt and economic conditions that cripple the soul, is a do-nothing religion, in need of new blood. Such a religion fails to realize that man is an animal having physical and material needs.[11]

King, like Niebuhr, contended that a human is in nature but at the same time above nature, because "man is a being of spirit."[12] Thought, memory, and imagination enable humans to transcend the lower animals; thought and language enable them to transcend space and time. Spirit is the realm of humankind's freedom, and that is what is meant by being made in the image of God.

> This is what the Bible means when it affirms that man is made in the image of God. The imago dei has been interpreted by different thinkers in terms of fellowship, responsiveness, reason, and conscience. An abiding expression of man's higher spiritual nature is his freedom. Man is man because he is free to operate within the framework of his destiny. He is free to deliberate, to make decisions, and to choose between alternatives. He is distinguished from animals by his freedom to do evil or to do good and to walk the high road of beauty or tread the low road of ugly degeneracy.[13]

In King's opinion, it is neither the material nature nor the spiritual nature that causes one to sin against God, but rather one's will, which is the center of one's being and the agency by which choices are made. Being created in the image of God should imply that humanity is basically good, but the truth, King discovered, is more complex. Because one is free one may choose to develop in accordance with the image of God or to reject that image and go one's own way. The latter tendency appears to be more prevalent in history than the former. In turning away from the Creator, a person engages in self-destruction. Self-destruction suggests the inability to relate meaningfully to others and to God. King had no doubt that such a state of affairs is the human condition. "Engulfing human nature is a tragic, three-fold estrangement by which man is separated from himself, his neighbors and his God. There is a corruption in man's will."[14] That is to say, King believed that we are sinners in need of God's grace. Like Niebuhr, he considered this fact to be no deadening pessimism but Christian realism.

But humanity is not ignorant of its sin. Because God is always related to humans, an inner voice gives them an uneasy conscience about what they know to be wrongdoing. Frequently, King used the parable of the prodigal son to describe humanity's chosen estrangement from God, its consequent self-destruction, and God's loving forgiveness, which was available to humankind whenever it should choose to return to its senses. Similarly, he was prone to describe every condition of evil in the world as an instance of humanity straying away from God's will. Hence, he could proclaim a moral and spiritual famine throughout Western civilization. "Man has strayed to the far countries of secularism, materialism, sexuality, and racial injustice. His journey has brought a moral and spiritual famine in Western civilization. But it is not too late to return home."[15]

An important implication of King's thought about God's will is that all humankind should acknowledge God's divine parenthood and its consequent kinship. The latter should affirm no superficial boundaries of race, nation, religion, status, or class. Such a relationship is the true end of humanity, and all alternatives are ultimately self-destructive. Evil in the world is a direct result of humankind's turning away from God's will. It is manifested in the various forms of individual disintegration and intergroup animosity.

King's vision of the kinship of humans as a direct corollary of the parenthood of God pervaded his entire thought. Only the divine principle of love can hold the diversity of humankind together in a harmonious community. That kinship of persons under the parenthood of God was, in King's mind, the kingdom of God, the true end of humanity, which could be partially realized in history. His fundamental ethical norm was the Christian understanding of love as presented primarily in the Sermon on the Mount and as symbolized most vividly in the cross on which Jesus died while forgiving his enemies. King viewed Jesus as the supreme manifestation of that religious and ethical principle.

> Throughout the centuries men have sought to discover the highest good. This has been the chief quest of ethical philosophy. This was one of the big questions of Greek philosophy. The Epicureans and the Stoics sought to answer it; Plato and Aristotle sought to answer it. What is the summum bonum of life? I think I have found the answer, America. I have discovered that the highest good is love. This principle is at the center of the cosmos. It is the great unifying force of life. God is love. He who loves has discovered the clue to the meaning of ultimate reality; he who hates stands in immediate candidacy for nonbeing.[16]

God wills human kinship, and those who work to that end King considered to be working in accordance with the divine purpose. However, those who worked against this relatedness were engaged in a combat against God, blasphemed God, and rendered themselves grossly immoral. It is not difficult to see why King saw the struggle for civil rights as a religious and moral problem threatening the heart of the nation's life. He believed that only God's way of combatting evil is ever permanently effective. Therefore, he sought a method for combatting evil that could be justified by an appeal to God's will.

Throughout his writings he constantly viewed the method of nonviolence as commensurate with the principle of love. In fact, he understood nonviolence as the vehicle or form that love should assume in the struggle of the oppressed against their oppressors. Chronologically and theologically, the priority of love is made abundantly clear in a passage written soon after the Montgomery episode.

> It was the Sermon on the Mount, rather than a doctrine of passive resistance, that initially inspired the Negroes of Montgomery to dignified social action. It was Jesus of Nazareth that stirred the Negroes to protest with the creative weapon of love.
>
> As the days unfolded, however, the inspiration of Mahatma Gandhi began to exert its influence. I had come to see early that the Christian doctrine of love operating through the Gandhian method of nonviolence was one of the most potent weapons available to the Negro in his struggle for freedom. . . . Nonviolent resistance had emerged as the technique of the movement, while love stood as the regulating ideal. In other words, Christ furnished the spirit and motivation, while Gandhi furnished the method.[17]

King admitted that at one stage in his life he was disillusioned about the effectiveness of the love ethic of Jesus in social reform. He had thought it appropriate only in interpersonal relationships. But after familiarizing himself with the thought of Mahatma Gandhi, he became convinced that it could be a powerful and effective force for constructive social change. The form love should take in social action would henceforth be a massive nonviolent resistance to evil. King's indebtedness to Gandhi is the latter's legacy of a method that could give an appropriate form to love in social action. The end of love is community, and nonviolence facilitates that goal. The opposite of love is hate, which aims at the annihilation of its object and the destruction of community. King affirmed that, existentially and theologically, love was the fundamental requirement of human existence. He thought it imperative that it be projected to the center of all human living. By *love* King meant Christian *agape*.

> When we speak of loving those who oppose us, we refer to neither *eros* nor *philia*; we speak of a love which is

expressed in the Greek word *agape*. *Agape* means understanding, redeeming good will for all men. It is an
overflowing love which is purely spontaneous, unmoti-
vated, groundless, and creative. It is not set in motion
by any quality or function of its object. It is the love of
God operating in the human heart.[18]

Agape expresses the nature of God. It is thoroughly
disinterested. That is to say, it is in no way conditioned by reciprocity. It aims at loving others for their
own sakes alone. It is entirely other-directed. It makes
no meaningful distinction between friend and enemy.
It fulfills human personality; hate destroys human personality. Consequently, King would argue that since
the personalities of whites are greatly distorted by hate
in the form of racial segregation, the love of God needs
to be conveyed through Black folk in order for whites
to be saved from certain self-destruction. Blacks are
confronted with an imperative from God to love white
persons because they need that love. Pathological fears
and insecurities can only be overcome by this kind of
love. King spoke unceasingly about Jesus' command
to the disciples, in the Sermon on the Mount, to love
their enemies. Love of enemies was, in King's mind,
one of the clearest manifestations of *agape*, since it
could not expect anything good in return.

Over and over again King reminded his followers
that *agape* was for the strong and the courageous and
not for the weak and the cowardly. In spite of persecution or even death itself, *agape* works diligently and
untiringly for the realization of community—the restoration of the separated into a harmonious whole.

> *Agape* is not a weak, passive love. It is love in action.
> *Agape* is love seeking to preserve and create commu-
> nity. It is insistence on community even when one
> seeks to break it. *Agape* is a willingness to sacrifice in
> the interest of mutuality. *Agape* is a willingness to go to
> any length to restore community. It doesn't stop at the
> first mile, but it goes the second mile to restore commu-
> nity. It is a willingness to forgive, not seven times, but

seventy times seven to restore community. The cross is the eternal expression of the length to which God will go in order to restore broken community. The resurrection is a symbol of God's triumph over all the forces that seek to block community. The Holy Spirit is the continuing community creating reality that moves through history. He who works against community is working against the whole of creation. Therefore, if I respond to hate with a reciprocal hate I do nothing but intensify the cleavage in broken community. I can only close the gap in broken community by meeting hate with love. If I meet hate with hate, I become depersonalized, because creation is so designed that my personality can only be fulfilled in the context of community.[19]

King believed strongly in the idea that all people are related to one another, because God is the parent of all. Further, it was his view that community with one another and with God was the end for which humankind was intended by its creator. It follows, therefore, that those who act for the destruction of such a community not only violate God's will but become involved in their own self-destruction as well. In other words, since we are all kinspeople, the degree to which I harm that relationship in any way I harm myself. My personhood is integrally tied to the kinship of all. Thus, the agent of the harm as well as the one harmed are victimized and are in need of liberation. This line of thought led King to espouse an important principle: Those who work for community must resist those who work against it. Love resists evil passionately but according to its own laws. In the final analysis, King thought that only love could achieve a lasting victory over hate. Since God works in the world in order to restore broken community, God's followers can do none other.

King's understanding of evil is clear. Since humans were made in the image of God and for communion with God and others, all efforts to destroy that image and to disrupt that communion are antithetical to

God's will and are the essence of human evil. Those who cooperate with such evil become agents in the destruction of God's creation. It is important to note that those who would follow the love ethic of Jesus must resist evil in a loving way, since there can be no Christian virtue in using methods contrary to love in order to gain the end for which love strives. Because the end is always present in the means, the means must be commensurate with the desired end. When love resists evil it does so for the sake of the desired restoration of community. Therefore, it must love the persons from which it is estranged inasmuch as it aims at an eventual reunion. This line of thought led King to say, "While abhorring segregation, we shall love the segregationist. This is the only way to create the beloved community."[20] The utilization of destructive methods can never result in restored community. Hate and violence can only lead to increased hate and violence or, at best, a fleeting and temporary peace. For these reasons King opposed violence in every form and viewed it as necessarily opposed to the love ethic of Jesus.

King's commitment to Christian realism caused him to frequently couple the theological view of the love ethic with a practical concern. Not only was love in the form of nonviolent resistance in accord with God's will, but, he claimed, it was the most effective means available to the oppressed in their fight against injustice. Indeed, he contended that there would be no permanent solution to the race problem until oppressed people developed the capacity to love their enemies. King clearly affirmed the theological doctrine of love as an effective principle of social change.

The cross of Christ symbolized, for King, suffering and victory. Christ, the personification of *agape*, suffered an ignominious death because he dared to live consistently the life of love. In that event, history witnesses the sacrificial element implied by love. Love is no guarantor against persecution and suffering. In confronting evil it risks the possibility of suffering and death. The end it seeks is the means it employs. And so, Christ died praying for his executioners, thereby manifesting the community his life and mission exemplified. Although he was crucified, love had not been destroyed, even in its darkest hour. And that is the victory the cross symbolizes. Those who love may suffer at the hands of injustice, but injustice cannot destroy the love of God, which is always redemptive. King justified nonviolent resistance to evil by an appeal to that kind of suffering.

> One may well ask: "What is the nonviolent resister's justification for this ordeal to which he invites men, for this mass political application of the ancient doctrine of turning the other cheek?" The answer is found in the realization that unearned suffering is redemptive. Suffering, the nonviolent resister realizes, has tremendous educational and transforming possibilities. "Things of fundamental importance to people are not secured by reason alone, but have to be purchased with their suffering," said Gandhi.[21]

And on the occasion of the bombing of his home, he recalled:

> At home I addressed the crowd from my porch, where the mark of the bomb was clear. "We must not return violence under any condition. I know this is difficult advice to follow, especially since we have been the victims of no less than ten bombings. But this is the way of Christ; it is the way of the cross. We must somehow believe that unearned suffering is redemptive."[22]

King considered love to be the supreme religious and ethical principle that aims at the restoration of community between people and God and between person and person. Kinship can only be achieved by acknowledging the parenthood of God and by making a commitment to God. Time and again King rebuked those humanists who relied only on the efforts of people to achieve peace and harmony. He castigated those who waited for God to establish the kingdom and who believed that there was nothing humankind could do about it. The former attitude he associated with the Renaissance view of humanity; the latter with the Reformation.

> The doctrines of justification by faith and the priesthood of all believers are towering principles which we as Protestants must forever affirm, but the Reformation doctrine of human nature overstressed the corruption of man. The Renaissance was too optimistic, and the Reformation too pessimistic. The former so concentrated on the goodness of man that it overlooked his capacity for evil; the latter so concentrated on the wickedness of man that it overlooked his capacity for goodness.[23]

Dialectically, King took a third position, which included the limited truths implied in each. Humanity must cooperate with God in eradicating evil from the world. It cannot do it alone without excluding God from history and thereby deifying itself. God will not act as a divine monarch and destroy humankind's freedom by imposing good on the world from without. Humanity and God must work together in order to preserve the true nature of both. It is God's nature to struggle against evil in God's own way since the universe was created with a moral structure. God created humans in God's own image, thereby bestowing upon them dignity and worth and freedom. Humanity has sinned against God, but the sin has not been absolute. The *imago Dei* has not been completely destroyed. Therefore, humankind has the capacity (though difficult to energize) to discern the presence of evil and to confront it. When it does so, God is on its side. "In our sometimes difficult and often lonesome walk up freedom's road, we do not walk alone. God walks with us. He has placed within the very structure of this universe certain absolute moral laws."[24]

In King's opinion, it was important not to lose sight of the fact that God supported those who combatted evil only when they acted in love and for the sake of the restoration of kinship. The strength and courage needed for such an enterprise came from God's grace, and the agents became renewed persons fighting for a divinely righteous cause.

> Admitting the weighty problems and staggering disappointments, Christianity affirms that God is able to give us the power to meet them. He is able to give us the inner equilibrium to stand tall amid the trials and burdens of life. He is able to provide inner peace amid outer storms. This inner stability of the man of faith is Christ's chief legacy to his disciples. He offers neither material resources nor a magical formula that exempts us from suffering and persecution, but he brings an imperishable gift: "Peace I leave with thee." This is that peace which passeth all understanding.[25]

One important implication of King's God-centered ethic is that humanity's ultimate loyalty ought to be to God and not to any human-made construct.

> Living in the colony of time, we are ultimately responsible to the empire of eternity. As Christians we must never surrender our supreme loyalty to any time-bound custom or earth-bound idea, for at the heart of our universe is a higher reality—God and his kingdom of love—to which we must be conformed.[26]

King could speak of the righteousness of the nonconformist who was imbued with the spirit of God. But more important, a certain amount of conflict exists in the heart of God, namely, opposition to evil. King made it amply clear that the gospel of Christianity is one that seeks social change religiously and morally. This twofold function of the gospel is what he thought the church frequently had ignored.

> Yet the Church is challenged to make the gospel of Jesus Christ relevant within the social situation. We must come to see that the Christian gospel is a two-way road. On the one side, it seeks to change the souls of men and thereby unite them with God; on the other, it

seeks to change the environmental conditions of men so that the soul will have a chance after it is changed. Any religion that professes to be concerned with the souls of men and yet is not concerned with the economic and social conditions that strangle them and the social conditions that cripple them is the kind the Marxist describes as "an opiate of the people."[27]

King contended that those who know the will of God ought to oppose evil whenever they see it, because that is the will of God. Such people must risk everything in order to be faithful. Being moral means acting to realize God's will, and such action must take precedence over social conformity and respectability. In the face of evil, King called the Christian church to assume a prophetic posture and rebuked it whenever it was slothful, impatient, or neglectful. He considered the church to be the moral conscience of the nation. Unfortunately, its failures are legion.

The church must be reminded that it is not the master or the servant of the state, but rather the conscience of the state. It must be the guide and the critic of the state, and never its tool. If the church does not recapture its prophetic zeal, it will become an irrelevant social club without moral or spiritual authority. If the church does not participate actively in the struggle for peace and for economic and racial justice, it will forfeit the loyalty of millions and cause men everywhere to say that it has atrophied its will. But if the church will free itself from the shackles of a deadening status quo, and, recovering its great historic mission, will speak and act fearlessly and insistently in terms of justice and peace, it will enkindle the imagination of mankind and fire the souls of men, imbuing them with a glowing and ardent love for truth, justice and peace.[28]

Now that we have seen in broad outline the major structure of King's theological and political thought, let us look more closely at the several issues that were highlighted in chapter 1, in order to see why King assumed the position he did on each of them.

Civil Disobedience

Martin Luther King's respect for the law is well known. He constantly sought to convince his followers that nonviolent direct action did not imply any disrespect for the just laws of the land, inasmuch as it was always practiced for the sake of legal justice. Further, the method is justified by the Constitution of the United States, which provides for legal protest as the means for the redress of grievances. King opposed all forms of anarchy with a passion similar to that with which he opposed tyranny. Since he considered the fundamental problem in America to be the moral cleavage between the national practice and the law of the cosmos, and since the civil rights movement was intended to be the agent for moral reform, he advocated a method for that reform that he could justify by an appeal to the moral law of the universe. He deemed it significant that the Constitution was a document that described truths in accord with that moral law. However, he viewed the nation's customs and practices as contradictions of that law, and consequently, he had no difficulty in appealing to the Constitution as a source for justifying many of his actions since that law was commensurate with the universal moral law. In his estimation, just laws ought always to be obeyed.

But during the Birmingham campaign King came face to face with the attempt of the legal enforcement agencies to use the moral arm of the law for immoral practices, namely, to impede the progress of a moral social reform movement. Such a tactic had been used before (most effectively in Albany, where King had been released suddenly from a forty-five–day jail sentence which, to dramatize the demands of the Black community, he had chosen to serve instead of paying a fine)[29] and had crippled the movement to such a degree that virtually none of its goals could be realized. The movement frequently searched for a means of counteracting injunctions that were cloaked in legal framework but that were aimed at the perpetuation of injustice. Therefore, when the decision was finally made to take an audacious new step in the history of the movement, much prayer and deliberation preceded such a move. That is to say, King did not undertake acts of civil disobedience in a casual way.

> We did not take this radical step without prolonged and prayerful consideration. Planned, deliberate civil disobedience had been discussed as far back as the meeting at Harry Belafonte's apartment in March. There, in consultation with some of the closest friends of the movement, we had decided that if an injunction was issued to thwart our demonstrators, it would be our duty to violate it. To some, this will sound contradictory and morally indefensible. We, who contend for justice, and who oppose those who will not honor the law of the Supreme Court and the rulings of federal agencies, were saying that we would overtly violate a court order.[30]

The reasons King gave for justifying such civil disobedience are, in the first place, practical:

> The injunction method has now become the leading instrument of the South to block the direct-action civil-rights drive and to prevent Negro citizens and their white allies from engaging in peaceable assembly, a right guaranteed by the First Amendment. . . . This has been a maliciously effective, pseudo-legal way of breaking the back of legitimate moral protest.[31]

Second, the justification was based on the conviction that the injunction served immoral ends and, therefore, was itself immoral. At the same time King insisted on a distinction between anarchy and incidental civil disobedience. The former represents a political philosophy, while the latter is contextually strategic. "We were not anarchists advocating lawlessness, but . . . it was obvious to us that the courts of Alabama had misused the judicial process in order to perpetuate injustice and segregation. Consequently, we could not, in good conscience, obey their findings."[32]

Later, in the "Letter from a Birmingham Jail," King appealed to Augustine as an authority for offering a theological justification for civil disobedience.

> The answer lies in the fact that there are two types of laws: just and unjust. I would be the first to advocate obeying just laws. One has not only a legal but a moral responsibility to obey just laws. Conversely, one has a moral responsibility to disobey unjust laws. I would agree with St. Augustine that "an unjust law is no law at all."[33]

Since King had advocated time and again that those who acquiesce to evil participate in promoting evil and are, therefore, as much the agents of evil as the initiators themselves, he concluded that one could not be moral by obeying immoral laws. But the troublesome question for many who have debated the issue is how one knows when a law is unjust. King answered that question in the following way:

> How does one determine whether a law is just or unjust? A just law is a man-made code that squares with the moral law or the law of God. An unjust law is a code that is out of harmony with the moral law. To put it in the terms of St. Thomas Aquinas: An unjust law is a human law that is not rooted in eternal law and natural law. Any law that uplifts human personality is just. Any law that degrades human personality is unjust. All segregation statutes are unjust because segregation distorts the soul and damages the personality. It gives the segregator a false sense of superiority and the segregated a false sense of inferiority. Segregation, to use the terminology of the Jewish philosopher Martin Buber, substitutes an "I-it" relationship for an "I-thou" relationship and ends up relegating persons to the status of

things. Hence segregation is not only politically, economically and sociologically unsound, it is morally wrong and sinful. Paul Tillich has said that sin is separation. Is not segregation an existential expression of man's tragic separation, his awful estrangement, his terrible sinfulness? Thus it is that I can urge men to obey the 1954 decision of the Supreme Court, for it is morally right; and I can urge them to disobey segregation ordinances, for they are morally wrong.[34]

In the above passage, which represents his best reasoning on the subject, King appealed to the authority of Catholic, Protestant, and Jewish theologians to support his understanding of how one identifies unjust laws. He gave certain examples:

An unjust law is a code that a numerical or power majority group compels a minority group to obey but does not make binding on itself. . . .

A law is unjust if it is inflicted on a minority that, as a result of being denied the right to vote, had no part in enacting or devising the law. . . .

Sometimes a law is just on its face and unjust in its application.[35]

King contended that the breaking of unjust laws must be done in the spirit of love and with a willingness to accept the penalty. The latter attitude demonstrates a high regard for law in principle.

One who breaks an unjust law must do so openly, lovingly, and with a willingness to accept the penalty. I submit that an individual who breaks a law that conscience tells him is unjust, and who willingly accepts the penalty of imprisonment in order to arouse the conscience of the community over its injustice, is in reality expressing the highest respect for law.[36]

Occasionally, King called upon biblical and historical examples to strengthen his justification of civil disobedience: the refusal of Shadrach, Meshach, and Abednego to obey the laws of Nebuchadnezzar be-

cause of their loyalty to a higher moral law; the refusal
of the early Christians to compromise their faith with
the laws of the Roman Empire; the refusal of the
Greek philosopher Socrates to compromise his principles with the conflicting laws of the state; the refusal of
the American revolutionaries to be taxed without representation.

School Boycotts

Most of the common arguments opposing school
boycotts were based on the premise that schoolchildren should not be encouraged to oppose the school
system, lest they lose respect for school authorities and
become disillusioned about the educational process.
King, on the contrary, supported school boycotts that
were undertaken self-consciously in the spirit of love
and nonviolence. In his understanding, nobody, including children, should be encouraged to cooperate
with evil. It was, he believed, that quiet acquiescence
in which Black folk had been nurtured since childhood
that had given them a false sense of inferiority. He
thought it infinitely more noble to stand up and resist
evil. Characters formed in that mode of action, if
guided by love and aimed at the realization of kinship,
would manifest the kind of dignity and worth and freedom that all persons ought to embody. The use of children in demonstrations also had a practical effect; it
aroused sympathy on the part of national observers,
who often saw them harassed and beaten by the perpetrators of racism. King was able to say, "Looking back,
it is clear that the introduction of Birmingham's children into the campaign was one of the wisest moves
we made. It brought a new impact to the crusade, and
the impetus that we needed to win the struggle."[37]
In King's mind, the movement represented the embodiment of the moral law. He could conceive nothing
evil in children participating in such a moral struggle.
Rather, he praised those who did and strongly heart-
ened others. The only alternative they had was to go

on submitting to an evil system and, in the process, to have their characters formed by immoral and self-defeating action. Children going to jail for a righteous cause was a manifestation of morality itself.

> A significant body of young people learned that in op-posing the tyrannical forces that were crushing them they added stature and meaning to their lives. Negro and white youth who in alliance fought bruising engage-ments with the status quo inspired each other with a sense of moral mission and both gave the nation an example of self-sacrifice and dedication.[38]

Over and over again King reminded his audiences that children have often been used for evil purposes in history and that they have usually been the most dam-aged victims of social injustice. The civil rights move-ment chose to employ the energies and imaginative creativity of children and young people for construc-tive, moral purposes. King was convinced that the ef-forts of Black children inspired the emergent white youth to take to the streets to protest immorality. Fur-ther, he viewed the participation of Black youth in the movement as a source of inspiration for the founding of the Peace Corps. The movement provided a chan-nel for the anger of youth to be utilized constructively and afforded a vehicle for the development of disci-pline and moral virtue. The youth know that the Black and the poor live in a cruelly unjust society. If their anger is not channeled positively, it will explode in the form of violence. But if they be committed to the use of nonviolence, they will aim their attack against in-justice and not against the lives of the persons who are their fellow citizens. They will fight against structures of injustice and not against people.

King had no problem supporting school boycotts in New York or in Chicago once he became convinced that the problem was segregation and/or discrimina-tion and that the participants in the boycotts were committed to the philosophy of nonviolence as the principal mode of action.

Civil Rights Legislation

Much of King's activity was aimed at the more proximate goal of effecting legislative change, chiefly at the federal level, in order to establish and protect the civil rights of Black people. Many of his critics considered his emphasis on legislative change to be far too great. King, however, was not persuaded, in spite of his knowledge of the limitation of law and law enforcement. He was never deluded into thinking that laws can change the hearts of people or that the existence of just laws is in itself sufficient for the emergence of the community of kindred human beings. However, he did believe that just laws and their enforcement could alter the behavior of citizens. Just laws in any state become necessary conditions for the eventual emergence of the association of related individuals. King actually thought in terms of two goals for society, one being justice and the other kinship. Justice is manifested in just laws, and the presence of the latter is a necessary step to the final goal of kinship. Just laws are the means to the goal of love. Justice is commensurate with love, because it works for the end of love by uplifting the welfare of the society and the personhood of individuals. Insofar as the structural framework of a society fosters justice, it performs the work of love.

It was King's opinion that the problems of racial segregation and discrimination were rooted in the legal framework of southern society. He acted, therefore, to cause the federal government to correct those legal injustices by enforcing existing laws and by enacting new ones wherever necessary. Since the federal government was always slow to act constructively for civil rights, King engaged in direct nonviolent confrontation with the local forces of evil in order to coerce the government to see the gravity of the problem and to act effectively for its resolution. Because the rights of persons in the United States have been understood largely in political and civil terms, finding their clearest expression in

the Declaration of Independence and in the Bill of
Rights of the Constitution, King constantly referred to
those two documents to support his claims regarding
the rights of Black folk. He regarded such rights to be a
person's due. Black people were not asking for anything
special. They had been denied their constitutional
rights for too long. Inasmuch as the rights of people
were determined by law, King found it appropriate to
aim his action at the law in order to attain those rights.
The actualization of just laws, however, was only a
means to that final goal King envisioned, namely, the
universal kinship of humankind. Just laws would aim
at effecting desegregation, but desegregation ought not
to be confused with integration. The relationship between love, justice, and law is nowhere described more
clearly than in the following:

> We must admit that the ultimate solution to the race
> problem lies in the willingness of men to obey the unen-
> forceable. Court orders and federal enforcement agen-
> cies are of inestimable value in achieving desegregation,
> but desegregation is only a partial, though necessary,
> step toward the final goal which we seek to realize, gen-
> uine intergroup and interpersonal living. Desegregation
> will break down the legal barriers and bring men to-
> gether physically, but something must touch the hearts
> and souls of men so that they will come together spiri-
> tually because it is natural and right. A vigorous en-
> forcement of civil rights laws will bring an end to
> segregated public facilities which are barriers to a truly
> desegregated society, but it cannot bring an end to
> fears, prejudice, pride, and irrationality, which are the
> barriers to a truly integrated society. These dark and
> demonic responses will be removed only as men are
> possessed by the invisible, inner law which etches on
> their hearts the conviction that all men are brothers and
> that love is mankind's most potent weapon for personal
> and social transformation. True integration will be
> achieved by true neighbors who are willingly obedient
> to unenforceable obligations.[39]

Thus, King understood justice as providing the formal structures for the good society, the substance of which would be provided by love. Love, however, needs the just structures, and the just structures provide the vehicle through which love expresses itself. In the present struggle, King believed the end of justice to be desegregation and that of love to be the integrated society.

> The word *segregation* represents a system that is prohibitive; it denies the Negro equal access to schools, parks, restaurants, libraries and the like. *Desegregation* is eliminative and negative, for it simply removes these legal and social prohibitions. Integration is creative, and is therefore more profound and far-reaching than desegregation. Integration is the positive acceptance of desegregation and the welcomed participation of Negroes into the total range of human activities.[40]

King observed that love and justice are compatible. Their relationship is similar to the relationship between desegregation and integration or that relationship between the just laws of the state and the ultimate goals of kinship. He was always cognizant of the limitations of government action and of the federal judiciary, but seeing their limits did not blind him to their importance. More important, he was never satisfied with the action of the government, which he considered too slow and quite insufficient. As a result, he was never able to endorse any particular presidential candidate, although he admitted that had John F. Kennedy lived he probably would have supported him. King's critical stance with respect to the seriousness of America about effecting racial equality through legislative reform and enforcement continued to the end of his life. "Every civil rights law is still substantially more dishonored than honored."[41] He contended that to be true of education, the franchise, open occupancy, employment, and practically all other goals that civil rights groups have attempted to effect. One of his most

extreme statements about the failure of the legal structures is contained in the following:

> The legal structures have in practice proved to be nei-
> ther structures nor law. The sparse and insufficient col-
> lection of statutes is not a structure; it is barely a naked
> framework. Legislation that is evaded, substantially
> nullified and unenforced is a mockery of law. Signifi-
> cant progress has effectively been barred by the cunning
> obstruction of segregationists. It has been barred by
> equivocations and retreats of government—the same
> government that was exultant when it sought political
> credit for enacting the measures.[42]

King's experience in the civil rights movement
taught him that significant social change in race relations would not happen easily or with a minimum
amount of suffering. He came to see that freedom is
won and not given, that the privileged do not give up
their privileges freely. Rather, those privileges must be
wrested from them. It was not easy for him to spend a
decade struggling to effect legislative change only to
see the laws formally written in the records but inade-
quately enforced. The struggle for Blacks seemed un-
ending at times. Their many and daring marches and
the suffering endured in most of them were necessary
to get what formal changes did occur. More and more
direct nonviolent demonstrations became necessary in
order to effect the enforcement of the law. This, for
King, was a sad commentary on American life, but he
refused to give up hope, because he believed that hope
was virtually the vitality of life. And that hope is sustained only by continued action against evil.

Black Power

One of the great traumas of King's career was the
emergence of Black Power, hailed by many as a political and cultural symbol that implied a new orientation
for Black people in America. Its agents, in the main,

were dissident young followers of King. Its rhetoric took the form of a new idiom or, at least, one distinctly different from that of King. Its proponents openly disassociated themselves from the love ethic of King and the philosophy of nonviolent resistance. They advocated power instead of love and self-defense instead of nonviolent resistance. The ethic of turning the other cheek was anathema to them. They advocated Black separatism and opposed the presence of whites in their movement.

In 1967 King wrote *Where Do We Go from Here: Chaos or Community?* seemingly for the purpose of answering the advocates of Black Power by demonstrating its errors in the light of his own philosophy. The book was King's public admission of an ideological split within the movement. King justified nonviolence by an appeal to love and, therefore, viewed it as intrinsically moral and in opposition to its alternative, violence. Time and again he buttressed the moral argument for nonviolence with a pragmatic concern that violence in the struggle for civil rights would be self-defeating. Further, King's belief in the ultimate goal of the kinship of all people in the blessed community prevented him from entertaining any argument whatsoever that would bar whites from participation in the movement. He agreed that the leadership of the movement ought to be in the hands of Blacks but strongly disagreed with any move toward racial separation. After all, racial togetherness was the moral goal of the movement and the ultimate goal of society. He repeatedly admonished his followers that the means must be commensurate with the ends. Hence, if racial togetherness be the ultimate end, then that end ought to be manifested in the means. Since King's theological position on racial togetherness was so dominant in his understanding of society and politics, it was virtually impossible for him to grant value to any proposition that would affirm racial separation.

King was convinced that the concept of Black Power was basically an emotional one and, therefore, was unsuitable to be a slogan for the movement. He considered it an unfortunate combination of words because of its implications connoting domination, violence, and racial chauvinism. In fact, he perceived it to be the antithesis of his movement and ideology. He tried to demonstrate how the positive tenets of Black Power were embodied in his philosophy, thus attempting to weaken its importance as a viable alternative.

First, he viewed Black Power as a negative slogan arising out of disappointing and frustrating experiences with the instigators of injustice. "It is necessary to understand that Black Power is a cry of disappointment. . . . So in reality the call for Black Power is a reaction to the failure of white power."[43]

King had no difficulty in agreeing with the charge that whites in positions of power acted inconsistently and faintheartedly on issues pertaining to the welfare of Blacks. He agreed with the apparent intransigence of racial injustice in the South, the irritating gradualism of the federal government and its timidity in enforcing civil rights laws, the plight of Blacks in urban ghettos, and much more. On the descriptive level he agreed that Blacks have suffered innumerable disappointments and agonizing frustrations because of the great gap between America's promises and its practices. But, in his mind, disappointment can lead easily to a loss of hope, which is the state of despair, and despair is the bedrock of hate and bitterness. "But revolution, though born of despair, cannot long be sustained by despair. This is the ultimate contradiction of the Black Power movement. . . . It rejects the one thing that keeps the fire of revolutions burning: the ever-present flame of hope."[44]

King believed that one ought to acknowledge the reality of disappointment but not succumb to despair because of it. Hope is the vitality of life. One must cling to hope in spite of the crushing blows of disappointment; one must do that in order to preserve the moral integrity of oneself. Bitterness, hatred, self-pity, and fatalism are self-destructive.

Our most fruitful course is to stand firm, move forward nonviolently, accept disappointments and cling to hope. Our determined refusal not to be stopped will eventually open the door to fulfillment. By recognizing the necessity of suffering in a righteous cause, we may achieve our humanity's full stature. To guard ourselves from bitterness, we need the vision to see in this generation's ordeals the opportunity to transfigure both ourselves and American society.[45]

Second, King affirmed Black Power's call to Black people to amass sufficient power to realize political, economic, and social goals via legitimate means. No one knew better than he the plight that powerless Black people have endured throughout their history in this country. Further, no one knew better than he the importance of power to effect meaningful change in any and all dimensions of social life. Indeed, he had viewed nonviolent resistance to evil as that power necessary to effect such change. The concept of power, therefore, did not trouble him, but rather, he rejected any force that was alienated from the principle of love. The influence of Paul Tillich is unmistakable as King describes the relation of power, love, and justice.

Power, properly understood, is the ability to achieve purpose. It is the strength required to bring about social, political or economic changes. In this sense power is not only desirable but necessary in order to implement the demands of love and justice. One of the greatest problems of history is that the concepts of love and power are usually contrasted as polar opposites. Love is identified with a resignation of power and power with a denial of love. . . . What is needed is a realization that power without love is reckless and abusive and that love without power is sentimental and anemic. Power at its best is love implementing the demands of justice. Justice at its best is love correcting everything that stands against love.[46]

King feared that Black Power was launching out to

do battle against racism by an immoral use of power. Such an enterprise would involve its proponents in the contradiction of using immoral means to attain a moral end. However, insofar as Black Power advocated the need to strengthen Black political power by bloc voting and to strengthen economic security by massive federal programs and consumer and product boycotts, King saw no problem, since he himself had supported such measures for many years.

However, King and the Black Power espousers were irreconcilably divided on the issue of coalitions with whites. The Black Power bloc was rigidly opposed to any such coalitions; King felt that Blacks could gain nothing in isolation from whites. He considered racial isolationism morally and practically unsound.

> Any program that elects all black candidates simply because they are black and rejects all white candidates simply because they are white is politically unsound and morally unjustifiable. The basic thing in determining the best candidate is not his color but his integrity.[47]

King was convinced that no group could make it in a pluralistic society in isolation. Political power, economic power, and social power can only be attained by virtue of wise and realistic coalitions between Black people and white liberals. "To succeed in a pluralistic society, and an often hostile one at that, the Negro obviously needs organized strength, but that strength will only be effective when it is consolidated through constructive alliances with the majority group."[48] King's arguments for coalitions were often grounded by practical considerations, but their moral foundation was always implicit. He believed in power for Blacks but never absolute power or even the quest for absolute power. Even if Blacks were able to acquire power in isolation from whites, he regarded such as being morally wrong because of the socially interdependent nature of humans, which is empirically perceived and morally necessary. In short, isolationism could never lead to the ultimate end of community and kinship, which is the end love seeks.

Black Power was understood by King to be an attempt to radicalize one side of reality. Its tenets regarding Black personhood, racial pride and solidarity and self-respect, and economic and political capacity to determine one's destiny were considered by him to be praiseworthy only if they were conceived in the context of the kinship of all persons. He had no delusions about the innate moral integrity of Black people. Rather, he believed that they could be as capable of opportunism, human exploitation, and racial injustice as were white people. Most of all, he perceived in Black Power and in its backers an implicit attempt to make violence a virtue. Violence, based on hatred and bitterness, can never lead to kinship but only to increased personal and social disruption. He perceived deep down within the courageous efforts of slave insurrectionists, the urban riots, and other forms of Black violence a pathological desire for self-destruction and suicide. King abhorred violence and thought it wrong on both practical and moral grounds.

> The beauty of nonviolence is that in its own way and in its own time it seeks to break the chain reaction of evil. With a majestic sense of spiritual power, it seeks to elevate truth, beauty and goodness to the throne. Therefore I will continue to follow this method because I think it is the most practically sound and morally excellent way for the Negro to achieve freedom. . . .
>
> Occasionally in life one develops a conviction so precious and meaningful that he will stand on it till the end. This is what I have found in non-violence.[49]

He considered nonviolence to be the new kind of power the world so desperately needed. Further, he felt that the discipline of nonviolence would mold the kind of character in people that alone will save the nation and the world. It was his observation that the violence implied by Black Power was virtually a regress to a primitive law of retaliation and was totally contradictory to the moral law of the universe.

The Goodness of America

Whenever King had an occasion to speak about the virtues of America, he usually began by enthusiastically praising the Declaration of Independence and the Constitution. Foremost in his theological understanding was the Christian view of the nature of humanity, namely, the fact that people were created with dignity and worth—beings free to choose their own destiny. He believed the worth of human personality to be one of the major affirmations in the American creed. "America is a great nation, offering to the world, through the Declaration of Independence, the most eloquent and unequivocal expression of the dignity of man ever set forth in a socio-political document."[50] Similarly, King frequently extolled America's immense technological achievements, which have made it one of the most productive nations in the world. But one of his most severe judgments on America was that it had virtually deified productivity, choosing a way of life governed by a practical materialism that is more interested in things than in values, in profits than persons. In a like manner he judged the entire Western civilization and attributed the fall of nations to such moral decay. In short, King was very circumspect about his praise of America. On the one hand, America is based on a constitution that depicts ideals that are praiseworthy. But, on the other hand, for purposes of economic gain, America suffered millions of Africans to be held in a system of brutal slavery for several centuries. When slavery was finally abolished, the United States adopted a new system of oppression called racial segregation. In both instances, the moral law of the universe was violated by depriving human beings of their freedom, which alone is the prerequisite for personhood and kinship. By such deprivation the United States, for the most part, has lost its own true nature, which can only be recovered by a loving coercion and a willing choice.

> Ever since the signing of the Declaration of Independence, America has manifested a schizophrenic personality on the question of race. She has been torn between selves—a self in which she has proudly professed democracy and a self in which she has sadly practiced the antithesis of democracy. The reality of segregation, like slavery, has always had to confront the ideals of democracy and Christianity. Indeed, segregation and discrimination are strange paradoxes in a nation founded on the principle that all men are created equal.[51]

King frequently spoke about an objective moral law in the universe. He also spoke about the forces of evil that caught up persons and nations. In his view, the United States had been so entrapped. He contended that in that entrapment, it had constructed institutions and systems of injustice to perpetuate evil. As a result of these feelings, he wrote about the crisis in Montgomery as being initiated by and evidence of the struggle between cosmic forces of good and evil.

> The crisis was not produced by outside agitators, NAACP'ers, Montgomery Protesters, or even the Supreme Court. The crisis developed, paradoxically, when the most sublime principles of American democracy— imperfectly realized for almost two centuries—began fulfilling themselves and met with the brutal resistance of forces seeking to contract and repress freedom's growth.[52]

King repeatedly mentioned the necessity for a revolution in order to eradicate the evil of racism. Indeed, he considered the civil rights movement to be that necessary revolution. He grieved over the fact that racism had shaped the character of the American people. "The strands of prejudice toward Negroes are tightly wound around the American character."[53] King believed that racism was present in the American consciousness long before there were significant numbers of Blacks on these shores. The policy of genocide toward the Indians marks that fact. The corruption of the national ideals and the American character is very deep. That depth must be illumined before there can be meaningful change. "This long-standing racist ideology has corrupted and diminished our democratic ideals. It is this tangled web of prejudice from which many Americans now seek to liberate themselves, without realizing how deeply it has been woven into their consciousness."[54]

King acknowledged that America was potentially a good nation but had grievously sinned against God and its citizenry by attempting to enable one part of the nation to live in freedom while the other part is forced into servitude. America's customs and mores and institutions are corrupted by the sins of racism. America is in a moral dilemma. On the one hand, it espouses freedom and dignity for all; on the other hand, these rights are denied to a full 10 percent of the population. "Overwhelmingly America is still struggling with irresolution and contradictions."[55]

It was King's belief that some Americans wanted significant social change in race relations but that the vast majority, although uneasy in their consciences about racial injustice, supported only formal changes that were lacking in substance. By remembering such formal changes with nostalgic pride, white America participates in a process of self-delusion and false vanity. That delusion evidences the fact that the consciences of white Americans burn only dimly. Although acute brutality is frowned upon, no justice at the deepest level can be expected short of the coercive and creative force of Black people engaging in nonviolent resistance. Succinctly, King considered white America psychologically incapable of initiating justice. Therefore, he saw the purpose of Blacks in the civil rights movement to be twofold: self-liberation and the liberation of white people.

King was not deluded about the moral virtue of the nation's founders, in spite of the fact that he often spoke of them as great persons—but great only in certain respects. They also were entrapped by the evils of racism, and they assisted its progress by constructing a social order that is systemically racist. Racism inhered in the souls of America's originators and in the political, economic, and religious institutions of the land. "Virtually all of the Founding Fathers of our nation, even those who rose to the heights of the Presidency, those whom we cherish as our authentic heroes, were so enmeshed in the ethos of slavery and white supremacy that not one ever emerged with a clear, unambiguous stand on Negro rights."[56] From the beginning King felt that America had manifested an ambivalent attitude on the question of racial justice. Racism has been institutionalized in a thousand different ways. The systems of law have been allowed to be corrupted by the practice of a dual enforcement method. That is to say, those laws that protect the civil liberties of Blacks are usually not enforced. Further, institutions of law that are themselves based on morality have been often used for immoral purposes, namely, to perpetuate injustice on Blacks. In the South, in particular, courts of law and law enforcement agencies provided ample evidence of this fact. And so, the fundamental conflict in American life penetrates the heart of the nation. Theoretically, the nation is committed to the kinship of all. Practically, it is oriented to keeping Blacks subservient in all phases of the social order. Democratic ideals and fascist practices exist in contradiction with each other. Therefore, since America is systemically racist, King called for forms of social action aimed at systemic change.

At no time did King possess an extreme pessimism toward America. He believed in the possibility of social change, because he believed that America's sin had not completely destroyed its potential for good; the good could be reclaimed. As with the prodigal son, it was not yet too late for America to change and construct a more just social order. America still had a conscience that could be appealed to for effective change.

The racism of today is real, but the democratic spirit that has always faced it is equally real. The value in pulling racism out of its obscurity and stripping it of its rationalizations lies in the confidence that it can be changed. To live with the pretense that racism is a doctrine of a very few is to disarm us in fighting it frontally as scientifically unsound, morally repugnant and socially destructive. The prescription for the cure rests with the accurate diagnosis of the disease. A people who began a national life inspired by a vision of society of brotherhood can redeem itself. But redemption can come only through a humble acknowledgement of guilt and an honest knowledge of self.[57]

King's theological description of America's sin is nowhere presented more graphically than in the following:

America has strayed to the far country of racism. The home that all too many Americans left was solidly structured idealistically. Its pillars were soundly grounded in the insights of our Judeo-Christian heritage: all men are made in the image of God; all men are brothers; all men are created equal; every man is heir to a legacy of dignity and worth; every man has rights that are neither conferred by nor derived from the state. They are God-given. What a marvellous foundation for any home. What a glorious place to inhabit. But America strayed away; and this excursion has brought only confusion and bewilderment. It has left hearts aching with guilt and minds distorted with irrationality. It has driven wisdom from the throne. This long and callous sojourn in the far country of racism has brought a moral and spiritual famine to the nation.[58]

King's Baptist tradition had taught him that whenever one wishes to be redeemed from sin one must, first of all, become knowledgeable about the nature of that sin and consciously repent and seek forgiveness. So, too, with the nation. He believed that the entire civil rights movement was aimed at giving America some self-consciousness about its sin in the hope that when the evil was clearly seen, the nation would respond by casting it out. Therefore, he felt justified in his speeches and writings to describe in vivid terms the nature of the country's sin. It was done in love, however. As he instructed his followers to love the sinner while hating the sin, so his posture toward America was one of love for the nation and of resistance to its evil. The desired goal would be a victory over neither persons nor the nation but over evil in its various expressive forms. When the evil has been eradicated, then all persons will have a chance to realize their potentiality in a national community of kinship that would partially manifest the blessed community of God.

Struggle Against Poverty

At the time of his assassination King was engaged in planning a Poor Peoples' Campaign, to take place in Washington, D.C. Some viewed this as a new issue in King's program. But that was not the case. As early as the Montgomery bus boycott, King had expressed his thoughts about the close relationship between racial segregation and poverty among Blacks. Segregation, he believed, deprived Blacks not only of their civil and political rights but also of the opportunity to acquire economic security. In his mind, all forms of human subjugation were instances of injustice. Early in his life he was bewildered by the affluence of the few and the poverty of the many. Although he never became a Marxist, his study of Marxism caused him to see the dangerous problems inherent in traditional capitalism. His understanding was that some kind of synthesis between capitalism and Marxism was required in order to gain justice in the economic domain. Once again his reasoning on this subject is marked by Tillich's influence.

> My reading of Marx also convinced me that truth is found neither in Marxism nor in traditional capitalism.

Each represents a partial truth. Historically capitalism failed to see the truth in individual enterprise. Nineteenth-century capitalism failed to see that life is social and Marxism failed and still fails to see that life is individual and personal. The Kingdom of God is neither the thesis of individual enterprise nor the antithesis of collective enterprise, but a synthesis which reconciles the truths of both.[59]

Since the reality of poverty is evidence of economic injustice, King affirmed that one ought to struggle against such injustice in a creative way. To cooperate with injustice would be to participate in the perpetuation of evil; this would necessarily be wrong. He constantly reminded the church of its important responsibilities in the area of relieving suffering wrought by injustice. Time and again he chastised the church for its laziness, its indifference, and, most of all, for its historical support of the agencies and institutions in the society that were bent on maintaining various forms of injustice. Insofar as the church complies with injustice, it blasphemes its Lord.

> The Christian ought always to be challenged by any protest against unfair treatment of the poor, for Christianity is itself such a protest, nowhere expressed more eloquently than in Jesus' words: "The Spirit of the Lord is upon me, because he hath anointed me to preach the gospel to the poor; he hath sent me to heal the brokenhearted, to preach deliverance to the captives, and recovering of sight to the blind, to set at liberty them that are bruised, to preach the acceptable year of the Lord."[60]

Further, because a human being is a unity of body and soul, King judged it incumbent on the church to be as concerned about bodily and material needs as it appeared to be with the needs of the soul. "Only an irrelevant religion fails to be concerned about man's economic well-being. Religion at its best realizes that the soul is crushed as long as the body is tortured with hunger pangs and harrowed with the need for shelter."[61]

King viewed economic justice as a necessary structural framework for the ultimate end, the blessed community. He went so far as to argue that the egalitarianism so eloquently set out in the Constitution implied economic justice for its citizenry as well as political justice. One looks in vain in King's writings to discover any emphasis on the Horatio Alger myth, which says that the autonomous person is the author of his or her own socioeconomic development. In relation to the condition of Blacks, it is reasonable to say that he did not consider it applicable, since Blacks had been forced into poverty by the structures of racial injustice. In some of his writings he actually came close to advocating some form of reparations for Blacks who have been excluded from so much in American society for so long. He considered the Marshall Plan, unemployment compensation, Social Security, occupational training, and the GI Bill as examples of the society's recognition of the necessity of granting compensation to those who have lost time in preparing for economic participation or to those who have been forced out of the marketplace through no fault of their own. Further, he noted that common law has always justified the legitimacy of such practices.

> No amount of gold could provide an adequate compensation for the exploitation and humiliation of the Negro in America down through the centuries. Not all the wealth of this affluent society could meet the bill. Yet a price can be placed on unpaid wages. The ancient common law has always provided a remedy for the appropriation of the labor of one human being by another. This law should be made to apply for American Negroes. The payment should be in the form of a massive program by the government of special, compensatory measures which could be regarded as a settlement in accordance with the accepted practice of common law.

Such measures would certainly be less expensive than any computation based on two centuries of unpaid wages and accumulated interest.[62]

King often described the debilitating effects of poverty in ways similar to his treatment of the victimizing effects of racism: both are destructive of human personality; both are disrespectful of persons and treat them as things. The attempt to make persons into things is, in King's thinking, prime evidence of gross immorality. The victims of racism and poverty are entrapped creatures who are deprived of freedom and personal dignity. King viewed racism and poverty as moral problems that could be resolved. However, he did not think the resolution would come easily. Those in power rarely alter the scale in favor of social justice without pressure. Hence, King became convinced that the struggle for economic justice necessitated direct confrontation between the haves and the have-nots. Since such an ethical appeal must employ ethical means, he advocated the method of nonviolent confrontation through demonstrations, boycotts, and negotiation. King was impressed with the labor movement, even though it had many limitations, especially on the question of racial justice. Despite those limitations, he was convinced that the economic problems facing Blacks could not be solved without a strong alliance with organized labor. He viewed the methods of organized labor to be effective and, if tempered by nonviolence, advisable. He recognized that mere ethical appeals for justice without the pressure of coercion were ineffective. Effective pressure would be needed to wage a successful fight against racism and poverty. "In the case of organized labor, an alliance with the Negro civil-rights movement is not a matter of choice but a necessity. . . . Nothing would hold back the forces of progress in American life more effectively than a schism between the Negro and organized labor."[63] He saw Operation Breadbasket, the economic

arm of the SCLC, as the institutional embodiment of
the combined techniques of organized labor and nonviolent resistance.

King felt that the federal government had a central
and decisive role in the struggle to effect economic justice. This was demonstrated most graphically in his
proposed Poor Peoples' Campaign in Washington,
D.C. He was very critical of the government's unwillingness to act decisively. Frequently, he proposed a
Bill of Rights for the Disadvantaged and similar major
policies in order to make the question of economic
justice a major domestic priority so as to gain the necessary resources to solve the problem. He praised the
theoretical construction of the War on Poverty but was
critical of the meager resources allocated to it. Toward
the end of his life he perceived the three major
problems in America to be racism, poverty, and militarism. He believed all of these were closely related
and required the power of government to eradicate.
But he was fully aware of the kind of pressure needed
to force the government to act constructively.

Since he viewed economic injustice as a moral problem, he viewed its solution as a means to restore broken community. Not only Blacks were poor; many
whites were poor also, and many other minority
groups suffered from poverty. King's efforts in the area
of economic justice were aimed at poverty everywhere
in the land and not just at poverty among Blacks.
Time and again he declared that injustice anywhere is
a threat to justice everywhere, thus reminding the nation of the social interdependence of all peoples. He
thought that many social problems manifested in varying forms of crime, personal and family disintegration,
and social animosity would be alleviated if people
could gain a new sense of personal dignity and worth
by being liberated from the threat of economic inse-
curity. Racism, poverty, and militarism were looked
upon as evils that destroy the possibility for the goal of
community and kinship. Therefore, it was incumbent
on all people of goodwill to struggle against them with

all the moral and the spiritual power they could muster. In such an endeavor one would have the support of all that is moral in the universe, including the moral law of Love, which is rooted in the Christian God of history.

Photo courtesy of the Library of Congress

4

Adam Clayton Powell, Jr.

Powell's Theological Understanding

Powell never considered his dual roles of minister and politician as contradictory. Rather, he viewed his politics as an outcome of his religion. That is to say, his public speeches, actions, and deeds (the stuff out of which politics is made) were judged by him to be compatible with the imperatives of the Christian faith. However, there was one difference. In his thinking, religion pertained to absolute values while politics pertained to relative values. That is not to say that either religious institutions or persons actually embody those absolute values, but it does mean that true religion is grounded in absolute truth. "For us God is a God of truth and that truth is absolute."[1]

Powell often referred to himself as a mystic. By that reference he implied that religion was always a profoundly powerful experience between the spirit of humanity and that absolute Spirit which rules the universe. In his understanding, God was absolute in all respects and did not at all reflect the image of humanity. Indeed, all who would make God in their image destroy the image of God: "Where there is anthropomorphism there is no God."[2] But even though God is absolute, Powell did not believe that God was unattainable by humankind. Rather, God,

being absolute in goodness, truth, and beauty, was related in history to those people and occasions wherein
goodness, truth, and beauty appeared.

Powell was not an orthodox Christian thinker. He
did not believe in the traditional concepts of heaven
and hell. "There is no heaven or hell in the sense that
they are places to which one goes after death. The
heaven or hell to which one goes is right here in the
span of years that we spend in this body on this
earth."[3] Neither did he believe in the Bible as the infal-
lible word of God.

> We do not believe in the Bible as the word of God. It is
> too filled with contradictions. We believe in the
> Thomas Jefferson Bible. Carefully, that brilliant Found-
> ing Father cut from the New Testament only those
> words that Jesus spoke. Then in logical and chronologi-
> cal order, he put them together until he had created a
> new Bible, a new Bible of old words, only the words of
> Jesus himself. This is the Bible from which I preach. I
> love the prophetic atmosphere of the Old Testament, I
> love the lyrical witness of Paul, but there is only one
> word that I feel is of God; and that is the word of the
> Son of God as it was recorded in Matthew, Mark, Luke,
> and John: "This is my Bible." I reject all else, even the
> other words of Matthew, Mark, Luke and John; and all
> of the Bible from Genesis to Revelations must be mea-
> sured in terms of the words of Jesus Christ alone.[4]

Powell did not always limit his preaching to the
words of Jesus alone, but it is clear that the teachings
of Jesus were normative for all of his preaching. He
felt that although the Bible was inspired, there are degrees of inspiration. Some inspiration does not reveal
the final truth, and some is so wrongfully received that
it reveals no truth. The spirit of God, however, still
lives and moves in the world such that as people become increasingly sensitive and aware of God they are
privileged to receive flashes of inspiration and to
speak those absolute truths. He allowed that, in a
sense, the Bible is still being written, even as it has

been down through the centuries, and that belief enabled him to experience in his preaching the kind of freedom from dogmatism and legalism that he greatly cherished.

In his thinking, religion is personal, speaking first of all to the inner being, making that personality aware of its sinfulness, convincing it that sinfulness is wrong, and pointing it to an awareness of God as the only way to salvation.

> I preach a strong personal gospel, which begins by trying to get man to have a sense of sin. Each of us knows when he is doing wrong or right. There is an Inner Voice that speaks through conscience and gives us all the correct evaluations of our thinking, of our thoughts, and of our sins. But we try to suppress this Inner Voice, to rationalize our wrongdoings, so the first thrust of my preaching is to give man a sense of sin—to preach that no man is better than any other man, that every human being is a sinner, that we are constantly in the process of sinning, that we sin by omission, we sin by commission, and we sin by permission. . . .
>
> When one has received the sense of sin, it is necessary to have a sense of conviction. Not just to accept that one is a sinner and that all people sin and are likely to continue, but to have conviction that sin is wrong, that there is no such thing as partial sin; that sin is sin, and that there is no such thing as one's sin being greater than another's.[5]

Powell avowed that an awareness of God is the only way to salvation. Further, God is beauty, goodness, and truth, and wherever those virtues manifest themselves God is present. "So what we preach is an awareness of these things: beauty, truth, and goodness—then we are opening up the way to the awareness of God."[6]

Although Powell felt that all people were sinful, he did not believe in their total depravity. On the contrary, he affirmed that deep within every person there was some goodness and truth and beauty that could respond to God. Indeed, he believed that an awareness of God in one's inner life changed the way one viewed the outer world. That is to say, a person is equipped with the resources to see through the relative truths of this world to the absolute truth implied by them.

> When one knows Him in His fullest sense, not only from reading and teaching but also from agonized searching, then one can walk through the world looking for beauty in all things. For all things have within them some element of beauty. One can also look and listen for truths, not the truths that the world proclaims as truths, for these truths are relative, but the truths that are absolute, the truths that one must find because only through finding the absolute can one be free. These absolute truths lead one into the ways of goodness.[7]

Powell was convinced that the absolute truth of God as seen in Jesus Christ is the truth that makes people free, and therefore, it stands in opposition to those relative truths that hold people captive. Indeed, he viewed this as the fundamental religious problem that confronts all humankind. That struggle between liberating truth and unliberating truth marks the pilgrimage of the religious person from bondage to freedom. "This is the eternal struggle of man against the unliberating truths that are self-evident, and toward the freedom-giving truths that must be agonizingly sought after."[8] It is important to note that Powell regarded the wrongs, the injustices, and the false truths in history as self-evident. He recognized that they were apparent to conscience, the "inner voice" that bothers every person, even though most reject its dictates and, at best, live lives of pretense, which he condemns as hypocritical. Indeed, he considered much of the life of the organized church in America to be hypocritical and, therefore, guilty of the same sort of sin of which Jesus accused the Pharisees.

Powell argued that when a person becomes conscious of the fact that he or she is a sinner and is convinced that sin is wrong, and when a person develops the sensitivity to become aware of God as the source of his or her salvation, then that person becomes a recipient of the kind of freedom humanity was intended to experience. But there is one condition necessary for the attainment of that blessed awareness of God. A person must be cleansed of all hatred toward his or her neighbors. It is at this point that Powell leveled his severest criticism against what he calls the "white man's religion."

> This drawing near to God, this increasing awareness, cannot be accomplished, nor even the initial steps be taken, until one has purged himself of all hatred toward all fellow men. This is why I view askance the average white man's religion; and in this religion of his I include not just his church but the whole priesthood of believers and of preachers, his institutions of theological learning and his outer projection of his religion into community and world life. There is absolutely no Christianity of any type in any church where there is not active and equal participation at every level of church life and every level of religious institutions by all the sons of God. When for any reason whatsoever any participation of any member of the family of God is prohibited at any level, then there is no Christianity present, regardless of pretensions.[9]

In Powell's understanding, the principle of love as exemplified by Jesus illumines the personal and the social dimensions of the gospel by demonstrating their interdependence. To choose to make the religion of Jesus either personal or social is a distortion, since either dimension is destroyed when alienated from the other. Further, any and all attempts to do so would necessitate a process of limiting God, who transcends all limits.[10]

Powell viewed Jesus' understanding of love as one of the major ethical contributions of his teaching. Love of God implies a personal dimension of religion, but its integral relation to the second commandment of Jesus to love one's neighbor conjoins the personal

and the social. Further, he believed that love functioned as a reflexive principle. On the one hand, love
for one's neighbor is a necessary condition for an
awareness of God, while on the other hand, an awareness of God leads one inevitably to a love for one's
neighbor. He also believed that to attempt to say or to
do otherwise would be an attempt to put Jesus in
bondage. From the proposition that Christ is unlim-
ited, Powell derived the position that no creed, doctrine, ritual, custom, or anything else could ever be
imposed upon Christ, since all such efforts necessarily
reduce this freedom and transcendence. Further, efforts to limit Jesus are themselves expressions of idolatry. Powell contended that anything that threatens to
disrupt the love of Christians for their kindred human
beings must be considered evil by God, whether it be
creeds, doctrines, rituals, or whatever. In this argument Powell established religious grounds for his condemnation of racism. Racism separates people on the
bases of prejudice and hatred. Racism compels
churches to betray their God by becoming living ves-
sels of hypocrisy and idolatry.

> Therefore, America is not a Christian country. It is a
> country of pretensions, of "churchianity," where the in-
> stitution of Christianity has been perverted into an in-
> strument to perpetuate, if not to propagate, directly and
> indirectly, anti-Christian doctrines of segregation and
> discrimination. The only Christian churches in the
> United States are those churches that, at all levels, wel-
> come and encourage the participation of all the sons of
> man. . . . I say that any church that in any way
> preaches or practices anything that will exclude anyone
> from membership is negating the power of Christ.[11]

Powell repeatedly preached from the passage in
John's Gospel, "Ye shall know the truth, and the truth
shall make you free" (John 8:32, KJV). Obviously, the
truth and the freedom about which the verse speaks
are of God. Powell's concern for freedom was paramount in his religious thought and in his political

thought. He greatly appreciated the fact that the framers of the Declaration of Independence recognized the religious basis of freedom by acknowledging that liberty was a right of every person, bestowed by God. Hence, he argued that the nation's founders did not bestow liberty upon the citizenry. They merely recorded it as a fact of human nature bestowed by the Creator. Freedom is of God and is not of humans.[12]

Powell's understanding of the absolute goodness of God and of the relative goodness of people and their works led him to propound a doctrine of two kingdoms: the kingdom of God and the kingdom of this world. He considered the two to be in conflict. In the kingdom of God, God's will is done. In the kingdom of humankind, humanity's will is done. The two are rarely harmonious. One should note that Powell did not envision the kingdom of God as suprahistorical but, rather, capable of realization in history if humanity should become aware of its sinfulness and of its need of God for salvation. God's will is humankind's true end.[13] Hence, Powell believed that the break between the will of God and the powers and structures of humanity meant simply that God was in no way controlled by human will. Further, it meant that none of the superficial conditions and boundaries constructed by humanity applied to God. Humankind has lost sight of its true destiny, because it has strayed away from the will of God. The task of the Christian church ought to be that of leading people back to that true way by persuading them to commit themselves to the God who is raceless, classless, regionless, and absolutely free.[14]

Powell had no difficulty in discerning when the will of God was being done and when the will of people was in control. Evidence for the will of God being done is marked by the presence of beauty, peace, love, and harmony.[15] Suffice it to say that all instances of personal or social discord evidenced for Powell the fact that the will of humans was taking precedence over the will of God.

Thus, in Powell's understanding, sin is the human attempt to declare oneself absolutely autonomous. By doing this one fails to see the relative, temporary, and superficial aspects of all one's works. Instead, he argued, the mark of the true Christian is an ability to look beyond the things of this world and the values of this world and to grasp the complete significance of the values of God. Further, Powell taught that the church is the family of God, although its life has been marred by prodigality. Its sin has been instanced by the many barriers to harmony and peace that it has erected and maintained. Time and again Powell spoke of the unity of the family of God as one of its essential characteristics.

Powell felt that the mission of the Christian church and the end of all true preaching should be the attempt to usher in the kingdom of God here and now in this world. Wherever there is discord and hatred among the peoples of the world, the Christian has a mandate from God to work for healing and reconciliation. The task of bringing about that healing is the political side of the religious goal.[16]

Our examination of the major aspects of Powell's religious thinking has led us to the question of politics. It was stated at the outset that Powell's politics was viewed by him as an outcome of his religion. Let us look more closely at his political thinking in order to see how he reasoned about that relationship.

Powell's Political Understanding

Before presenting a description of Powell's political thought, I will include a brief biographical sketch in order to put the man, his church, and his activities into a context that must be assumed at every point.

For over a quarter of a century the names Abyssinian Baptist Church and Adam Clayton Powell, Jr., were virtually household terms throughout Black America. In many respects the religious institution and its pastor had come to symbolize the political struggle for racial justice in this country. That struggle manifested itself in the quest for a maximization of legitimate power in the political process to effect social change. The power that accrued to both was understood by Powell to be religiously based and utilized for the purpose of expanding racial justice for Black Americans.

All his life Powell had been opposed to all forms of racial injustice. Basically, he understood racism to be a demonic power bent on the perpetual control of a captive people. Like his father, to whom he always remained greatly indebted for much of his religious and political learning, he believed that Blacks should participate with whites in the realization of their goals but from an independent base. In his autobiography he revealed the depth of that independence as it had evidenced itself in the leadership of Abyssinian Baptist Church.

> At one time $60,000 was needed to pay off the balance of the indebtedness. John D. Rockefeller, Jr., a staunch Baptist and the major contributor to the Riverside Baptist Church, agreed to give the entire amount, but on the condition that one member of the Board of Trustees be appointed by him. My father brought this news back to the United Boards of the church, which turned it down unanimously. Within four and a half years the church was free and clear of any mortgage and also from any outside control.[17]

In spite of his major emphasis on personal and institutional independence for Blacks, Powell was never a Black separatist. He had been brought up in a church that enjoyed a long and distinguished history as a nonsegregated religious institution. It had been founded in 1808, when a group of visiting Abyssinian dignitaries sought a place to worship one Sunday morning. Upon entering what turned out to be the only Baptist congregation in the city of New York, they were ushered promptly to the segregated section. In protest they walked out. "The Reverend Thomas Paul, a liberal white preacher educated at Harvard, left with them."[18]

Soon thereafter they bought property and established the first Baptist church in the North that had an integrated membership from the beginning. At the time of its centenary, when Adam Clayton Powell, Sr., became its minister, his son, the younger Adam, was an infant. The child's first teacher was his father. As a result of this instruction, together with the influence of the church, he was nurtured in a firm belief that racial harmony was designed by God and that it was the noblest end of a democratic state. Further, Adam C. Powell, Jr., took great pride in the fact that in this country the Black church first made possible the appearance of racial harmony.

The elder Powell worked zealously to make Abyssinian Baptist Church conscious of its social responsibilities to the people in its midst. In the early years of the Great Depression, his son effectively concretized that zeal and caused the institution to gain a new measure of respect and praise from the entire Black community of Harlem and from most outsiders who learned of its mission. Many were surprised by his particular style of ministry. Here was a man who had spent his early life insulated from poverty and hardship of any kind. The crushing blows of racism so frequently inflicted upon the Black masses had not touched him. In the early 1930s he began to learn for the first time about the sufferings of the people—Black and white. When forced into a leadership position, he responded with amazing organizational skills and political insight.

When he succeeded his father as senior pastor of Abyssinian in 1937, he already had a citywide reputation as a fighter for racial justice. By then he had become a master of such direct confrontation tactics as mass rallies, demonstrations, boycotts, and marches aimed specifically at the eradication of racial discrimination in employment. His successful campaigns against the merchants of Harlem, the Harlem Hospital, Consolidated Edison utility company, and others resulted from his skillful leadership in founding the

Greater New York Coordinating Committee for the Unemployed. But the greatest victory in his early years of public leadership was the campaign against Mike Quill, the Irish Catholic leader of the Transport Workers Union, which barred Blacks from employment. In 1940, Powell organized a massive bus boycott, which, in time, forced the bus company to negotiate and reach a favorable agreement. This undoubtedly was the first significant employment victory for Blacks anywhere in America.

In 1941 he was elected to the New York City Council as an independent. In 1943, when congressional reapportionment made Harlem a congressional district, he was elected to Congress. His incessant attacks on all forms of bigotry soon caused him to be viewed by Black America as "our congressman." He always considered himself to be a representative of the masses, with a mandate to fight vigorously for the correction of racial wrongs. Let us now examine more closely his political thinking in order to see how it related to his religious thought and why he took the positions he did on the issues raised in chapter 1.

One can certainly say of Adam Clayton Powell, Jr., that he was an independent. In his private life and in his public life he displayed a rigorous independence of thought and action. He considered himself unconstrained by theological dogma, religious institution, political party, or economic power group. At all times and in all situations he exhibited an indomitable spirit of freedom. His critics were legion. In large part, the criticism pertained to and was influenced by both his personal style of life and his outspoken brashness, neither of which was consonant with customary practice. Many viewed him as an extremely inconsistent person. They could not understand how he could threaten to leave the Democratic party in 1952 and again in 1960 and then fail to carry out the threat. They could not understand how a Democrat could campaign for Eisenhower in 1956 and still remain a Democrat. They could not understand how he could repudiate Lyndon

Johnson at one time, only to prefer him as president to John F. Kennedy in 1960. They could not understand how he could insist on his famous Powell Amendment as a civil rights rider to a bill for a federal grant to aid local school construction in 1956, when the amendment put the liberals in an awkward position and forced them to vote against the bill, thus forfeiting the support of Southerners. There were numerous seeming contradictions in the political life of Powell that baffled and frustrated many observers, causing them to judge him not only inconsistent but irresponsible.

Yet I contend that Powell was often unjustly maligned by his critics, chiefly because they failed to understand the nature of his political thinking. That is to say, they failed to grasp those principles on which he acted consistently in all his political activity and to distinguish them from his day-to-day strategies and tactics. Powell knew how to be expedient and how to compromise, yet certain major political principles were always unnegotiable.

He believed unquestionably in the principle of democratic government as the best possible political system.[19] The only alternatives to it that he saw were anarchy and totalitarianism. He viewed the former as a mere eccentric and academic pastime; he abhorred the latter. He revered the Constitution of the United States, but from the beginning of his official political career, he deplored the daily injustices to Black people that were upheld by that constitution. In 1945, when he stood on the floor of the House of Representatives and took the oath to uphold the Constitution, he was vividly aware of the contradiction officially sanctioned by the federal government in having a segregated armed forces fighting to preserve democracy at home while trying to create a new world of freedom overseas.

> This, then, was our country fighting a war to preserve democracy, but with an undemocratically segregated Navy, Army, and Air Force. Abroad the United States was preaching "the century of the common man" and

the "Four Freedoms," yet it was denying any of these freedoms at home, even in the nation's capital. America was talking about the creation of a new world while its conscience was filled with guilt.[20]

Powell loved the truth, because he believed the teaching in John's Gospel that knowing the truth was a condition for freedom—the inner freedom of one's spirit as well as the outer freedom of participation in the body politic. He held the view that political freedom was the goal envisioned by the framers of the Constitution and that it made up the substance of the American dream. During the Fourth of July weekend in 1956 he proposed to attach his famous Powell Amendment to the Kelly Bill, which supported federal aid for school construction. He concluded that speech with a characteristic description of the American dream, which he believed should be the governing principle for all voting on all bills passed by the United States government. "We have before us the American dream. It is a dream of one nation, indivisible, with liberty and justice for all, and I believe that you should vote according to that American dream."[21]

Powell thought the American dream to be good, because it aims at the quality of nation that is commensurate with his understanding of God's purposes. The actualization of a state exemplifying the virtues of freedom and justice, unity and peace would be, in his opinion, the highest possible attainment of human beings. Such a state would be classless, raceless, and regionless, thus exhibiting those qualities that, in their absolute realization, he attributed to God.

Powell's constant fight to enact into law the civil rights of Black people and to seek the enforcement of such laws was not considered by him to be a racial fight but a democratic one. Although he was often judged by his critics to be inconsistent, he fought unceasingly for consistency between the government's ideals and its practices. Moreover, he battled for consistency between certain precedents established by the government and their implications for present and future action. His justification for attaching the Powell Amendment to the Kelly Bill illustrated his attempt to do precisely that: to force the legislative body to acknowledge and yield to the action of the judicial body, a practice he considered to be long established in the American political system. That is to say, he was striving to make the political body publicly consistent with the judiciary.

> And in reply to the stand that "we should not implement the Supreme Court decision by legislative action," I stated: "I am sure that we all agree that whenever there is a constitutional executive order, judicial decision, or legislative action, immediately it is encumbent [*sic*] upon all other branches of the government to yield to whatever that decision, order, or law may be. We implemented the Supreme Court decision for fifty-seven years in Plessy against Ferguson, which was the doctrine of separate but equal. We in this House and in the other body passed amendments to the draft bill, the Hill-Burton Act, the Federal school lunch program, implementing the Supreme Court decisions. Now we come to a new decision, a decision of integration, and this is the first test of whether we are going to abide by the Supreme Court decision as a legislative body. This is not a racial amendment."[22]

In that amendment and in all his subsequent actions in the United States Congress, Powell tried his best to be faithful to the oath he first took in that assembly, namely, to uphold the Constitution. He contended that that oath implied the making and enforcing of laws that would guarantee the realization of democratic practices throughout the land and for all citizens.

Not only at home did he fight for democracy but also abroad. When he acted independently and against the judgment of the State Department and the Congress in 1955 by attending unofficially the Bandung Conference (the first international assembly of inde-

pendent Asian and African countries),[23] he later felt
that that act was justified, because he believed God
had willed him to be there and because he sensed that
his presence there had resulted in a victory for democracy over communism.

> Nevertheless, the United States did win a victory at
> Bandung which it did not deserve to win, which it did
> nothing toward winning and deliberately tried to lose.
> We won at Bandung only because the idea of democ-
> racy triumphed over the idea of Communism. I played
> a small part in this but only because God willed that I
> should be there.[24]

Powell's commitment to democracy was so complete
that he refused to be a partner with the Communists
and others at Bandung when they sought to condemn
the United States for its racist practices toward Black
Americans. In a surprising counterattack, made during
a largely attended news conference, he proclaimed that
racism in America was on its way out and chided
members of other delegations for various kinds of discrimination and segregation that were present in their
respective countries.[25]

Powell's commitment to democracy is further evidenced by his relations with Fidel Castro soon after
the fall of the Cuban dictator Fulgencio Batista. He
openly criticized the United States for its acts of du-
plicity vis-à-vis Batista and for the unjust treatment
Castro was receiving from the government and from
the press in this country. He believed that Castro was
willing to cooperate with the United States, and he
worked vigorously to effect such an end. But, in the
final outcome, Castro had become committed to communism, and Powell could no longer see any virtue in
trying to maintain communications.[26]

Powell's second major political principle might be
called *participatory power for the masses*. Perhaps a
second thing that could be said for certain about Powell is that he was a leader of the masses. Since the days

of the Depression, when he led thousands of Blacks in protest marches for economic justice in Harlem, the Black masses have never ceased to love him. During the 1930s, '40s, and '50s, he was, for the masses of Harlem and the rest of Black America, the Black Knight in shining armor. Fearlessly and unabashedly, he gained a reputation in white America of being outrageous, mainly because he told the truth the way he saw it and in a manner that only the common people could appreciate. Symbolically, he was Harlem's king and the ambassador *extraordinaire* for Black America.

By 1941, while yet a young man, he had become Harlem's most powerful leader. His massive relief program of free meals for the hungry was destined to be the precursor to New York City's welfare agency. His Coordinating Committee for the Unemployed had won many victories under the slogan "Don't Buy Where You Can't Work." His weekly column in Harlem's newspaper, *The Amsterdam News*, defined the problems accurately and contributed to the task of unifying the people. His preaching attracted the young and the unchurched, because he focused on the real problems of life with graphic force. Their admiration of him was also increased by their ability to identify with his life-style. Powell shocked many of the old church members with his frequent escapades in "doing the town." When he decided to run in the city election as an independent, the people gave him a resounding victory. They never let him down thereafter. He became one of the few representatives in Congress who seldom had to campaign in order to maintain his seat.

Powell's style of life bore many of the outward marks of affluence and of Epicurean tastes. But the inner being, the spirit of Powell, was always in tune with the problems and the desires of the average folk. That communion was apparent in his speeches and in his political deeds. Consequently, the masses found no fault with him, and in their eyes even his flamboyant life-style took on the appearance of protest. In fact, Black Americans long admired Powell's flamboyancy and his daring arrogance in ridiculing white attitudes toward Blacks. So, in a very real sense, Powell's style of independence, pretentiousness, and arrogance, coupled with an attitude that seemed to tell whitey to go to hell, enabled the Black people to identify with him vicariously. But this identification was not free of political significance. Powell's legislative power, given to him by the masses, was for empowering the masses.

It is important to note that Powell's commitment to the people was not simply a matter of political expediency or of skillful manipulation for personal self-aggrandizement. True, he was interested in his own ambition, but he was more deeply interested in helping the masses to realize their ambitions. In the political arena there was a chance of realizing both. His distinguished record bears testimony to the fact that his self-interest did not overshadow his responsibility to the public interest. More important, his belief in the masses, and especially in the Black masses, was grounded in his religious perspective. Indeed, he often came close to considering the commonplace people as the true people of God. In a sermon entitled "What a Day to Live In," Powell stated that those leaders who have resisted inequality and injustice have always been from the masses. The mighty and the noble are never the agents of liberalism. Rather, they represent those forces of oppression that are overwhelmed by the good deeds of the poor, the despised, the people of low estate—those with whom Jesus easily identified.[27]

Powell considered his constituency to be not only the Black masses of Harlem but also the nation at large. More significant, he viewed himself as representing the downtrodden and the oppressed, whomever they might be, regardless of race or citizenship. In spite of the fact that his major priority was that of representing the Black masses, as early as his first congressional election he publicly promised to protest the defamation of any group while working for victories that would be prolabor and prominority.

In my platform I outlined that I would push for fair racial practices, fight to do away with restrictive covenants and discrimination in housing, fight for the passage of a national Fair Employment Practices Commission and for the abolition of the poll tax, fight to make lynching a Federal crime, do away with segregated transportation, undergird the Thirteenth, Fourteenth, and Fifteenth Amendments to the Constitution, protest the defamation of any group—Protestant, Catholic, Jew, or Negro—fight every form of imperialism and colonialism, and support all legislation, one hundred percent, to win the war, to win the peace, pro-labor and pro-minority.[28]

In fighting for constitutional justice and for participatory power for the masses, Powell believed that both could be effected through Christian leadership. Indeed, he believed that the only way of guaranteeing democracy's continuance was by acting to improve it, to change those practices that thwart its purpose. This, he felt, could be done by Christian leadership instead of the leadership of those who are elected to legislate pork barrels rather than morality.[29]

Closely akin to Powell's belief that Christian leadership should be the agency for effecting constructive change in the democracy in order to rid itself of its hypocritical practices was his belief that the source of that agency would be the Black church. Many of his critics have analyzed the role Abyssinian Baptist Church played in his political career, concluding that it was simply a political power base similar, in their estimation, to most other monolithic power bases. However, these analysts have failed to grasp the religious significance that gave Powell's political base a meaning quite different from other political organizations. In the first place, although Powell asserted that Blacks were no better than whites, he considered their awareness of God to be more genuine. The latter he attributed to their implicit belief in the fundamental unity of all humanity and to their historic experience of continuously seeking God as a means of liberation from oppression.[30]

Second, Powell regarded Christ as the only true Savior for humankind. It follows, therefore, that the true disciples of Christ must be those who aid in effecting humanity's salvation. Since he looked on the white Christian church as being hypocritically fraudulent because of its history of sanctioning the racist customs of segregation and discrimination, it is not difficult to see why he viewed the Black church the way he did. Indeed, his opinion of the role of the Black church should be understood as a precursor to what is now commonly called Black Theology.[31] He called his own Abyssinian Baptist Church a memorial to those who dared to attack the corrupters of Christianity. Abyssinian in particular and the Black churches in general have *kept the faith* by opposing slavery and colonialism, by protesting the unequal citizenship of Black Americans.[32]

To summarize Powell's political understanding it is important to state that he remained faithful to two major political principles: constitutional democracy and participatory power for the masses. Their integral relation to his religious perspective has been demonstrated, perhaps nowhere more clearly than in his understanding of the role of Black Christian leadership, with the Black church as its base. The task of healing the ills of democracy was given religious significance by him. Politics clearly was viewed as an outcome of religion and was justified by his appeal to true religion, Christianity, as the only source for authentic salvation—not Christianity as it is practiced by white Christians, however, but Christianity as it was intended by the Lord Jesus Christ. Now we are ready to look more closely at the positions Powell took on the issues raised in chapter 1 and to see how his religious and political understandings justified those positions.

The Supreme Court Decision of 1954

Throughout his public career Powell vigorously opposed racial discrimination and segregation on moral and on legal grounds. At the outset of his congressional career he fought forcefully against segregation as practiced in the use of congressional facilities; the rampant segregation in the nation's capital; segregation in the armed forces, the veterans hospitals, the draft, the Naval Academy; segregation practiced by the Daughters of the American Revolution; the appropriation of federal funds to support discrimination in education; and so on. Consequently, he welcomed the Supreme Court decision that declared that segregation in public schools was unconstitutional. He said that that decision had changed the tide of American thought concerning civil rights. He had only one regret: Congress had failed to speak out in support of the Supreme Court decision. He soon became aware of the fact that numerous states were acting in defiance of the court order. He sought to make Congress more responsible in that matter. After much thought about what he might be able to do, he decided in 1955 to attach a civil rights amendment to all bills that had to do with education. He fought vigorously for the passage of his amendment, because he believed that neither the president of the United States nor the Congress had assumed the moral and the legal leadership that was necessary following the Supreme Court decision. He thought his amendment would be an effective device for coercing Congress to legislate the enforcement of the Supreme Court decision. That amendment created many problems for Congress. Because the majority of the House opposed the amendment, it took several years for any federal aid bill for school construction to pass. Powell pledged to do all in his power to force the government to ensure that all legislation would be compatible with the decisions of the supreme judiciary. In that task he viewed himself not as a sponsor of racialist legislation but as a backer of democratic legislation for the purpose of upholding the Constitution. He deplored the fact that a decree from the Supreme Court was being defied by the states and virtually ignored by both the executive and legislative branches of the government.

As Powell fought on the legislative side of the problem, he was always conscious of its moral dimension. In a sermon preached at the time the Supreme Court was considering the case, he said that racial segregation was more than a racial problem or a national problem or a constitutional problem; it was a moral problem destined to shape the moral justice of the world.[33]

In Powell's thinking, moral problems pertained to the quality of relationships that existed between people. The right to liberty is bestowed by God and not by people. When persons deny others that right, they thwart the purposes of God and must necessarily become involved in self-destruction. Discrimination and segregation, together with all forms of colonialism and imperialism, aim at the destruction of humanity. In fact, Powell believed that no other national problem, including that of harnessing nuclear power, was more important to America's moral nature than that of granting first-class citizenship to Blacks.

Further, Powell viewed the results of segregated education as immoral. He argued that it produced poor instruction for Blacks, and consequently, millions were condemned to a destiny of poverty, ignorance, and immeasurable suffering. As late as 1963 Powell contended: "Regardless of how fine school buildings may be, how dedicated and educated the teachers may be, you can never have good education without integration."[34] He never departed from that position.

Civil Disobedience

The issue of civil disobedience never became a major practical problem for Powell. He did not advocate it as a rule, although he formed working alliances with such diverse supporters of civil disobedience as Martin Luther King, Jr., and Malcolm X. But his alliances never implied that he totally accepted the philosophy of either. Yet if he did not promote civil disobedience as a moral principle, neither did he fear it. Indeed, in the immediate aftermath of the tragic killing of two students in Jackson, Mississippi, *Jet* magazine reported that Powell had admonished Blacks to "go without food if necessary and buy a gun."[35] But, in the light of his whole thinking, Powell maintained that such an imperative was justified on the grounds of self-defense alone. He had always believed in nonviolence as a realistic, practical approach for effecting social change. In an interview with Robert Penn Warren he said, "The day the Negro changes from non-violence to violence, he is finished, and the Black Revolution has to start all over again, at some future date."[36] He affirmed it not only for practical reasons but also for religious reasons. In fact, he took it for granted that nonviolence was of God and therefore instructed his people to practice it as a Christian virtue.

Although Powell neither advocated nor feared civil disobedience, in his understanding the relationship between the laws of human beings and the law of God made civil disobedience justifiable in certain circumstances. Time and again, he preached about the character of God in terms of absolute goodness, truth, and beauty. In comparison, humanity's will was regarded as contrary to that of God. Thus, when humankind's laws contradict the laws of God, Powell upheld the necessity of disobeying the former. Such disobedience, however, did not imply violence. In his thinking, the law of God was the final and complete good. In his attempt to harness the good implied by the Black Power movement and to control its radical implications, he spoke of Black Power as a significant way for Blacks to gain their freedom provided violence played no part in its realization.[37] Nevertheless, in the face of unjust laws, he considered civil disobedience a morally good act.

Black people must continue to defy the laws of man when such laws conflict with the law of God. The law of God ordains that "there is neither Jew nor Greek, there is neither bond nor freedom [*sic*], there is neither male nor female: for ye are all one." Equal in the eyes of God, but unequal in the eyes of man, Black people must press forward at all times, climbing toward that higher ground of the harmonious society that shapes the laws of man to the laws of God.[38]

Clearly, Powell distinguished between violence and civil disobedience. However, I admit that there is some ambiguity as to what he meant by "defying the laws of man." At times there was an unmistakable implication that defiance of the laws of humanity involved fighting for their correction. Obviously, when one seeks to correct a law, one does so because one is against that law. Now, that opposition can express itself in legitimate ways and in illegitimate ways. The latter pertains to civil disobedience. Powell spent much of his public career battling for social change via legitimate processes. Possibly, he deliberately chose to be ambiguous on this matter in order to maintain his alliance with those who advocated civil disobedience as well as with the moderates in the civil rights struggle.

But the ambiguity is lessened when one views the characteristic pragmatism Powell stood for vis-à-vis the means he was prepared to utilize in order to realize his goals. The goals were always justified by appeals to political and religious principles; the tactics used by him were justified only in terms of their utility for effecting the desired end. Given the limitation placed on the function of principle, it appears that Powell's religious and political beliefs did not hinder him from giving tacit support to certain forms of civil disobedience. Rather, he was able to do so on utilitarian grounds.

It is important to note, however, that Powell's backing of civil disobedience could never be extended to actions that were aimed at the wholesale destruction of

institutions. When he was asked whether or not he upheld the Rev. Milton Galamison's statement that the
public school system should be wrecked if it refused to
become integrated, he said, "I don't subscribe to that
anymore than I can subscribe to the white segregationists destroying the public school system rather than
obeying the Supreme Court."[39] Wanton and aimless
outbursts of anger and frustration were, in his judgment, unjustified. Although he was no revolutionary in
the sense of advocating the overthrow of the present
social order, he had no difficulty in supporting such a
measure as a proposed stall-in at the World's Fair in
New York on the grounds of practical utility. With
regard to the stall-ins, he said, "It's an overreach, but I
was in favor of the stall-ins because to me any form of
demonstration that's nonviolent necessarily quickens
the thinking of people in the power structure."[40]

It appears clear that Powell could not tolerate any
kind of civil disobedience based on violence. But once
a group was committed to nonviolence toward persons
and institutions, he saw no meaningful distinction between legitimate and illegitimate means for effecting
the correction of social injustice. Nowhere is this
made more explicit than in his interview with Robert
Penn Warren.

> WARREN: In nonviolent demonstrations, is there a
> distinction between legitimate and illegitimate?
> That is, with reference to the effect on society?
> Say the stall-ins as contrasted with picketing or
> sitting-in?
> POWELL: I don't think there's any difference. I say
> that any form of nonviolence has its effects.
> WARREN: Violence has an effect, too.
> POWELL: Yes, but I don't believe in it.
> WARREN: What about the difference between dem-
> onstrations that have a specific target, as con-
> trasted with those that are merely expressions of
> anger or discontent?

POWELL: I believe in demonstrations directed at
specific targets, because when you have demonstrations of just bitterness and frustration, with no
goal, then you're on the edge of something that
could turn into violence.[41]

Civil Rights Legislation

Even a casual observer of Powell's public career
could not mistake the fact that he was an avid believer
in the importance and effectiveness of civil rights legislation. The most obvious evidence of this is his legislative career. During most of his public life, long before
the public emergence of Martin Luther King, Jr., he
was the congressman who had earned the reputation of
being Mr. Civil Rights. During the times when he
could not muster sufficient power in Congress to cause
a bill to be passed, he eagerly crusaded for the protection of the civil rights of minorities in all proposed
legislation. He described himself as the "First Bad
Nigger in Congress" and devoted a chapter in his autobiography to that title. He became known as a trouble-
maker, but the trouble he made was usually associated
with his ability to grab headlines by embarrassing the
Congress and the country about civil rights issues. He
considered effective legislation a necessary means for
ridding the nation of racial discrimination and segregation. Early in his congressional career he came to see
himself as a Black congressman who represented not
only Harlem but all of Black America. Reflecting on
that period in his life, he wrote the following perceptive commentary on the limitations of individual action in Congress:

> There was only one thing I could do—hammer relent-
> lessly, continually crying aloud even if in a wilderness,
> and force open, by sheer muscle power, every closed
> door. Once inside, I had to pierce the consciences of
> men so that somewhere someone would have to answer;

somewhere something would have to be done ... for
there is no way for an independent man who fights for
what he thinks is right to succeed in passing legislation.[42]

Those early years were frustrating for him. His presence on the floor was always dramatic and exciting,
but he longed for results. He came to see that the real
substance of political power lay in the powerful House
committees and was quick to discern that power
therein was determined entirely by the seniority system. It took two years before he discovered a method
of forcing Congress to seriously consider civil rights
legislation. In 1946 he introduced his Powell Amendment, "forbidding Federal funds to those who sought
to preserve segregation, and wherever I thought there
was an opportunity that it could be passed, or wherever the opportunity arose to defeat bad legislation,
there I would introduce it."[43] That same year it was
first used effectively, in the bill pertaining to free
school lunches. "From then on I was to use this important weapon with success, to bring about opportunities
for the good of man and to stop those efforts that
would harm democracy's forward progress."[44]

At the 1952 Democratic National Convention, Powell threatened to bolt the party if the presidential candidate did not accept a strong civil rights plank in his
platform. Powell said, "My position on civil rights is
much more important than my seat in Congress."[45]
Although opposed by many Black moderates, including Congressman William L. Dawson, he firmly insisted that Adlai Stevenson's platform be strengthened
vis-à-vis civil rights before Powell would give his endorsement. Stevenson did so two months following the
convention, and Powell rightly took credit for forcing
that issue to its effective conclusion.

During Eisenhower's first term of office as president,
Powell, realizing that he could not cause significant
legislation on civil rights to emerge out of Congress,
spent considerable time in correspondence with the
president concerning civil rights. He was able to gain

some changes by virtue of presidential order—for example, desegregation of Washington, D.C., desegregation in Veterans Administration hospitals, and desegregation in the armed forces. Powell was so pleased with Eisenhower's performance on civil rights in contrast with Stevenson's refusal to carry a strong civil rights plank in his platform during the 1956 election campaign that he was moved to do the unprecedented—to endorse a Republican for president and to campaign for him without resigning from the Democratic party.

It was not until he became chair of the powerful Education and Labor Committee, in 1960, that he began to realize many of his long-desired legislative goals. He became the most effective legislator in Congress and received high praise from House Speaker John McCormack and Presidents Kennedy and Johnson. "On my fifth anniversary as chairman, the record showed that I had guided to passage from my committee sixty major laws."[46] Five years earlier few people in the country thought Powell capable of effectively chairing the Education and Labor Committee. His record is an astounding contradiction to that opinion.[47] He was able to say of himself and of his work: "After so many years of a do-nothing Education and Labor Committee, I was now seeing many of my dreams and goals made into law."[48]

Powell never completely lost faith in the possibility of democracy's full realization in this land. He knew that governments are structured by people and that the laws denote that quality. But he was not deluded into thinking that formal laws were sufficient in themselves. Rather, he knew that they required rigorous enforcement and implementation in order to manifest the substance of a morally good nation. He realized also that lawmaking is an art that necessitates appropriate alliances in order to maximize the power needed to achieve the desired results. He mastered that power without forsaking his characteristic function of "fighting to squeeze a little more justice from the system, not for myself but for those downtrodden or discriminated against for skin color or other irrelevant causes."[49]

Powell believed that racism was a great evil akin only to colonialism and imperialism. He was convinced that its existence violated the spiritual vision of national unity because it mutilated its citizenry by exploitative means. But he was also convinced that the will of a people to be free is inherently spiritual and always transcends those who seek its destruction.[50]

In Powell's thinking, civil rights was viewed as a moral problem, and all efforts aimed at effective legislative guarantees for the civil rights of every person were seen as forms of moral action. He also thought of morality as an outgrowth of religion.[51] Therefore, as he frequently preached, the job was not to put politics into religion but to put religion into politics. He considered himself to be doing precisely that when he lobbied, cajoled, threatened, and used whatever means he could to effect civil rights legislation.

School Boycotts

Like the issue of civil disobedience, school boycotts never became a major problem for Powell. He had used the boycott technique effectively in the 1930s to wrench some measure of increased justice out of the business enterprises that flourished in Harlem. Under the slogan "Don't Buy Where You Can't Work" he was the first to use the technique successfully against racial discrimination in employment. Since that time he had always considered the boycott justified when it aimed at correcting racial injustices nonviolently. Powell was impressed with its effectiveness, and his pragmatism concerning means was another reason for his support of the technique. In his opinion, the boycott is similar to the labor union strike. The one withholds its labor power; the other withholds its buying power. In other words, both withhold their participation in the exploitative system.

In 1963 Powell supported Galamison's proposal for

a widespread boycott of public schools in New York, because it was aimed at destroying segregation in the public schools. In a sermon he declared it to be mandatory.[52] He also supported such boycotts because they generated courage in people who were fighting against racism. In fact, he viewed courage as indispensable to the struggle and frequently ridiculed those Blacks who were lacking in that virtue.[53]

More important, Powell's belief in the complete rightness of school boycotts is grounded in his religious understanding. He was convinced that God wills racial integration for the world and denounces all forms of racism as necessarily evil. In proclaiming God as the final voice in what humanity should do, Powell limited the power of all voices advocating the maintenance of racism, including those of science, finance, and technology. All voices must be judged by that final voice that decrees racial harmony. While concluding a sermon on Galamison's school boycott, he reaffirmed his faith in a God who will one day conquer the voice of the white backlash and will be manifested as being classless and raceless—one who desires a classless and raceless world.[54]

Powell contended that the absolute classlessness and racelessness of God is the ultimate norm for all human activities that would make class or race a force for exploiting others. If boycotting schools could be an effective method for correcting racial injustice, then Powell's unqualified support could be depended upon. He justified school boycotts by the end they sought. That end was not only religiously sound but was also politically sanctioned by the Constitution, the 1954 Supreme Court decision, and all subsequent civil rights legislation. He had no difficulty whatever in justifying civil disobedience of that kind.

The Goodness of America

Powell respected and loved the Constitution. He deplored the American practice of racism—a practice he

considered contradictory to the nation's constitutional
ideals. He viewed racism as a betrayal of God, of democracy, and of humanity. His entire public life was
dedicated to the task of seeking to bring America's
practices into harmony with its ideals. When he first
went to Congress, he was made vividly aware of the
way in which the capital city itself symbolized the contradiction.

> In that capital, along the banks of the quiet and muddy
> Potomac, witness and testimony were given by night
> and by day to the emasculation of the Bill of Rights and
> the Constitution that I had sworn to uphold, even when
> there was no upholding being done by those in high
> places. The dream of the Founding Fathers was becom-
> ing a faint mirage and "these truths" were no longer
> self-evident because truth had been banished from the
> land. There was evil there in Washington on January 3,
> 1945—the evil that comes when one preaches and fails
> to practice, when one proclaims and does not act, when
> the outside is clean and the inside is filled with filth.
> This was Washington, D.C.—capital of the "sweet land
> of liberty."[55]

Powell judged hypocrisy to be one of the worst
forms of evil, because of its deceit and cowardice.
More specifically, since it pretends that reality is something other than what it is, it denies truth. Powell's
love for truth was largely the center of his religion. He
believed that God was the absolute truth and the ultimate norm for all relative truths and the supreme
judge of all falsity. He was never more prophetic than
when he would pour out his stinging criticism on
America for its hypocrisy. "High above Washington
on the great dome of the Capitol, was the statue of
Freedom, and yet below that statue there was no freedom for people with the 'wrong skin color.' "[56]

He was convinced that the contradictions and hypocrisy that characterized America would lead to its
destruction if allowed to continue indefinitely. He was
completely persuaded of this when he returned from

the Bandung Conference in 1956. In spite of his fight at that conference to uphold the image of America in the face of the various communist onslaughts, his thinking on the problem of racism had changed. He began to view it not as a Black problem but as an American problem and as one that, if left unchecked, could destroy the nation itself. He had come to see that racism at home is linked with the international problem of colonialism. The Bandung Conference had stepped up the timetable for freedom. America had to lend its support or history would surely pass it by. He described the impact of Bandung thus:

> Bandung had completely changed my thinking. It made me over into an entirely new man. Before the Bandung Conference I could have been called, with some justification, a nationalist. Nearly everything I had done was aimed at obtaining more rights for the Negro people. . . . Whereas previously I had thought of civil rights in terms of rights for Negroes only, I now thought of civil rights as the sole method by which we could save the entire United States of America.[57]

He had come to the conclusion that the problem of civil rights in this country was integrally connected with the nation's salvation. Bandung represented the uniting of the nonwhite peoples of the world against the white colonialists and imperialists. America was condemned because of its internal racist policies.

In fits of anger Powell often leveled blanket statements of condemnation at America. But he never repudiated his oath to uphold the Constitution. When abroad he was never ashamed of his citizenship and frequently displayed defensiveness in his desire to protect America from foreign attacks. He took great pride in being a congressman. In none of his criticism did he ever repudiate the promised substance of American democracy. Even when he identified himself publicly with the Black Power movement, he defined it carefully in order to preserve its militancy while lessening its radical implications. He was neither extremely op-

timistic about America nor extremely pessimistic. He
was a faithful and severe critic, blessing American ideals, deploring American hypocrisy, while seeking to
discover a way whereby America's practice might become commensurate with its ideals. He felt that there
was evidence that some goodness and some justice was
a reality in America and that it was possible to discover effective means within the system to maximize
that goodness and that justice. The experience at the
Democratic National Convention in 1952 would re-
peat itself many times in Powell's political career. He
said of it: "There were those who stood forthright for
the kind of civil rights platform I knew would save the
nation and our party, and others who wanted no civil
rights plank whatsoever, who were interested in the
triumph of sectionalism rather than the salvation of
America."[58] He was able to form alliances with the
former group and to fight unceasingly in opposition to
the latter. From time to time victories would be won,
and with each victory his confidence in America would
increase. He deemed it possible to purge the American
political scene of its decadence. Discovering the means
and maintaining the power to do so, however, was always problematic.

Black Power

The emergence of Black Power as a cultural symbol
and as a political ideology greatly frightened white
America *and* Black America. Most militant and moderate civil rights leaders quickly went on record as disassociating themselves from it. Powell feared some of
its radical implications, but instead of running against
the new tide that had found ready acceptance among
the masses, he characteristically sought a way to ally
himself with it. Such an attempt was characteristic of
the way he had always encountered new left-wing
forces in the Black community.

Powell was not unprepared, however, for this event.
As a child he had developed a respect for many of the

things taught by Marcus Garvey and in later years wrote appreciatively of Garvey's notable contribution to Black American self-respect. During the '30s Powell had formed practical alliances with many nationalist groups, religious and political, in Harlem. Even the Communists were not beyond the pale.[59] When Malcolm X became an important force in Harlem and elsewhere, Powell cultivated a working relationship with him that was mutually satisfying. As with most of his alliances, there was a measure of mutual respect between the parties, although Powell was seldom in complete accord with their respective philosophies. Philosophical agreements were not important to him. He believed that groups representing differing philosophies could unite in their opposition to the common enemy, racial segregation, and could thereby realize some desired objectives in that fight. In his various confederations one sees advocates of differing philosophies and ideologies uniting around some practical goal that was desired by all. Further, Powell believed that one should join forces to combat common problems, thus affirming a variety of means short of violence and wanton destructiveness. That is to say, given the common goal—the destruction of segregation—many diverse groups could and should submerge their philosophical differences until the practical victory was won. He had mastered well that particular political art within the halls of Congress and among various outside organizations.

Powell had always been an independent. Although he was a member of the Democratic party and although he had accepted financial contributions from many whites, no person or party could control him. In all his activities he displayed enviable freedom. Hence, the cry of Black Power advocates for Black control of Black institutions was no new thing for him. He had always demanded such control of his own organizations, and during the preparatory stages of the 1963 March on Washington, he had strongly criticized Black civil rights organizations for allowing them-

selves to be controlled by white liberals. Such principles as Black self-determination, Black self-initiation,
Black self-reliance, Black self-development, Black racial pride, Black responsibility, and Black self-respect
had been affirmed by him throughout his public career. Not many were surprised that he should be the
one to call the first national conference of Black Power
in an attempt to give it definiteness. Subsequently, he
read into the congressional record his Black position
paper,[60] thus putting to death the idea that Black
Power was necessarily subversive. Indeed, he could
say that his position on Black Power had been the philosophy on which all his thinking and action had been
based during a quarter of a century of public life. "In
those 25 years, a philosophy which has guided my
thought and my every act has evolved out of my life
experiences as minister, politician, Congressman, and
man from Harlem. This philosophy is summed up in
what I call my 'Black Position Paper.' "[61]

Powell's Black position paper clearly upheld the
democratic creed and the principle of participatory
power for the masses. His many bills under the War on
Poverty program are considered integrally contribu-
tory to the economic and political empowerment of
the masses. Clause 11 of that report admonishes that
all demonstrations and protest activities must continue to be nonviolent.

Obviously, he saw much potential for good in the
Black Power movement, and in order to legitimate it,
he sought to harness it within the confines of his own
philosophy. For various reasons Powell's actual association with the leaders of the Black Power movement
was destined to be minimal, partly because people like
Stokely Carmichael were suspicious of any Black
leader who had worked and who resolved to continue
working with the Establishment, and partly because
his own personal and political problems with respect
to his continued tenure in the House preoccupied his
time and his energies. Further, Powell had never been
one who could become enmeshed in long philosophi-

cal discussions. His position on the matter provided a basis for some tactical alliances had they become necessary. But in his thinking, that was all he needed to do, given his position as congressman and civil rights leader. That is not intended to imply that Powell's position on Black Power was merely a tactical one. As stated above, he viewed his entire political philosophy as commensurate with the Black Power thrust save for its implications regarding violence, wanton destructiveness, and hostility toward whites. "Black Power is not antiwhite. Black Power simply reaffirms the integrity, dignity and self-respect of Black people. White supremacy denies them."[62]

Theologically, Powell looked on Black Power as consistent with the will of God. In fact, he viewed all power used for the actualization of God's will in the affairs of humans as inspired by God. Hence, he declared that Black Power and divine power are not dissimilar.[63]

In a baccalaureate sermon preached at Howard University in 1966 he called for an "audacious power" in order to realize the human rights that are God-given. "To demand these God-given human rights is to seek black power, what I call audacious power—the power to build black institutions of splendid achievement."[64] But, once again, that audacious power must be directed by God; Powell made that point abundantly clear. "I call for more arrogance of power among Black people, but an arrogance of power that is God-inspired, God-led and God-daring."[65]

For a long time Powell believed that America would be saved by the Black people, because the whites did not appear to have the moral capacity to take the initiative in guaranteeing racial justice. He held a dim view of the many Black leaders who were controlled by whites; he was more optimistic about the Black masses. He saw Black Power as the means of empowering the masses and of putting them in control of their destiny. He regarded the masses and their power—Black Power—as God-inspired and God-led.

In his thinking, that was vitally important, because once a people loses sight of God it then seeks to make the world over in its own selfish image. That, he believed, is what had happened to white America.

Struggle Against Poverty

Powell's public career began during the 1930s, when the situation of rampant misery and suffering in Harlem forced him to fight for economic justice in behalf of the masses. Blacks in New York were victims of racial discrimination and segregation in public and in private spheres of employment. Many businesses flourished in Harlem, but they rejected Black employees save for the most menial jobs. Through mass rallies, protest marches, boycotts, and other forms of agitation, Powell made significant progress in breaking down Jim Crow practices. Salesclerks, bus drivers, telephone operators, and many others owed their jobs in the '40s and '50s to the unstinting efforts of Adam Clayton Powell. Throughout his life he considered the problem of poverty among Blacks a direct outcome of racial discrimination and segregation.

Powell fought valiantly for a Fair Employment Practices Commission during his first term as congressman, but it was destined to take four years before that dream passed into law. When he became chair of the Education and Labor Committee, he successfully guided most of the bills pertaining to the War on Poverty through the House. His one criticism regarding that massive bulk of legislation was that insufficient funds had been allocated to the program. Further, he felt that much could be done by private corporations and foundations on a tax-free basis to win a permanent victory against poverty, but unfortunately, they were not interested. Although funds were limited, Powell took great pride in the War on Poverty programs, because he believed they were aimed at providing the substance that made desegregation meaningful to the masses. He continually emphasized that Blacks must have political power and economic advantage in order to participate meaningfully in the American society.

He contended that the economic problems facing Blacks could be solved, in large part, by effective legislation. In his judgment, Blacks would need to become more intelligent politically in the future and would have to devise effective ways of putting representatives with character and intelligence into public office, with a clear mandate from the people to effect legislation that would be economically significant to them. In the late '60s he criticized Black leaders who failed to see the necessity of helping the masses to develop political power through racial solidarity, which alone could lead to economic empowerment.

Although Powell was intensely interested in helping Black Americans to become economically sufficient, he was also conscious of the moral decadence that frequently accompanies economic security. Consequently, he often reminded his people that their real salvation lay in obedience to God and not to money, technology, or selfish pleasures. As he charged the church to stress participation in politics as a religious vocation, he charged it to accept its social obligation at all times: to challenge constantly all actions that deny respect for personality, a basic moral principle. But in all of this, he advised the church to constantly warn its members not to sell their souls in the process of gratifying physical desires. The Christian spirit must prevail, else Black America might inherit the crisis in values presently being experienced by white America—a crisis that could easily lead to self-destruction. In the main, however, Powell regarded his legislative efforts as the means for eliminating poverty among Blacks. Since he was of the opinion that poverty was caused by racism, civil rights legislation opposing racism was at the same time legislation for economic empowerment.

Photo courtesy of the Library of Congress

5

Malcolm X

The Theological
and Political Thought
of Malcolm X

It is necessary to state at the beginning of this chapter that neither orthodox Islam nor the Nation of Islam makes any meaningful distinction between theological thought and political thought. Neither acknowledges any cleavage between the sacred and the secular dimensions of life. Indeed, the religion of Islam presupposes a sacred nation founded on the truths of Allah and structured in obedience to the law of Allah.

For most of his public life Malcolm X was a trusted disciple of the Honorable Elijah Muhammad, the supreme authority of the Nation of Islam in America.[1] During many years of public speaking Malcolm regularly attested to the immense personal indebtedness he felt to his leader and teacher. He had come to Elijah Muhammad with an eighth-grade education, years of involvement in the underworld of criminal activity in Boston and in New York, and a lengthy prison record. Phoenix-like, he was destined to rise from ignominy to great fame. He had read voluminously while in prison, and after a period of personal training by Elijah Muhammad, he quickly rose in the Nation of Islam to

become, in a few short years, its official national
spokesperson. Through him the Nation of Islam grew
rapidly and soon became nationally known. His national reputation paved the way for international recognition. Until 1963 he considered himself a mere
disciple propounding the teachings of the Divine Messenger. Because he considered Elijah Muhammad to
be the final Messenger of Allah, faithfulness to his
teachings was sufficient claim to truth. Malcolm had
accepted the Myth of Yacub, which depicted the creation of the white person by a mythical Black scientist
called Yacub. He unquestionably affirmed the content
of the myth, namely, that the white person was created
as a devil with the charge to reign over the earth for a
designated period of time, after which Allah would restore the kingdom to its rightful heirs, the original
Black people. The Yacub Myth is the center of the
Nation of Islam's beliefs. In it the Black-white problem in America is given mythical structure by Elijah
Muhammad, and that structure is decreed to be absolutely true, known by the whites but hidden for centuries from Blacks. Indeed, the myth states that Blacks
have been scientifically brainwashed by whites. Since
the latter are devils by nature, they have no capacity
for morality. At best, they are tricksters and can never
be trusted. At worst, they are capable of indescribable
brutality. Time and again Malcolm correlated the animal analogy of fox and wolf with the liberal and conservative whites respectively. He considered their
goals to be identical and only their methods to be different. The fox (white liberal) is crafty and clever and
bent on serving only its own interests. The wolf (white
conservative) is cruel and unequivocally but equally
bent on serving only its own interests. Black people
were believed to have no true knowledge of themselves
so long as they remained outside the teachings of the
Nation of Islam. Their historic past, their language,
names, culture, and so on had been destroyed by the
devil white person. Salvation rested in their regaining
that true knowledge of self, of God, and of the other,

which God had given to Elijah Muhammad through
Wallace D. Fard, founder of the Nation of Islam. Malcolm described the true knowledge with the clarity
that was destined to become characteristic of his public discourses.

"The true knowledge," reconstructed much more briefly
than I received it, was that history had been "whitened"
in the white man's history books, and that the black man
had been "brainwashed for hundreds of years." Original
Man was black, in the continent called Africa where the
human race had emerged on the planet Earth.

The black man, original man, built great empires and
civilizations and cultures while the white man was still
living on all fours in caves. "The devil white man,"
down through history, out of his devilish nature, had
pillaged, murdered, raped, and exploited every race of
man not white.

Human history's greatest crime was the traffic in
black flesh when the devil white man went into Africa
and murdered and kidnapped to bring to the West in
chains, in slave ships, millions of black men, women,
and children, who were worked and beaten and tortured as slaves.

The devil white man cut these black people off from
all knowledge of their own kind, and cut them off from
any knowledge of their own language, religion, and past
culture, until the black man in America was the earth's
only race of people who had absolutely no knowledge of
his true identity.

In one generation, the black slave women in America
had been raped by the slavemaster white man until
there had begun to emerge a homemade, handmade,
brainwashed race that was no longer even of its true
color, that no longer even knew its true family names.
The slavemaster forced his family name upon this rape-
mixed race, which the slavemaster began to call "the
Negro."

This "Negro" was taught of his native Africa that it
was peopled by heathen, black savages, swinging like

monkeys from trees. This "Negro" accepted this along with every other teaching of the slavemaster that was designed to make him accept and obey and worship the white man.[2]

Race is a central category in the Yacub Myth.[3] The Black person is said to be the original human, while the white person originated as the evil product of a deviant experiment undertaken by a Black scientist who was embittered with Allah. Yacub created a devil in the form of the white person, who, in turn, has polluted the world with deceit and cruelty and tyranny. The persuasive appeal of that mythical knowledge is that it correlates with and tends to explain for the masses of Black people the reality they experience. To perceive actual human experience in a religious and mythical framework in such a way as to clarify that experience is a liberating event. For Malcolm it was a religious conversion.

> I do not now, and I did not then, liken myself to Paul. But I do understand his experience.
>
> I have since learned—helping me to understand what then began to happen within me—that the truth can be quickly received, or received at all, only by the sinner who knows and admits that he is guilty of having sinned much. Stated another way: only guilt admitted accepts truth. The Bible again: the one people whom Jesus could not help were the Pharisees; they didn't feel they needed any help.
>
> The very enormity of my previous life's guilt prepared me to accept the truth.[4]

Malcolm X was converted by what appeared to be the religious truths that were propounded by the Nation of Islam by the authority of its religious sage, Elijah Muhammad. The latter had given religious meaning to the history of Black people in the world. According to him, the racial conflict in America originated several thousand years ago, when white people were created. Devils by nature, they have always sought the total destruction of Black people through lies, deceit, hypocrisy, and a scientific brainwashing process. The fundamental task of the Nation of Islam is to awaken Black people to a true knowledge of themselves, God, and country. That knowledge must compel them to separate themselves from evil and from its source. True knowledge and moral purification is necessary in order to prepare the Black people to submit themselves completely to Allah, who will destroy the white people in the great eschatological battle of Armageddon.

A commitment to this true knowledge changed Malcolm's entire life; courageously and unequivocally, he proclaimed it far and wide. His powerful oratory and undeniable sincerity were effective in bringing thousands into the ranks of the Nation of Islam. In proclaiming the fundamental religious truths of Elijah Muhammad, Malcolm could be most persuasive whenever he illustrated their veracity by an appeal to the actual historical experience of Blacks with whites in this country.

Malcolm's pilgrimage to Mecca in 1959 resulted in a second major change in his life. The Mecca experience alone, however, was not the sole cause of the change, for Malcolm's intellectual curiosity had already led him to inquire about the relationship between the Nation of Islam in America and so-called "orthodox" Islam. Further, his experiences in being treated as a human being, with respect and dignity, in France, Germany, and Cairo enabled him to see for the first time that the race problem, so pervasive in America, did not exist everywhere.

> Back at the Frankfurt airport, we took a United Arab Airlines plane on to Cairo. Throngs of people, obviously Muslims from everywhere, bound on the pilgrimage, were hugging and embracing. They were of all complexions, the whole atmosphere was of warmth and

friendliness. The feeling hit me that there really wasn't any color problem here. The effect was as though I had just stepped out of a prison.[5]

Throughout the trip his experience of genuine kinship with the Muslims was unforgettable. In describing the flight from Cairo to Jedda he writes: "Packed in the plane were white, black, brown, red, and yellow people, blue eyes and blond hair, and my kinky red hair—all together, brothers! All honoring the same God Allah, all in turn giving equal honor to each other."[6]

Having been born and raised in the cradle of the world's most pernicious evil—racism—Malcolm experienced in Mecca the kind of genuine kinship among all races of humankind that he believed was made possible only by absolute submission to the will of Allah. No longer could he avow that white people were, by nature, racists. In a letter to his immediate friends and to the press he said:

America needs to understand Islam, because this is the one religion that erases from its society the race problem. Throughout my travels in the Muslim world, I have met, talked to, and even eaten with people who in America would have been considered "white"—but the "white" attitude was removed from their minds by the religion of Islam. I have never before seen *sincere* and *true* brotherhood practiced by all colors together, irrespective of their color.

You may be shocked by these words coming from me. But on this pilgrimage, what I have seen, and experienced, has forced me to *re-arrange* much of my thought-patterns previously held, and to *toss aside* some of my previous conclusions. This was not too difficult for me. Despite my firm convictions, I have been always a man who tries to face facts, and to accept the reality of life as new experience and new knowledge unfolds it. I have always kept an open mind, which is necessary to the flexibility that must go hand in hand with every form of intelligent search for truth. . . .

> We were *truly* all the same (brothers)—because their belief in one God had removed the "white" from their *minds*, the "white" from their *behavior*, and the "white" from their *attitude*.
>
> I could see from this, that perhaps if white Americans could accept the Oneness of God, then perhaps, too, they could accept *in reality* the Oneness of Man—and cease to measure, and hinder, and harm others in terms of their "differences" in color.
>
> With racism plaguing America like an incurable cancer, the so-called "Christian" white American heart should be more receptive to a proven solution to such a destructive problem. Perhaps it could be in time to save America from imminent disaster—the same destruction brought upon Germany by racism that eventually destroyed the Germans themselves.[7]

The major change this experience brought about in Malcolm's thought was that white people were not necessarily incurable racists. He had come to believe that they might be saved from their characteristic racism by submitting themselves to Allah. He hoped that the white youth in colleges and universities might respond to this solution.

> But as racism leads America up the suicide path, I do believe, from the experiences that I have had with them, that the whites of the younger generation, in the colleges and universities, will see the handwriting on the wall and many of them will turn to the *spiritual* path of *truth*—the *only* way left to America to ward off the disaster that racism inevitably must lead to.[8]

These new thoughts were diametrically opposed to the teachings of Elijah Muhammad, since they challenged the truthfulness of the Yacub Myth.

But these thoughts did not lead Malcolm to become an integrationist, as so many have hastened to conclude. Rather, I contend that up to the time of his assassination he continued to believe that most whites in the Western world were incurable racists bent on

the destruction of the humanity of the dark peoples of
the world. Malcolm steadfastly repudiated any and all
suggestions of integrating with the enemy. Such could
be only an exercise in self-annihilation.

In one respect, Malcolm always regretted his break
with Elijah Muhammad. He felt that Black people
should avoid fighting one another publicly, because
that made them indirect participants in the oppressor's strategy of divide and rule. Unfortunately, the
break was inevitable. In Malcolm's opinion, the Nation of Islam was too narrowly confined in terms of its
religious thought and in its unwillingness to engage in
political action. He described his private feelings:

> If I harbored any personal disappointment whatsoever,
> it was that privately I was convinced that our Nation of
> Islam could be an even greater force in the American
> black man's overall struggle—if we engaged in more *ac-
> tion*. By that, I mean I thought privately that we should
> have amended, or relaxed, our general non-engagement
> policy. I felt that wherever black people committed
> themselves, in the Little Rocks and the Birminghams
> and other places, militantly disciplined Muslims should
> also be there—for all the world to see, and respect, and
> discuss.[9]

I contend that the break with Elijah Muhammad
represented a change in Malcolm's theological understanding of the nature of humanity and of the origins
of racism. However, that change did not imply that
Malcolm's political understanding had become less
radical. It is clear that after Mecca he could no longer
affirm the mythical explanation of white racism as ex-
plicated in the Yacub Myth. Obviously, therefore, he
could no longer be a disciple of Elijah Muhammad. In
spite of that, his political understanding continued to
be shaped by the master-servant model of society,
whereby the whites in Western society were viewed as
the inevitable masters over Blacks. Whether in
America or in other parts of the world, white domination of darker peoples characterized, in Malcolm's

view, the nature of political and social and economic arrangements. Malcolm had come to see that racism in America was part of a worldwide exploitation and domination of darker peoples by Western whites. Because the problem seemed to be worldwide, it implied goals that were not simply national goals. Therefore, he advocated human rights rather than civil rights—the former applying to all humankind while the latter is applicable only within a specific state. Malcolm no longer preached that the white person was evil by nature, but even on that subject one should not assume that his thought had softened greatly. He continually claimed that he was not indicting a whole race, although he admitted that the historical evidence indicts most of it. As late as January 1965, in what had by then become a typical manner, he skillfully fell short of indicting the whole white race:

> Any man who will know the level of civilization that we started out on, and came from, any man who knows the criminal creeds that were done to us by his people to bring us to the level that we've been on for the past three hundred years, knows he is so deceptive, so deceitful, so criminally deceitful, that it is almost beyond his nature or desire to come up with anything meaningful that will undo what has been done to us over the past three hundred years. It is absolutely necessary—anything that is done for us, has to be done by us.[10]

Since the debate about his cleavage with Elijah Muhammad has centered so completely on the nature of Malcolm's ideological changes and their concomitant implications for political action, it is important to note that up until March 1964 Malcolm had spoken about politics from within the framework of Elijah Muhammad's religious perspective. For many months prior to that date his speeches dealt primarily with the social problem of human rights facing the nation and the world. During that time he did not speak about the religious myth per se, although it could easily have been assumed by the audience, since the break had not yet become public. "But around 1963, if anyone had noticed, I spoke less and less of religion. I taught social doctrine to Muslims, and current events, and politics."[11]

What I want to convey is that a careful analysis of Malcolm's sociological analysis and political ideology will reveal that both remained fundamentally the same after his break with the Nation of Islam. That is to say, his religious thought changed in the sense that Elijah Muhammad's myth could no longer be affirmed in the light of orthodox Islam. His political thought, however, did not change in principle. For indeed, he had been teaching such political doctrines even while giving public assent to the Nation of Islam, whether implicitly or explicitly. But it was clear that he would advance no new focus in that organization without Elijah Muhammad's tacit permission. It appears that nothing in his encounter with orthodox Islam threatened his perspective regarding Black nationalism. Malcolm had always considered his political thinking to be compatible with his religion while in the Nation of Islam and also later, when he formed his orthodox Islamic mosque. This was clearly seen in March 1964, when he declared his independence from the Nation of Islam and announced that he would found a mosque in Harlem that would give a religious and moral foundation to his political philosophy of Black nationalism.

> I am going to organize and head a new mosque in New York City, known as the Muslim Mosque, Inc. This gives us a religious base, and the spiritual force necessary to rid our people of the vices that destroy the moral fibre of our community.
>
> Our political philosophy will be black nationalism. Our economic and social philosophy will be black nationalism. Our cultural emphasis will be black nationalism.[12]

Initially, Malcolm had thought to incorporate the politics of Black nationalism into the Muslim Mosque and to allow it to be open and flexible to the participation of all Black people, whether or not they were Muslims. Three months later he saw the need for a distinctively political organization and founded the Organization of Afro-American Unity, which he considered compatible with the mosque but which allowed more freedom to those non-Muslims who participated. This is a clear illustration of the measure of openness he envisioned. The OAAU was constituted so that he could work cooperatively with non-Muslims for the goals of Black nationalism. This was a measure of expediency, since his break with Elijah Muhammad left him with a small constituency of actual followers.

In his declaration of independence Malcolm stated that he still believed in Elijah Muhammad's basic solution to the problem of racism: a return to Africa. He considered that proposal to be a long-range prospect, however, and in the meantime he felt that Blacks should act on certain more proximate goals, which he also judged to be compatible with the principles of Elijah Muhammad.

> I am and always will be a Muslim. My religion is Islam. I still believe that Mr. Muhammad's analysis of the problem is the most realistic, and that his solution is the best one. This means that I too believe the best solution is complete separation, with our people going back home, to our own African homeland.
>
> But separation back to Africa is still a long-range program, and while it is yet to materialize, 22 million of our people who are still here in America need better food, clothing, housing, education and jobs *right now*. Mr. Muhammad's program does point us back homeward, but it also contains within it what we could and should be doing to help solve many of our own problems while we are still here.[13]

For the remainder of his life Malcolm concentrated his efforts on that more imminent goal of Blacks: developing the power to control their destiny here in America. In keeping with his philosophy of Black nationalism, he advocated that Blacks should control the political, economic, and social institutions in their communities.[14] Later, however, he would be led to discover the philosophical difficulties implied by the nomenclature "Black nationalism," which excluded those true revolutionaries in Africa and elsewhere who were not Black. That presented a philosophical problem but not one that threatened the political position he had been advocating for Blacks in America.

Malcolm's newly found freedom from the controls of Elijah Muhammad enabled him to be more flexible in thought and in action. He sought some form of coalition with other leaders and organizations with which he might agree on selected matters. Intellectually, he allowed for the possibility that some whites could participate in the struggle to eradicate racism, but practically, he was not prepared to permit any to join either the mosque or the political organization. In his declaration of independence that point was made abundantly clear. "Whites can help us, but they can't join us. There can be no black-white unity until there is first some black unity."[15] He advised whites to develop their own programs and strategies for solving the problem of racism. Although he was often charitable and humane to whites as individuals, he was suspicious of those whites who wanted to join Black organizations or who sought some form of close association with Blacks. "America's racism is among their own fellow whites. That's where the sincere whites who really mean to accomplish something have got to work."[16]

Formerly, Malcolm had justified his thought and proposals by an appeal to the teachings of Elijah Muhammad. After the break his final appeal to truth was orthodox Islam, which he genuinely thought was capable of producing a society of love and humility and kinship while affirming a broad measure of diversity in its citizenry. "True Islam removes racism, because people of all colors and races who accept its religious principles and bow down to the one God, Allah, also automatically accept each other as brothers and sisters, regardless of differences in complexion."[17]

Malcolm was impressed with the practical possibility Islam offered for kinship among the races of humankind. He believed that submission to Islam on the part of whites could effect that desired end.

> If Islam can place the spirit of true brotherhood in the hearts of the "whites" whom I have met here in the Land of the Prophets, then surely it can also remove the "cancer of racism" from the heart of the white American and perhaps in time to save America from imminent racial disaster.[18]

He contended that Islam was needed by whites but more especially by Blacks, in whom he hoped for a more ready response. Further, he asserted that the establishment of a kindred spirit is not a legal task but a religious one.

> I am in agreement one hundred per cent with those racists who say that no government laws ever can *force* brotherhood. The only true world solution today is governments guided by true religion—of the spirit. Here in race-torn America, I am convinced that the Islam religion is desperately needed, particularly by the American black man. The black man needs to reflect that he has been America's most fervent Christian—and where has it gotten him? In fact, in the white man's hands, in the white man's interpretation . . . where has Christianity brought this *world?*[19]

Malcolm expressed the view that Islam was completely void of racism, and therefore, its objective of kinship was true and practical. But the religion of Islam is based on radical distinctions between truth and falsehood, good and evil. Further, the religion teaches its followers to work zealously for the realization of that religious end and never to compromise or shun the battlefield whereon the truth and goodness of Allah is threatened by infidels. At Malcolm X's funeral, Omar Osman, a representative of the Islam Center of

Switzerland and of the United States, spoke these words:

> We knew Brother Malcolm as a blood brother, particularly after his pilgrimage to Mecca last year. The highest thing that a Muslim can aspire to is to die on the battlefield and not die at his bedside. Those who die on the battlefield are not dead, but are alive.[20]

The battlefield has been prominent in the history of Islam, and a strong belief in self-defense is largely responsible for that fact. Time and again Malcolm would declare that he believed in the universal kinship of all peoples but saw no sense in wasting it on those who didn't want it. Further, he would say that he believed in peace, but peace is of no worth unless it can be defended against those who would destroy it. In his third and final lecture at the Harvard Law School Forum he said:

> I believe in the brotherhood of all men, but I don't believe in wasting brotherhood on anyone who doesn't want to practice it with me. Brotherhood is a two-way street. I don't think brotherhood should be practiced with a man just because his skin is white. Brotherhood should hinge upon the deeds and attitudes of a man. I couldn't practice brotherhood, for example, with some of those Eastlands or crackers in the South who are responsible for the condition of our people.[21]

In the same lecture he also spoke about his belief in peace. He was often forced to address himself to this matter, since the news media had created an image of him as a leader who advocated violence in opposition to nonviolence.

> The Organization of Afro-American Unity (to which I belong) is a peaceful organization based on brotherhood. Oh yes, it is peaceful. But I believe you can't have peace until you're ready to protect it. As you will die protecting yours, I will die protecting mine. . . . We believe that the O.A.A.U. should provide defense units in

every area of this country. . . . Such self-defense units should have brothers who will not go out and initiate aggression, but brothers who are qualified, equipped to retaliate when anyone imposes brutality on us, whether it be in Mississippi, Massachusetts, California, or New York City. The O.A.A.U. doesn't believe it should permit civil rights workers to be murdered. When a government can't protect civil rights workers, we believe we should do it. Even in the Christian Bible it says that he who kills with the sword shall be killed by the sword, and I'm not against it. I'm for peace, yet I believe that any man facing death should be able to go to any length to assure that whoever is trying to kill him doesn't have a chance.[22]

In Malcolm's thinking, true leadership was based on genuine religious foundations. Unfortunately, the white people had corrupted Christianity when it entered Western Europe and had simply used it as a device to draw other persons into their imperialistic schemes. Malcolm contended that people who have no spirituality become seekers after naked physical power; they exhibit the character that is germane to the brutes and lose the capacity to embody the humane virtues. "Mankind's history has proved from one era to another that the true criterion of leadership is spiritual. Men are attracted by spirit. By power, men are *forced*. Love is engendered by spirit. By power, anxieties are created."[23]

But Malcolm considered it a delusion to think that one could alter the behavior of one's enemies by spiritual acts of love. Those who live by power and force must be resisted by power and force. But within the community of kinship physical power has no rightful place. Malcolm was a practical man. He was interested only in those thoughts, actions, alliances, and associations that were able to produce the desired results. Using the strategy of nonviolence to combat the forces of evil made no sense whatsoever to him. He thought that it presented no threat to the forces of white op-

pression and that it was easily pacified by certain token benefits, which were granted for purposes of
furthering the objective of continued oppression. In an
interview conducted by Kenneth B. Clark, Malcolm
stated his position on the matter, a position that he
held to tenaciously for the rest of his life.

> Any Negro who teaches other Negroes to turn the other
> cheek is disarming that Negro. Any Negro who teaches
> Negroes to turn the other cheek in the face of attack is
> disarming that Negro of his God-given right, of his
> moral right, of his natural right, of his intelligent right
> to defend himself. Everything in nature can defend it-
> self, and is right in defending itself except the American
> Negro. . . . King is the best weapon that the white man,
> who wants to brutalize Negroes, has ever gotten in this
> country, because he is setting up a situation where,
> when the white man wants to attack Negroes, they can't
> defend themselves, because King has put this foolish
> philosophy out—you're not supposed to fight or you're
> not supposed to defend yourself.[24]

Thus, Malcolm affirmed the Islamic principle of kinship, which enabled and required its followers to defend this kinship whenever its security was threatened
and by any means possible. When one confronts evil
only the natural law of self-defense is justifiable. A
Muslim is strengthened by the confidence of being
blessed by Allah in that battle. When the enemy
threatens one's humanity, there is no common moral
ground to which one can appeal. Therefore, negotiation between the parties is meaningless, because doing
business with perpetrators of evil can only issue in
compromise, and the desired good is always distorted
in that process. Further, Malcolm could see no religious or moral virtue in choosing to suffer at the hands
of the evil one. When the latter is bent on one's destruction, one would do well only by destroying that
evil one by any means possible. To do otherwise would
be inhuman at best and subhuman at worst.[25] As an
activist primarily interested in solving the problem of

racism, Malcolm took comfort in a religion that affirmed a rigorous pragmatic approach to the problems of life. Consequently, he had no difficulty in defending himself when he was attacked for changing his tactics and strategies from time to time. A pragmatic approach does not require fixed principles that guide all action but rather the ability to be flexible in accordance with time and circumstance. "The reason you change your method is that you have to change your method according to time and conditions that prevail."[26] Further, Malcolm's political pragmatism went so far as to include Islam itself as a means of effecting the desired goal, since it had demonstrated capability in achieving certain liberating results among Black people in America.

> In New York we have recently founded the Muslim Mosque, Incorporated, which has as its base the religion of Islam, the religion of Islam because we have found that this religion creates more unity among our people than any other type of philosophy can do. At the same time, the religion of Islam is more successful in eliminating the vices that exist in the so-called Negro community, which destroy the moral fibre of the so-called Negro community.[27]

Consistent with his pragmatic orientation, Malcolm utilized minimum energy in discussing the nature of abstract principles and their justification. Major ethical principles became, for him, operationalized objectives. Their intrinsic value was assumed if they could be operationalized in the struggle. Nowhere does he engage in philosophical debate concerning them. The major problem he saw was that freedom, justice, equality, and human dignity were actualities for the oppressor but were denied to the oppressed. And because of that denial the oppressed stood in danger of losing their humanity. He contended that the struggle to preserve one's humanity is justified by reason, by nature, and by the Islamic faith. Freedom, justice, equality, and dignity could never be abstract princi-

ples for him. Rather, they were the basis of humanity,
and if they were threatened or denied, they could only
be meaningfully viewed as immediate goals that must
be struggled for with all one's being.

> Our objective is complete freedom, complete justice,
> complete equality, by any means necessary. That never
> changes. Complete and immediate recognition and re-
> spect as human beings, that doesn't change, that's what
> all of us want. I don't care what you belong to—you
> still want that, recognition and respect as a human
> being.[28]

It was Malcolm's opinion that Black Americans, in
large part, had lost their humanity. That is evidenced
by their apparent lack of resistance to the paralyzing
conditions they are forced to endure. In Malcolm's
thought, any person with a strong sense of self-worth
should fight vigorously against that which threatens it.
Freedom, justice, and equality can only become realities for and be preserved by self-respecting human beings. And self-respect implies self-defense. No one can
give an individual freedom, justice, equality; one must
demand them and claim them.

> There's only one way to be a first-class citizen. There's
> only one way to be independent. There's only one way
> to be free. It's not something that someone gives to you.
> It's something that you take. Nobody can give you inde-
> pendence. Nobody can give you freedom. Nobody can
> give you equality or justice or anything. If you're a
> man, you take it. If you can't take it, you don't deserve
> it. Nobody can give it to you. So if you and I want
> freedom, if we want independence, if we want respect,
> if we want recognition, we obey the law, we are peace-
> ful—but at the same time, at any moment that you and
> I are involved in any kind of action that is legal, that is
> in accord with our civil rights, in accord with the courts
> of this land, in accord with the Constitution—when all
> of these things are on our side, and we still can't get it,
> it's because we aren't on our own side.[29]

Malcolm delivered a considerable number of speeches that justified his call for revolutionary action by appealing to a series of historical precedents. America and all other nations of the world became independent by means of warfare and not by means of nonviolence. Since the freedom to be independent, self-respecting human beings is a basic value of all humans, Blacks, like countless millions before them, must be prepared to lay down their lives fighting for that freedom. In December 1964, while appearing with Fannie Lou Hamer and other representatives of the Mississippi Freedom Democratic party, Malcolm expressed sentiments he had reiterated many times before:

> I say that a black man's freedom is as valuable as a white man's freedom. And I say that a black man has the right to do whatever is necessary to get his freedom that other human beings have done to get their freedom. I say that you and I will never get our freedom non-violently and patiently and lovingly. We will never get it until we let the world know that as other human beings have laid down their lives for freedom—and also taken life for freedom—that you and I are ready and willing and equipped and qualified to do the same thing.[30]

Malcolm held the conviction that defending one's independence and self-respect by any means necessary was a basic requirement of humanity and, as such, was an act of self-defense. Further, he believed that a people gained respect from others only by demonstrating a willingness to defend themselves. Revolutionaries have always been repudiated by the oppressing powers, but history records that their own people regard them as virtuous heroes when the battle is won. He also asserted that such a commitment on the part of Black people would be effective in communicating with the oppressing powers in America, since it would use a language the oppressor has no difficulty in comprehending. Grudgingly, white oppressors would have more respect for Blacks who demonstrated their willingness to engage in a violent battle for their freedom than for those who nonviolently exposed themselves to additional doses of suffering or who went begging the oppressor for such token benefits as an integrated cup of coffee.

Most of Malcolm's thought about proposed policies for solving the race problem emerged out of his penetrating analysis of the nature of the problem. Being a practical man, he focused most of his speeches and writings on preparing Blacks to be effective agents of their own liberation. Indeed, he felt that the problem for America was so severe in this contemporary period that all scholarship should be for the purpose of uniting theory and practice to the end of emancipating Black people.

> What is actually meant by theoretical or academic education? The unity of theoretical education and the application of this wealth of knowledge to the practical requirements and demands of our liberation is a difficult challenge. In a freedom struggle such as the one that exists in Africa and America today the unity of thought and action must be the cornerstone of all of us who desire to work for the total emancipation of the black race.[31]

During his association with Elijah Muhammad and thereafter, Malcolm believed that before a people can move effectively toward genuine social change they must, first of all, have a clear and true understanding of themselves, the problem, and the enemy. Malcolm reasoned that the problem facing Blacks in this country was twofold. On the one hand, the whites were systematic oppressors, and that oppression had to be stopped by any means necessary. But, on the other hand, Blacks were victims of that oppression not only politically, economically, and socially but also in terms of their own self-understanding. He declared that during slavery the white masters had systematically and scientifically destroyed all characteristics of

the Black people's African identity. But he continued
to feel that some remnants of that African heritage had
survived in the form of music and in human sensitivity. Most Blacks had come to think that they had no
significant history prior to slavery. Accordingly, they
considered themselves as a people to be inferior, because they possessed nothing of their own in which to
have pride. Inasmuch as they had a false understanding of their history, they had no self-respect as a race.
Consequently, they were doomed to failure in attempting to solve the race problem, because they could only
think white thoughts and aspire to white goals. Malcolm regarded the educated Black bourgeoisie to be
the most brainwashed of all. The social isolation of the
Black masses from whites was a blessing in disguise,
since it prevented the manipulative process from being
completed. Malcolm was fond of drawing a sociological analogy between the house slave and the field slave
as a way of describing the nature of the "educated Negro" and the "uneducated Negro" respectively. Meta-
phorically, he condemned the former as Uncle Tom
and praised the latter as the rebel. In a like manner, all
the institutions and organizations founded by the "educated Negro" were considered to bear the marks of
that brainwashing process. For this reason Malcolm
decided that the first thing that needed to be done was
to reeducate the so-called Negroes about their true
identity and about the nature of their oppression.
Freedom for Blacks must begin with right thinking in
order to regain the sense of self-respect that had been
so skillfully destroyed by the oppressor. Every Black
person in America must overcome the Negro identity
(an identity forged by whites) and become an African-
American. "In short, in order that African-Americans
must become free they must reidentify themselves
with Africa, as do Jews, Irish, Germans and Italians
with the respective countries of their origin."[32]
　Malcolm stated that without true self-understanding
a person is not free but is a victim of ignorance or of
some external force. As a result, one's humanity is se-

verely compromised. She or he is a mere puppet who reflects the desires and values of the puppeteer. The primary objective of Malcolm X was to liberate Blacks from false thinking about themselves and about their world. This was considered a necessary condition for any meaningful action.

> This is the type of philosophy that we want to express among our people. We don't need to give them a program, not yet. First, give them something to think about. If we give them something to think about, and start them thinking in a way that they should think, they'll see through all this camouflage that's going on right now. It's just a show—the result of a script written by somebody else.[33]

Now that we have a sufficient overview of the major concerns and principles that shaped Malcolm's thought, we are ready to look at the specific issues set forth in chapter 1 in order to see why he took the positions he did.

Civil Disobedience

During the Birmingham campaign Martin Luther King's acts of civil disobedience created a major national issue. The matter was widely debated in the media, in civil rights organizations, and in colleges and universities. Malcolm's response to the issue was strongly affirmative, but his reasoning on the subject was that of a Black nationalist and was, therefore, quite different from King's reasoning and that of his followers and sympathizers. Malcolm believed that the rules governing the struggle against racism should be determined by Black people and not by whites. He contended that the way things are viewed by the oppressor is necessarily different from the way things are viewed by the oppressed. What appears reasonable and just to the one has the opposite appearance to the other. For the most part, Malcolm did not express much interest in that particular debate; he deemed it a very minor issue. He advocated revolution, and any true revolution must disobey the laws of the Establishment. His condemnation of the historic March on Washington was partly due to the fact that the Black leaders, in his estimation, were conned out of doing what they first said they intended to do, namely, to bring the capital city to a standstill. Had they done that they would have gained considerable respect from him, but instead, they allowed John F. Kennedy and other white liberals to dictate the terms on which the march would take place. Even certain speeches had to be edited by the white liberals, who possessed a veto. Malcolm wrote that the Black leaders had said

> that they were going to march on Washington, march on the Senate, march on the White House, march on the Congress, and tie it up, bring it to a halt, not let the government proceed. They even said they were going out to the airport and lay down on the runway and not let any airplanes land. I'm telling you what they said. That was revolution. That was the black revolution.[34]

In Malcolm's opinion, the initial intention of the march scared the white power structure to death. So they decided to integrate it, which was tantamount to infiltrating it; the resulting approval of the government and the churches and organized labor turned it into an Establishment occasion. In short, its militancy was killed. "It ceased to be angry, it ceased to be hot, it ceased to be uncompromising. Why, it even ceased to be a march. It became a picnic, a circus."[35]

Malcolm held the view that those who practiced racism against Blacks were in violation of the law. When one is a victim of another's violation of the law, one is justified in exercising the natural law of self-preservation. In other words, Malcolm argued that racism violated the law and that Blacks, therefore, were compelled to employ acts of self-defense in whatever ways possible. Civil disobedience, in the sense of violating an injunction, was trivial in comparison to what they might need to do. But Malcolm was capable

of confusing his own argument when he repeatedly likened civil disobedience to the tactics of the Ku Klux
Klan, saying that the only language the latter can understand is its own. He admonished his followers that
in the event they be attacked by the foe, they should
retaliate similarly in self-defense. The more radical
point he advocated, however, was that when Blacks
are hurt or killed by white racists, and when the government and its law enforcement officials refuse to
find and discover those who are guilty, then Blacks
should get revenge on behalf of their own people and
should enforce the law themselves. They should seek
out the guilty ones and punish them accordingly.
"When a government can't protect civil rights workers, we believe we should do it."[36] In stronger language
he said in the same speech,

> Racists know only one language, and it is doing the
> black man in this country an injustice to expect him to
> talk the language of peace to people who don't know
> peaceful language. In order to get any kind of point
> across our people must speak whatever language the
> racist speaks. The government can't protect us. The
> government has not protected us. It is time for us to do
> whatever is necessary by any means necessary to pro-
> tect ourselves. If the government doesn't want us run-
> ning around here wild like that, then I say let the
> government get up off its . . . whatever it's on, and take
> care of it itself.[37]

Malcolm viewed civil disobedience in the light of
his revolutionary thought. It was no mere isolated instance of whether or not a group should disobey a civil
injunction. Rather, it was a necessary aspect of orient-
ing oneself to the enemy. It is a life-or-death battle,
and if Blacks do not perceive it as such, their actions
will be ineffective. The laws of the land are racist. Law
enforcement officials use their power and position to
promote racism. When the battle lines are clearly
drawn between good and evil, then it is incumbent
upon Blacks to engage the enemy by any means neces-

sary in order to gain the desired victory. When it becomes necessary to break the law, then that is the single, uncompromising thing Blacks must do, for in breaking that law they demonstrate their independence from such racist controls. When Blacks are given the vote or any other legal right of citizenship, Malcolm felt that they should utilize that right justly and intelligently. But when they are not given the rights and protection of law, then that situation becomes a revolutionary one, and Blacks ought to take up arms and win those rights for themselves, even as the founders of independent America did vis-à-vis the English colonial powers.

School Boycotts

Most of the school boycotts that gained a measure of prominence in the mid-'60s were directed at effecting the implementation of the 1954 Supreme Court desegregation decision. In spite of the fact that Malcolm X viewed civil rights legislation for Blacks as having no substance, he was willing to support various kinds of school boycotts aimed at racial integration. On first impression, one discerns a contradiction in the man who advocated racial separation but who supported action leading to integration. Malcolm viewed it differently. He supported such moves because he was opposed to segregation and not because he affirmed integration.

> We will work with anybody, anywhere, at any time who is genuinely interested in tackling the problem head-on, non-violently as long as the enemy is non-violent, but violent when the enemy gets violent. We'll work with you on the voter registration drive, we'll work with you on rent strikes, we'll work with you on school boycotts—I don't believe in any kind of integration; I'm not even worried about it because I know you're not going to get it anyway; . . . but we will still work with you on the school boycotts because we're against a seg-

regated school system. A segregated school system produces children who when they graduate, graduate with
crippled minds. But this does not mean that a school is
segregated because it's all black. A segregated school
means a school that is controlled by people who have
no real interest in it whatsoever.[38]

Hence, Malcolm was able to work with those who
organized school boycotts even though he did not
agree with the ends they sought, namely, integrated
schools. Rather, he believed that Blacks should have
their own schools. However, separate schools were not
segregated schools. Segregated schools were forced
upon Blacks. Separate schools were chosen voluntarily
and were controlled by Blacks. Black control of the
institutions that shaped Black destiny was a major
goal of his political thought and action. Accordingly,
his support of school boycotts did not imply that he
shared a common philosophy with civil rights activists. Rather, he justified his participation on different
grounds. Further, such actions as school boycotts, rent
strikes, and voter registration drives, in his eyes, evidenced the fact that Blacks were moving forcibly
against segregated institutions, not in a manner of
moral suasion but by making demands and by employing force to effect those demands. It also demonstrated
Blacks using their own power to fight against the
power that oppressed them. The boycott was a method
that could be effective in closing down certain racist
institutions. Malcolm had no difficulty in participating
in those kinds of activities.

After his break with Elijah Muhammad, Malcolm
sought to unite all Black people around the principles
of Black nationalism. In order to effect that unity he
confessed a certain craftiness in his strategy, which he
glibly equated with the way Billy Graham relates to
the churches.[39] He decided that he would not threaten
the existence of any other organizations that might be
practicing Black nationalism. Indeed, he would cooperate with those programs that were directed at the

development of Black people and would encourage his followers to participate in those organizations that promoted such programs.

> Our gospel is black nationalism. We're not trying to threaten the existence of any organization, but we're spreading the gospel of black nationalism. Anywhere there's a church that is also preaching and practicing the gospel of black nationalism, join that church. If the NAACP is preaching and practicing the gospel of black nationalism, join the NAACP. If CORE is spreading and practicing the gospel of black nationalism, join CORE. Join any organization that has a gospel that's for the uplift of the black man. And when you get into it and see them pussyfooting or compromising, pull out of it because that's not black nationalism. We'll find another one.[40]

In his published statement of the basic aims and objectives of the Organization of Afro-American Unity, Malcolm gave the rationale for the importance of schools for Black children being controlled by Blacks and announced that if those demands were not acknowledged he would call upon the parents of schoolchildren to participate in school boycotts. The proposals call upon the Board of Education in New York City to turn over to the OAAU that 10 percent of the schools they confessed were unimprovable.

> Through these steps we will make the 10 percent of schools we take over educational showplaces that will attract the attention of people all over the nation. If these proposals are not met, we will ask Afro-American parents to keep their children out of the present inferior schools they attend. When these schools in our neighborhood are controlled by Afro-Americans, we will return to them.[41]

School boycotts organized by Blacks manifested the kind of independent action Malcolm appreciated. They were premised on uncompromising demands, and they represented real power in confrontation with

real power. They displayed a kind of hostility and re-
bellion that marked the first stage of the necessary revolution for solving the problems facing Blacks in this
country and around the world. They were organized
on the presupposition that the demands of Blacks were
not going to be met apart from an inevitable struggle
on a battlefield where the lines were clearly drawn between good and evil, friend and foe.

Civil Rights Legislation

Malcolm X was opposed to Black people fighting for
civil rights legislation. In the first place, he viewed the
strategy as a white liberal trick designed to make Blacks
think that they were achieving victories only to discover later that they had been deluded. In his third and
final lecture to the Harvard Law School Forum, December 16, 1964, he described the Supreme Court decision
on desegregation as the prime example of that conspiratorial strategy. Civil rights legislation is a farce since
there is no commitment to enforcing such laws.

> Because we began to cry a little louder, a new strategy
> was used to handle us. The strategy evolved with the
> Supreme Court desegregation decision, which was writ-
> ten in such tricky language that every crook in the
> country could sidestep it. The Supreme Court desegre-
> gation decision was handed down over ten years ago. It
> has been implemented less than ten percent in those ten
> years. It was a token advancement, even as we've been
> the recipients of "tokenism" in education, housing, em-
> ployment, everything. But nowhere in the country dur-
> ing the past ten years has the black man been treated as
> a human being in the same context as other human
> beings. He's always being patronized in a very paternal-
> istic way, but never has he been given an opportunity to
> function as a human being.[42]

While he was a follower of Elijah Muhammad, Malcolm had opposed civil rights legislation for Blacks.
That position remained unchanged. He had a pen-

chant for clarity; that is seen most graphically as he continually reasoned that, according to the Constitution, citizenship is bestowed automatically upon everyone by virtue of his or her birth on American soil. Since that is the case, then why should Blacks be forced to face beatings, imprisonment, and even death fighting for the passage of more laws to effect their citizenship. The whole matter appeared ludicrous and absurd to him.

Further, he contended that white Americans had no commitment whatsoever to giving Blacks citizenship rights, and, therefore, those Blacks who struggled for such were forced into a position of begging for something they would never get. He saw clearly that the basic value underlying the civil rights struggle was integration, and he spent the whole of his public career opposing that value. It was difficult for him to understand why anyone would want to integrate himself or herself into a morally corrupt society. He felt that only those who had been completely brainwashed, for example, Black civil rights leaders, could even entertain such a notion.

Further still, Malcolm believed that Black civil rights advocates were capable of being deluded by the conspiratorial scheme of white liberal Americans, because they had not been committed to doing for themselves what other peoples have had to do for themselves, namely, protect and project their humanity. Consequently, the civil rights movement had completely misunderstood the nature of the problem and could effect no lasting solution for it. In its very design, the civil rights movement was doomed to failure. Malcolm felt that it was obvious that America is not governed by law but by that which is expedient to the furtherance of its own interests. To that end it had tricked the civil rights leaders into thinking the problem was, in fact, a legislative one. The results of the Supreme Court decision of 1954 and subsequent civil rights laws should have made this point abundantly clear a long time ago.

> If the Federal government cannot enforce the law of the highest court in the land when it comes to nothing but equal rights to education for African-Americans, how can anyone be so naive as to think all the additional laws brought into being by the civil-rights bill will be enforced?[43]

Malcolm characterized the struggle for civil rights legislation as one whereby the victim of oppression requests the oppressor to cease oppressing. He considered such tactics futile. Freedom would never be gained that way.

> When you go to Washington, D.C., expecting those crooks down there—and that's what they are—to pass some kind of civil rights legislation to correct a very criminal situation, what you are doing is encouraging the black man, who is the victim, to take his case into the court that's controlled by the criminal that made him the victim. It will never be solved that way.[44]

Malcolm was also of the opinion that tricky white liberals had brainwashed Blacks into thinking that their problem was one of civil rights. Such a strategy succeeded in getting Blacks to consider their predicament as a simple domestic one, and as such no other country or association of nations had any right to interfere with a civil dispute. Long before he left the Nation of Islam, Malcolm attempted to teach his followers that the dilemma was not one of civil rights but of human rights. Blacks could be recognized as citizens only after they had first been respected as humans. Their human rights were threatened, and that threat was much more basic than the denial of civil rights. More important, if Blacks could think of their plight in terms of human rights, they would be justified in appealing to the United Nations for help. Since America is sensitive to world opinion and does respond to world pressure, he considered the United Nations a possible agency in forcing the nation to become more just in its dealings with Black people. To that end he spoke at the first meeting of the Organization of African Unity, in Addis Ababa, Ethiopia, and urged the African independent nations to bring the matter of American racism before the United Nations. His respect for the Organization of African Unity was so great that he organized his own philosophy of Black nationalism into an organization based on it and similarly named: the Organization of Afro-American Unity. Malcolm opposed civil rights legislation because he judged the problem of racism to be no civil matter. Civil rights legislation assumed that racism was an internal national situation. Malcolm had come to view it as an international matter, and as such he considered it necessary for the answer to come via an international agency. Malcolm deplored the struggle for civil rights legislation to the point of condemning the March on Washington, D.C., in 1963, by calling it a "one-day integrated picnic."[45]

Black Power

Malcolm X is certainly one of the patron saints of the Black Power movement. His several contacts with the Student Nonviolent Co-ordinating Committee (SNCC) are significant in understanding SNCC's gradual cleavage with King's SCLC. For many months prior to the Greensboro, Mississippi, event in 1966, the growing conflict between SNCC's leader, Stokely Carmichael, and Martin Luther King had become well known. For a time that conflict centered on SNCC's dissatisfaction with nonviolence as a strategy for opposing racism. Self-defense was considered the only meaningful alternative. Carmichael's cry for Black Power at Greensboro publicly symbolized the cleavage between the two organizations. But the symbolic slogan represented not only SNCC's rejection of nonviolence but also its affirmation of many elements hitherto associated with the political philosophy of Black nationalism. In many ways Malcolm's Organization of Afro-American Unity became the model for the

Black Power movement. That movement contributed one lasting legacy to Black America by persuading Blacks and by demanding that whites repudiate the slave name "Negro." All the principles set forth in Malcolm's philosophy of Black nationalism were adopted by the Black Power movement. Such major principles as Black control of institutions and organizations in the Black community, exclusion of whites from Black organizations, Black separatism as a major objective, Black self-development, Black self-respect, and the recovery of Black history became, in the Black Power movement, indisputable moral goals for determining action even as they were for Malcolm and his movement. In short, Malcolm X was, in many respects, the originator of the Black Power movement and was its major theoretician. Many saw themselves in the position of continuing his work. They did not accept his religion of Islam, and unwittingly, it would appear that Malcolm had made that possible by organizationally separating his religion from his politics. The two were related, to be sure, but he had made it possible in the beginning for one to participate in the OAAU without having to become a Muslim.

Malcolm's analysis of the emergence of the various independent nations in Asia and Africa focused on their ability to acknowledge the importance of power in the struggle against oppression. The oppressor is a power. In his understanding, power acknowledges only power. In the face of lesser power it gains power. In the face of more power it loses power. In his Black nationalist philosophy the category of power is all-important. It has its beginning in right thinking, and with that right thinking it is able to devise the kind of action necessary to become self-determining and to remain so until it is conquered and killed.

So, all these little advances were made by oppressed people in other parts of the world during 1964. These were tangible gains, and the reason that they were able to make these gains was they realized that power was the magic word—power against power. Power in defense of freedom is greater than power in behalf of tyranny and oppression because power, real power, comes from conviction which produces action, uncompromising action. It also produces insurrection against oppression. This is the only way you end oppression—with power.

Power never takes a back step—only in the face of more power. Power doesn't back up in the face of a smile, or in the face of a threat, or in the face of some kind of non-violent loving action. It's not the nature of power to back up in the face of anything but some more power. And this is what the people have realized in Southeast Asia, in the Congo, in Cuba, in other parts of the world. Power recognizes only power, and all of them who realize this have made gains.[46]

It is possible that Malcolm's entire mission might be summed up as a quest for the kind of power that could effect the liberation of Blacks from the control of white oppression. Right thinking would produce the necessary mental and psychological power for the construction of practical strategies to gain economic and political power. That power must not be considered as self-sufficient but must discover effective allies in order to maximize itself. Malcolm spent much time traveling in Asia and in Africa for the purpose of building that relationship so that the degree of power needed to conquer racism in America and in the world could be developed.

The Goodness of America

Malcolm X believed that America was morally corrupt from its beginning. That judgment focused on the way in which it has treated its Black citizens. He could have no respect for a nation that had robbed 22 million Black people of their humanity. Neither could he respect the nation's founders, who, he avowed, had come from the criminal elements of English society and who were intent on creating a nation based on crimes against humanity, namely, slavery.

> The founding fathers from England came from the dungeons of England, came from the prisons of England; they were prostitutes, they were murderers and thieves and liars. And as soon as they got over here, they proved it. They created one of the most criminal societies that has ever existed on the earth since time began. And, if you doubt it, when you go home tonight, look in the mirror at yourself, and you'll see the victim of that criminal system that was created by them.[47]

While he was a member of Elijah Muhammad's movement, Malcolm had seen that white persons, criminal by nature, could do none other than create a society in accordance with their own nature. The historical facts of cruelty and brutality toward Black people were used to demonstrate the white person's true nature. But after the break, he simply focused on the historical facts in order to show that everywhere the white person has gone it has involved the oppression of the darker peoples of the world. To be sure, that oppression has taken various forms, but the objective has always been the same—the systematic destruction of the humanity of Black peoples.

Malcolm's analysis of the history of slavery taught him that the current plight of Blacks in twentieth-century America is not radically dissimilar from slavery itself. In his famous "Message to the Grassroots," he depicted present-day America as a prison in which freedom for Blacks had been nullified. "That's what America means: prison."[48] Ten days after his declaration of independence from the Nation of Islam he delivered another of his famous speeches, "The Ballot or the Bullet." In that speech he spoke about the moral corruption that pervaded America's character and about the futility involved in trying to change that character.

Don't change the white man's mind—you can't change his mind, and that whole thing about appealing to the moral conscience of America—America's conscience is bankrupt. She lost all conscience a long time ago. Uncle Sam has no conscience. They don't know what morals are. They don't try and eliminate an evil because it's evil, or because it's illegal, or because it's immoral; they eliminate it only when it threatens their existence. So you're wasting your time appealing to the moral conscience of a bankrupt man like Uncle Sam. If he had a conscience, he'd straighten this thing out with no more pressure being put upon him.[49]

Malcolm considered it an undeniable fact that America has been involved continuously in devising various kinds of conspiracies to maintain its control and power over Blacks. He characterized the relationship of America to Blacks as a colonial relationship and its strategy as one of divide and rule.

So America's strategy is the same strategy as that which was used in the past by the colonial powers: divide and conquer. She plays one Negro leader against the other. She plays one Negro organization against the other. She makes us think we have different objectives, different goals.[50]

Malcolm's thinking about America led him to the inevitable conclusion about his own citizenship. He did not regard himself as an American but as a victim of Americanism. He admonished his followers to view themselves similarly. He reasoned that being born in this country did not imply citizenship for Blacks, else there would be no need of legislation to determine that citizenship. Since the various immigrant groups who have assimilated into the culture became citizens without having to wage struggles for special legislation, why shouldn't Blacks, who have been in this country much longer than most, be treated as citizens. One of his most unpatriotic statements was the following:

No, I'm not an American. I'm one of the 22 million black people who are the victims of Americanism. One of the 22 million black people who are the victims of democracy, nothing but disguised hypocrisy. So, I'm not standing here speaking to you as an American, or a patriot, or a flag-saluter, or a flag-waver—no, not I. I'm speaking as a victim of this American system. And I see America through the eyes of the victim. I don't see any American dream; I see an American nightmare.[51]

Malcolm's perspective on America condemned all the nation's major institutions, which he believed fostered the oppression of Blacks. Chief among those institutions was the government itself. In his opinion, it was completely void of moral virtue, as evidenced by its historical complicity with racism.

You and I in America are faced not with a segregationist conspiracy, we're faced with a government conspiracy. Everyone who's filibustering is a senator—that's the government. Everyone who's finagling in Washington, D.C., is a congressman—that's the government. You don't have anybody putting blocks in your path but people who are a part of the government. The same government that you go abroad to fight for and die for is the government that is a conspiracy to deprive you of your voting rights, deprive you of your economic opportunity, deprive you of decent housing, deprive you of decent education. You don't need to go to the employer alone, it is the government itself, the government of America, that is responsible for the oppression and exploitation and degradation of black people in this country.[52]

Malcolm saw no meaningful distinction between racism in the South and racism in the North. The only difference was in terms of its form. Similarly, he saw no meaningful difference between white liberals and white conservatives. Neither wanted Blacks to enjoy full citizenship rights, but liberals were more tricky than conservatives. Also, he viewed the Dixiecrats and the Democrats as adherents to the same basic principles.

Malcolm noted that America only made slight alterations in its policy of racism when forced to do so by external forces. Implicit in the following passage is an indictment of any who would assume a measure of goodwill on America's part regarding the question of racism.

> Never at any time in the history of our people in this country have we made advances or progress in any way based upon the internal goodwill of this country. We have made advancement in this country only when this country was under pressure from forces above and beyond its control. The internal moral consciousness of this country is bankrupt. It hasn't existed since they first brought us over here and made slaves out of us. They make it appear they have our good interests at heart, but when you study it, every time, no matter how many steps they take us forward, it's like we're standing on a . . . treadmill. The treadmill is moving backwards faster than we're able to go forward in this direction. We're not even standing still—we're going backwards.[53]

Malcolm's indictment of America as a racist nation was complete. He often said that he considered America worse than South Africa, because in the latter there was no hypocrisy and deceit. The government of South Africa made its position abundantly clear to all that in no way did it hold Blacks to be equal with whites. Toward the end of his life Malcolm looked upon America as the worst country in the world.

> This is the *worst* racist society on this earth. There is no country on earth in which you can live, and racism be brought out in you—whether you're white or black— more so than this country that poses as a democracy. This is a country where the social, economic, political atmosphere creates a sort of psychological atmosphere that makes it almost impossible, if you're in your right mind, to walk down the street with a *white* person and

not be self-conscious, or he or she not to be self-conscious.[54]

Racism in America, which has pervaded the nation's history and which is endemic to the national style of life, caused Malcolm to view this country as an evil nation, virtually incapable of responding positively to moral reform. If allowed to continue, America's evil would destroy the nation in time. Meanwhile, it was incumbent upon Blacks to view the enemy realistically and to struggle by any means necessary for the realization of their humanity. He taught that only a revolution could change America's racist posture in the world. He felt that if America were to give Blacks full citizenship rights, revolution could be effected without violence. For example, if Blacks in practice had voting rights equal to those of whites, their numbers alone would cause the removal of all racist elected officials in the nation, and a new day would have already dawned. But he did not expect America to do that, since it was so bankrupt in terms of moral sensitivity.

Struggle Against Poverty

Malcolm X was greatly concerned about the problem of poverty. It was implied in all dimensions of his thought and action. In fact, he viewed poverty among Blacks as an inevitable outcome of racism and poverty among the darker peoples of the world as the result of racism's twin, colonialism. In his understanding, capitalism necessitates poverty, because it always needs "blood to suck." Formerly, that "blood" had come from those territories which capitalism had been able to conquer and oppress. He believed, however, that as those territories achieve their eventual independence, capitalism will necessarily grow weak and gradually die.

It is impossible for capitalism to survive primarily because the system of capitalism needs some blood to suck. Capitalism used to be like an eagle, but now it's

more like a vulture. It used to be strong enough to go
and suck anybody's blood whether they were strong or
not. But now it has become more cowardly, like the
vulture, and it can only suck the blood of the helpless.
As the nations of the world free themselves, then capitalism has less victims, less to suck, and it becomes
weaker and weaker. It's only a matter of time in my
opinion before it will collapse completely.[55]

Malcolm frequently advised his followers to look to
the newly developing nations of the world if they would
discover a way to solve the problem of racism. In this,
the richest country of the world, there exist devastating
degrees of poverty. Obviously, capitalism cannot solve
that dilemma. Malcolm believed that the countries that
have solved it are not capitalistic. "What they are using
to solve their problem in Africa and Asia is not capitalism. So what you and I should do is find out what they
are using to get rid of poverty and all the other negative
characteristics of a rundown society."[56]

It is not surprising that Malcolm should analyze the
problem of poverty in terms of power arrangements,
whether in America or beyond its borders. He looked
upon politics and economics as being the basic forms
of power in America, since social power was derivative
from them. Further, he felt that political power was
prior to economic power, especially for the poor. "The
only real power a poor man in this country has is the
power of the ballot."[57] He was of the opinion that he
should fight for voter registration for Blacks and then
discourage Blacks from voting until they had been
properly trained in the philosophy of Black nationalism. Only then would they vote in an intelligent and
scientific way to serve the interests of the Black community. Black nationalism meant not only Black control of the political institutions in the Black
community but also Black control of the economic institutions in the Black community.

Economic exploitation in the Afro-American community is the most vicious form practiced on any people in

America: twice as much rent for rat-infested, roach-crawling, rotting tenements; the Afro-American pays more for foods, clothing, insurance rates and so forth. The Organization of Afro-American Unity will wage an unrelenting struggle against these evils in our community. There will be organizers to work with the people to solve these problems, and start a housing self-improvement program. We propose to support rent strikes and other activities designed to better the community.[58]

Malcolm believed that the philosophy of Black nationalism would enable Blacks to devise means for controlling those white economic institutions in the Black community and would prevent them from continuing their historic practice of exploitation. He was also aware that the situation was complicated by the fact that the Black community had become economically dependent upon the white community. He admonished his followers to become involved in self-development. He taught that Blacks should organize their own businesses and should patronize their own businesspeople, thus enabling the money to circulate in the Black community. In that respect, they would eventually be in a position to stop the process of going downtown to beg a white person for a job or a loan. Further, they would no longer be participating in the process of destroying the Black community economically by spending every dollar in the white community. As Blacks must shape their futures politically, so they must shape them economically. The power necessary to do this will not be given to them; it must be demanded and taken. Thus, in Malcolm's opinion, the question of poverty among Blacks is due to the problem of political oppression, and consequently, the solution must begin with the actualization of political self-determination.

PART THREE

Diversity in Unity

6

Theological and Political Understandings: Differences and Similarities

In chapters 2–5 the religious and political understandings of the selected figures were closely examined in order to discern their respective ways of justifying the particular stands each of them took on the issues raised in chapter 1. No attempt was made to relate those understandings to one another. That is the purpose of this chapter. A careful analysis of their relationship is necessary in order to determine how those understandings, separately or collectively, have hindered or might have fostered meaningful cooperative action.

However, at this point it is important to make clear what has been only implied up to now, namely, that human action is associational. That is to say, the particular form of human action about which I am concerned in this study is that kind of action that takes place among humans, whether it be aimed at the development or at the destruction of human association. There are many kinds of human association, but in this study we have concentrated on only two: religious and political. As operational definitions, I consider religious associations to be those that are formed for the purpose of ordering the relationship between humans and the source of their ultimate meaning; I consider thought about the nature of that relationship to be

theological. Similarly, I regard political associations to
be those formed for the purpose of structuring the relationship between humans in order to construct a human world; I regard thought about the nature of that
world to be political.

It has been shown that these four individuals became prominent leaders of associations that had religious purposes and political purposes and that each
had his own specific understanding of the nature of
those purposes and of how they should be related. It is
our task now to analyze carefully the differences and
similarities in their religious and political thought in
order to discern their respective relationships.

A careful examination of the thought of Jackson and
King has revealed that both derived their political
principles from their understandings of the Christian
faith. In fact, our analysis reveals that they believed
that their religious understandings underlay and
shaped their understandings of society in general and
of the problem of racism in particular. Both thought
that the kingdom of God as revealed in the Christian
gospel is the proper end toward which history and the
American nation should move. Both employed that
particular Christian concept as a principle of criticism
on all societal structures and as a standard for their
reform. Now, Jackson thought certain historical ante-
cedents forming the bedrock of the American nation
(for example, the Declaration of Independence and the
Constitution) were consonant with history's final end.
That is to say, Jackson believed that the kingdom of
God had been embodied (in part at least) formally and
substantively in the nation's body politic. In his view,
the nation per se is theologically significant. One could
even say that he had a sacramental view of American
political life. In other words, he viewed the nation as a
theocracy and saw its political leaders and citizens as
obligated to bear the awesome responsibility of being
custodians of sacred truths. In his thought, those sacred truths are manifested in the Constitution, which
is made efficacious by the various legal and judicial

structures established under it. Therefore, the first responsibility of all good citizens is to protect and preserve that which has been received already and which is in accord with the kingdom of God. Consequently, it is not difficult to understand why Jackson insisted on a vigorous patriotism as the means of uniting the nation and thereby fostering the realization of the good in human affairs.

Such a view of politics must necessarily be intolerant of other possible alternatives. Indeed, Jackson viewed such alternatives as heretical and frequently declared them to be anti-Christian and anti-American.

Jackson believed that the kingdom of God is the true and final end to which all of history is destined, and therefore, he viewed it as normative for all human activity. He concluded that the norm had been partly realized in America as evidenced in its constitution. He argued that all forms of action aiming at social change were justified only by manifesting that norm and by being commensurate with the Constitution. Further, since the kingdom of God is perfect harmony, all political activity must make harmony its primary goal and must be carried out in the spirit of love, goodwill, peace, and respect for the Constitution.

Jackson's thought on this matter was often reminiscent of the spirit of medieval Christianity. He viewed the nation as good because of the relationship he saw between its constitution and the Christian gospel. He admitted, however, the presence within its borders of enemies, of infidels, who desire to destroy the nation by instituting its contrary. Such people have been the perpetrators of racism and for a while have succeeded in leading a whole region—the South—astray from its aim as established by the founders of the nation. Presently, that enemy is neither Black nor white but both. It is composed of all those who speak disparagingly about the substance of the nation's life—who defy the law of the land by advocating civil disobedience, whose speeches are laden with military epithets of hate, bitterness, and malice—whose actions are prem-

ised on conflict and polarization—whose deeds result
in confusion regarding loyalty, faith, trust, and liberty—whose attitudes create dispositions that are ex-
cited by violence and pillage. In keeping with the spirit
of medieval Christianity, Jackson contended that enemies such as these ought to be dealt with as harshly as
the situation merits and even advocated capital punishment for such "treasonous" activities.

Jackson maintained that the struggle against racism
must proceed by means of the legal and judicial structures that are provided by the Constitution for the redress of grievances. Throughout his life he supported
voter registration projects in those areas where Blacks
were disfranchised and advocated firm support of the
federal government and of its enforcement agencies in
that enterprise. Similarly, he backed specific economic
boycotts against those who practiced racial segregation
and discrimination. At the same time, he diligently
urged Blacks to commit themselves to a doctrine of
self-development in all dimensions of their lives with
whatever resources they might have at their disposal.

It is clear that Jackson sought to demonstrate a close
alliance between Christianity and American politics.
In fact, politics is significantly joined with religion in
such a way that good politics is identical with good
religion. His theological views not only served as the
norm for his political views, but they also implied
initiative of a certain kind in the body politic. That
initiative is inspired by the awareness that something
of eternal worth is present in the Constitution of the
United States, and all good citizens are called upon to
improve the quality of the nation's life by building on
those constitutional values. In the face of difficulties
one is not justified in seeking revolutionary change;
rather, in patience and in long suffering one does what
is possible in the spirit of love and goodwill to improve one's condition via an ethic of self-development
and through varying kinds of service projects. The gospel is regarded under the principle of harmony; that
principle implies a consensual attitude to sovereign

authority. In the American context, loyalty and commitment to that authority are virtuous, while debate and controversy are destructive.

Clearly, Jackson's political and theological understandings were closely related. In his thought, the true end of humanity, of the nation, and of history is given by the Christian religion. Politics is and ought to be the means to that end. In his opinion, the good fortune of the American nation is that its constitution demonstrates the partial appearance of that end in history. The Constitution and its structures are vested with Christian significance and become normative for political action. The only way a citizen might be assured of doing the good is by acting in accordance with the Constitution and by preserving and increasing harmony in the nation.

On the face of it one might easily conclude that Jackson's political understandings were derived from his theological understandings. I do not hasten to do so, because it would be just as reasonable to conclude the reverse, namely, that his theological views were derived from his political understandings. That is to say, it is reasonable to hypothesize that Jackson emphasized those aspects of the Christian gospel that were congruent with his own views of the U.S. Constitution, the potential danger of the problem of racism, and his basic anthropological beliefs. At this point I do not intend to resolve the problem, only to avoid premature conclusions. It is clear, nonetheless, that there is a definite correlation between his understandings of religion and politics.

Now, let us reflect on the relationship of King's thought to Jackson's, since King also viewed Christianity as normative for his political views. In fact, many have contended that, like Jackson's, King's political involvement was motivated by his religious understandings. Others have argued that the religious understandings of both men were shaped largely by their social situation and by their political activities. Obviously, there can be no easy resolution of this vexing problem, and I do not seek one here. However, it is clear for whatever reasons that both men felt compelled to address the nation itself concerning the problem of racism. Similar to Jackson, King saw the kingdom of God as revealed in Jesus Christ to be the basic principle with which to judge historical matters. But the main difference between his thought and Jackson's is the way in which each surveyed the nation's relationship to that principle. As we have seen, Jackson considered the Constitution and all structures and values implied by it to be in basic accord with that principle. Therefore, opposition to racism is aimed not against the nation per se but against those alienated forces residing within and without the nation. Jackson declared that it was necessary to fight those enemies vigorously in order to preserve, to improve, and to develop the substance of the American way of life. In contrast, King looked on the kingdom of God as being potentially realizable in this nation but not yet significantly present. He had a deep respect for the Constitution, but he viewed it as an ideal that had not been realized in practice. Unlike Jackson, he concluded that the body politic lacks moral and spiritual substance. While Jackson saw the nation's historic past with a romantic nostalgia, King assessed the facts of history with unequivocal candor and judgment.

> Negroes no longer are tolerant of or interested in compromise. American history is replete with compromise. As splendid as are the words of the Declaration of Independence, there are disquieting implications in the fact that the original phrasing was altered to delete a condemnation of the British monarch for his espousal of slavery. American history chronicles the Missouri Compromise, which permitted the spread of slavery to new states; the Hayes-Tilden Compromise, which withdrew the federal troops from the South and signaled the end of Reconstruction; the Supreme Court's compromise in *Plessy v. Ferguson*, which enunciated the infamous "separate but equal" philosophy. These measures

compromised not only the liberty of the Negro but the integrity of America.[1]

King regarded the historic condition of Blacks in this nation as brutal and inhumane, and he considered their situation in his day to be intolerable and unendurable. In his view, the spirit of the masses of Blacks had arisen in righteous wrath against the perpetrators of racial injustice. He took no credit for inciting the race to rise up but tried only to lead and to direct that passion toward constructive social change via moral means. "It was the people who moved their leaders, not the leaders who moved the people."[2] More important, King saw a cleavage between the substance of the American nation and the Christian understanding of human nature and of society. He wrote at length about his search for a political principle that would be in accord with the Christian gospel and that would be adequate in effecting social change. The Christian understanding of love *(agape)* was the essence of the gospel, in his mind. But it took a long time before he could see it operationalized as a political principle.[3] In time he discovered the principle of nonviolence, which he believed to be in basic accord with the Christian faith. To be sure, he saw it as reflexive in nature. He taught that those who would dare to employ it consistently in the struggles for social justice would indeed discover that it could become a way of life for them, since the habitual practice of nonviolence leads to a corresponding state of character. Thus, an instrument of social change would effect a qualitative change in the character of its user. King felt that nonviolence was regulated by the ideal of Christian love effecting its good work in social outcome and in personal character. While Jackson affirmed a close relationship between the Christian gospel and the U.S. Constitution, King affirmed a close relationship between the Christian faith and the practice of nonviolent resistance. The former attached ultimate significance to the nation, while the latter attached it to a form of protest.

Unlike Jackson's, King's understanding of Christian love implied a politics of conflict rather than harmony. Since he judged the evil implicit in the American society as contradictory to the Christian gospel, and since it perpetuated itself by acts of violence, and since that evil was a profound threat to the well-being of the nation itself, King took comfort in his discovery of nonviolence as an instrument of resistance and as a way of life. He saw in nonviolence the Christian gospel actualizing itself in the body politic, and in the rhetoric of lamentation he frequently likened the sufferings of its bearers to the sufferings of Jesus. In contrast to Jackson, he argued that in the presence of evil Christianity must necessarily wage battle and that among the major threats to the preservation of the Christian message are those who are silent supporters of the status quo. Much of his famous "Letter from a Birmingham Jail" deals with that problem. King had no difficulty in surveying his movement as an army or in describing nonviolence as a "sword that heals."[4] His basic presupposition was that the Christian gospel must wage war against evil by employing its own methods of militant love through nonviolence and not by utilizing the instruments of the evildoers.

> We did not hesitate to call our movement an army. But it was a special army, with no supplies but its sincerity, no uniform but its determination, no arsenal except its faith, no currency but its conscience. It was an army that would sing but not slay. It was an army that would flank but not falter. It was an army to storm bastions of hatred, to lay siege to the fortresses of segregation, to surround symbols of discrimination. It was an army whose allegiance was to God and whose strategy and intelligence were eloquently simple dictates of conscience.[5]

King believed that struggle and conflict were necessary to effect the good that would liberate Blacks and the nation from the grip of racism. It was a redemptive conflict, because he contended that the nation had the capacity to respond to truth. That capacity was evidenced by the ideals most Americans espoused and by their uneasy conscience concerning their actual practice. "Yet there is something in the American ethos that responds to the strength of moral force."[6] The genius present in the struggle of love via nonviolent resistance was thought by King to lie in the fact that it vigorously fought evil practices and evil systems while affirming the personhood of their agents. Indeed, the end to be achieved was that of transforming the lives of the enemies by a reformation of those institutions that controlled individuals. "The enemy the Negro faced became not the individual who had oppressed him but the evil system which permitted that individual to do so."[7]

After wrestling with the accusation that he was an extremist, King began to take satisfaction in the indictment. He considered all the saints and prophets in the Bible to have been dubbed extremists; he himself thought that Lincoln, Jefferson, and others in American history had been rightly called extremists. But it made all the difference to him whether an extremist was one for hate or one for love. He asserted that Jesus was put to death because he was an extremist. Further, he taught that creative extremism is a goal to be desired if it be in keeping with the life and teachings of Jesus.

And so, like Jackson's, King's theological thought and political thought were closely related. In both cases it is difficult to separate political thought from theological thought. Each made prominent use of the symbols of the Christian gospel as norms for good public action. But each gave different meanings to those common symbols and, consequently, formulated different propositions concerning them and derived different implications from them concerning social action. Like Jackson, King viewed the kingdom of God as revealed in Jesus Christ as the supreme norm for political action. But unlike Jackson, he saw the nation's relationship to that norm as problematic. He had no quarrel with the ideals that America espoused, but he considered the nation's institutional practices as contradictory to those ideals. In his opinion, those practices were not only problematic for the body politic but were also an offense to the Christian gospel. Further, King's understanding of the gospel was that it wages a redemptive war against evil, destroying the evil itself while preserving and saving the evildoer.

Both King and Jackson grounded their political norms in their theological understandings. Although their theological opinions were different, they appealed to commonly named Christian symbols. But their different understandings of those symbols enabled them to justify alternative modes of political action. Further, their understandings of how the nation is related to those theological propositions differed. Jackson surveyed the nation's ethos and basic institutions as manifesting in significant ways the substance of the Christian faith. King viewed the nation's institutional practices as a denial of its fundamental ideals and of the Christian faith. The political implication of Jackson's thought is that one builds on the good that is already present, while the implication of King's thought is that one must rid the social order of a basic contradiction. Jackson's thinking leads to programs of a developmental nature; King's thinking leads to societal reformation.

Now, let us look again at Powell's theological and political understandings in order to discern how they are related to the above. In chapter 4 the way in which Powell viewed religion was described as a mystical experience. In his understanding, religion pertained to things that are absolute in all respects. Consequently, he believed that nothing in the affairs of humans could merit such a status. Thus, the quality of all human activity must necessarily be ambiguous. That is to say, insofar as the absolute enters into human affairs it is only relatively present and can never be taken for granted. Goodness, beauty, and truth are signs of the divine presence whenever they are experienced.

Whenever one posits absolutes and relativities, the question of their relationship inevitably arises. Powell was rather unclear about that relationship. He stated that religion is personal and that its locus is the inner person. The inner person who strives for absolute truth attains some perception of it only by what Einstein called "the inspired leap."[8] The point of contact between the individual and the absolute is inexplicable, although she or he knows it to be present within. An attempt to explicate that inner locus is an exercise in assertions and, on occasion, analogical argumentation based on humanity's experience with nature.

> There is something within me that I cannot explain— all that I know is there is something within. This benign growth of the spirit has given me the power to speak what I have been told to say, regardless of whom it offends. It has given me a tremendous stability and security that makes it totally impossible for any power or combination of powers of man to disturb. It has come to me oftimes [*sic*] in life with increasing frequency, with a touch of prophecy.[9]

In Powell's understanding, the things pertaining to God are absolute, while those pertaining to humanity are relative. He affirmed that there were two kingdoms: the kingdom of God and the kingdom of humankind. In the former the will of God is done; in the latter the will of humanity predominates. He had no doubt that the will of God as seen in the historical revelation of Jesus Christ is the true end of humanity and of history. Humans have strayed away from that true end, and the road they have chosen leads to certain doom. Nevertheless, he believed that they had the capacity to return to their true end and to work constructively in the task of building a world that conformed with God's will. The will of God being done was evidenced by the presence of beauty, peace, love, and harmony in human affairs. Their opposites demonstrated the fact that the will of humans was being exercised. The great human sin was the temptation to

consider oneself and one's works as completely autonomous and thereby to refuse to see that all human
works are temporal and superficial. He felt that the
kingdom of God was partially realizable in history. Although his writings lacked a systematic statement on
this problem, he did believe that the absolute resides
in history and in some mysterious way affects the good
that humans are able to accomplish. Similar to Jackson and King, Powell asserted that the will of God was
normative for history and insisted that it was discern-
able in all experiences of beauty, goodness, peace, and
kinship. That norm liberates, because it sets humans
free from all forms of conformism and enables them to
speak the truth and to act for the sake of God's will
regardless of the consequences. God's absolute will as
the norm for history gave Powell a radical principle of
criticism of history. By employing it he was able to see
the possibilities and limitations inherent in all things,
including the U.S. Constitution, the American way of
life, the civil rights movement, the Black radical move-
ments, and communism, for example. On many important issues his position constituted a dialectic in
that he would affirm certain aspects of the issue while
negating others. That fact was frequently misunderstood, and in the eyes of many he appeared as a cha-
meleon, since it was always difficult to predict from
day to day how he would evaluate even his own associational alliances. A radical affirmation of the will of
God as normative for humanity was, for him, the basis
of freedom and the ultimate ground of his loyalties.

Powell's profound belief in the capacity of the inner
person to be touched by the absolute and to be inspired to seek God's will in human affairs distin-
guishes him greatly from Jackson and King. Unlike
Jackson, he had no unquestioned belief in the fact that
the absolute inhered unambiguously in the structures
and in the basic values of the American society. Unlike King, he had no unquestioned belief in the absolute virtue of any particular strategy, principle, or

technique for governing human affairs. That fact enabled him to exercise his biting criticism on the Constitution and on the philosophy of nonviolence whenever
he felt it necessary to do so. And he did so notwithstanding the fact that he loved America and its constitution and upheld the virtues of nonviolence over the
vices of violence. However, he did not seek to give
either the Constitution or nonviolence the status of
religious principles. In relation to the absolute will of
God they were only relatively good. Powell's commitment to democracy as the best possible form of government and to nonviolence as the most appropriate
means of acting in the body politic were political judgments and not religious affirmations. His belief in the
goodness of the American dream is perhaps the one
place in his thought where the political vision of the
nation is viewed as being in accord with the will of
God. The vision of a state wherein freedom and justice, peace and friendship among all peoples would be
actualized was, in his view, the highest possible attainment of human beings. But that vision had the character of religion in that its form transcended time and
space, and its desired alterability was unthinkable to
Powell. And since its truth is unambiguous, it could
not be equated with the Constitution or with any other
existing political form.

In Powell's thought, the end of humankind is given
by God, and politics must be for the sake of helping
humankind to attain that end. Similarly, the source of
moral and spiritual strength is God. When humans use
their power to destroy the moral and spiritual powers
of their kinspeople, they thwart the will of God, and
their actions lead inevitably to self-destruction. Powell
believed that these truths were stamped on the inner
nature of humans and were either affirmed or denied
voluntarily. He was convinced that it was the responsibility of people of conscience to use whatever means
possible short of violence to correct social injustices.
As one who had spent most of his public life in the

U.S. Congress, he utilized all the power he could amass legitimately to effect those corrections. Negotiation, alliances, compromise, and various forms of off-the-record manipulations were part of the common culture in that political arena. He adjusted himself to that culture and employed its techniques for the sake of Blacks and the nation. He viewed racism as a democratic problem that would severely threaten the well-being of the nation should it be permitted to continue unsolved. Insofar as the subject matter of politics is morality, good relationships among persons, he considered it religiously significant, since the will of God is the norm for those relationships.

Thus, we see that Powell's political understandings were related to his religious understandings in the sense that he believed that politics is concerned with morality and that the moral norm is given by God. Hence, politics was thought to serve that moral norm. He regarded the relativities of the human condition to be used well only insofar as they aimed at the realization of the will of God in history. At that point his thought was similar to that of Jackson and of King. But it differed from theirs in one significant way. Jackson and King expended great amounts of energy in demonstrating how their political principles, strategies, and tactics were grounded in the Christian gospel. Powell, however, viewed humankind's chief end as given by God but saw political principles, strategies, and tactics as constructed by human beings. Accordingly, he did not consider political matters to be religious in any specific way, but nevertheless, he thought that they ought to be exercised for the sake of humankind's religious end. Further, Powell made no attempt to justify his political principles or actions by appeals to theological categories. Rather, their adequacy was determined by prudential judgment alone.

Now, let us turn our attention to Malcolm X. As we have seen, he was a faithful follower of Elijah Muhammad, and his religious and political thought coincided on all crucial points with that of his master teacher. In the Nation of Islam no meaningful distinction is drawn between the sacred and the secular. Since followers in the Nation of Islam affirm that Elijah Muhammad is divine, his teachings are accepted as absolutely true. Malcolm was no exception in that respect. He had said, "Mr. Elijah Muhammad is our divine leader and teacher here in America."[10] For as long as Malcolm accepted that doctrine he judged the Nation of Islam to be God's solution for Blacks in America. In other words, he thought that through Elijah Muhammad God had become set against the American way of life and its evil practices of racism and that God's divine initiative would be decisive in human affairs. "Now, today, God has sent Mr. Elijah Muhammad among the downtrodden and oppressed so-called American Negroes to warn that God is again preparing to bring about another great change, only this time it will be a final change. This is the day and the time for a complete change."[11]

The notion of a complete change is significant, because it designates the point of continuity between the earlier and the later Malcolm. It is evident to all who hear the Myth of Yacub that its explanation of the origin of racism is set forth in political concepts and symbols that are primordial in nature. Further, it is clear that the final resolution of that cosmological problem is destined to be political in nature. That is to say, in the final battle of Armageddon the Black race will regain its rightful place of dominance in the world. The religion of the Nation of Islam is revolutionary. It aims ultimately at the complete destruction of the present systems of power and at the constitution of a new nation.

When Malcolm finally broke away from the discipline of the Nation of Islam, that break entailed his rejection of the Myth of Yacub and his denial of the divine status of Elijah Muhammad. He continued to use the political concepts and understandings that he first discovered in the Nation of Islam, however. To be sure, their primordial nature was denied, but the polit-

ical goal of racial separation and the desired establishment of a Black nation were maintained. Thus, in the
later Malcolm, political understanding was no longer
grounded in Elijah Muhammad's Myth of Yacub. That
does not mean that Malcolm ceased to be a religious
person. On the contrary, he founded his own orthodox
mosque at the same time that he founded the Organization of Afro-American Unity. His reasons for forming the two organizations do not necessarily imply any
philosophical split between his religious and political
thought. Their separation appears to be primarily a
matter of function rather than one of principle. It is
clear, however, from his later writings and speeches
that he continued to view Islam as the only solution
for the world problem of racism in spite of the fact
that he no longer sought to demonstrate the relationship between his nascent orthodox mosque and Black
nationalism. Perhaps he took that relationship for
granted and decided, for strategic reasons, not to dis-
cuss it in public. The separation of his OAAU from the
mosque appears to have been motivated at least by a
desire to effect a broader base of participation than
was possible in the Nation of Islam. That is to say, one
no longer had to become a Muslim in order to participate in the goal of nation-building. In that respect,
Malcolm felt liberated from the constraints imposed
upon him by the Nation of Islam.

In the early Malcolm one discovers a man whose
political understandings are integrally connected with
and derived from the religious myth of Elijah Muhammad. At that time it was his habit to speak and write
entirely from within that perspective. Accordingly, his
teachings were extremely critical of everything outside
the pale of the Nation of Islam. The Myth of Yacub
operated as a revolutionary principle of criticism of
white people and of all their constructs. Further, it
functioned as a severe principle of criticism on the
total experience and action of Blacks in this country.
In his later writings there is a concern for a wider umbrella under which Blacks could be encouraged to par-

ticipate in the task of building a Black nationalism in education, politics, economics, and all dimensions of Black societal life. The decisive change in Malcolm following his break with Elijah Muhammad was his decision that Blacks need not become Muslims in order to be full members of the OAAU. He had come to believe that the principles of Black nationalism could be efficacious without being integrally connected to Elijah Muhammad's religion or, for that matter, even to orthodox Islam.

Once again we arrive at certain preliminary conclusions. King and Jackson were bent on persuading their followers that their political principles were derived from their religious (theological) understandings of the kingdom of God and other related symbols. In both we see a common view, to wit, the conviction that their respective theological understandings of the Christian faith are the only valid justification for political action. That is to say, both felt themselves obligated to demonstrate that their political understandings were commensurate with their understandings of the kingdom of God. But their understandings of the kingdom of God differed in the way each saw its relationship to the American society. Jackson viewed the American nation as one that had constructed its fundamental law and way of life in harmony with the precepts of the Christian faith. In form and substance the nation manifested, in part at least, important elements of what it ought to be according to the Christian understanding of human history. In his perspective, conflict between the citizens and the state was a detriment that had to be arrested as quickly as possible in order for harmony (the good) to be reestablished. He emphasized that the appropriate stance for citizens to take was one of unquestioned loyalty to the state, a devotion to self-development under the aegis of the state, and a utilization of the channels provided by the state for the redress of grievances.

In the thought of King we see a reverent respect for the U.S. Constitution, which he looked upon as a formal manifestation of certain prominent Christian precepts. But, unlike Jackson, he considered the basic institutional practices of the American society to be antithetical to its formal ideals. Indeed, he saw a dilemma between America's ideals and its practices. He thought that such a dilemma violated the original intentions of the nation's founders and the conscience of the American citizenry and, if left unchecked, would result inevitably in self-destruction. He believed that the religious principle of love could be translated into a political principle for social change. He affirmed that love could not be passive in the face of evil, nor could it merely be celebrative of the good that people experience while ignoring the evil they encounter, nor does it imply that a people should endure hardship. Rather, he asserted that it aggressively struggles against evil by employing its own methods. In that struggle love enables the enemy and the actor to be affirmed as persons and to be reconciled. And so, at the heart of King's interpretation of the Christian symbols and their relationship to society, we see a transformative style of action emerging, premised on conflict but aimed at the resolution of that conflict in the reconciliation of all God's children. That goal is not distant but is made present in the actual methods of the struggle.

Thus, King and Jackson had similar understandings of the kingdom of God as a theological symbol. Yet they had different understandings of the way that symbol is related to the American society and of its implications for the struggle against racism. Hence, on the basis of two differing theologies of culture, they offered two differing views of social change: the one developmental within the conditions of the society and the other transformative of those societal conditions.

We have seen that Adam Clayton Powell's theological understanding explicates the true end of human history. His theology pertains to things absolute, while the affairs of humankind are viewed as always relative. Accordingly, the norm for history is the will of God, which partially manifests itself wherever beauty, goodness, truth, and kinship appear. The will of God is made known by certain kinds of human experience, and all human activity should aim at the actualization of the will of God. This circularity of thought was characteristic of Powell, although he expended no energy in trying to demonstrate that his political activity was in harmony with the will of God. He assumed that social injustice is a self-evident reality and that working for its correction is morally good. Thus, it is significant that he pledged his support and allegiance to the American government for whose constitution he had great admiration and worked diligently within the framework of the law to preserve, consolidate, and change the law in the interest of justice for all peoples, especially for those who are downtrodden and victimized by various power structures. He viewed his political activity as part of his service to God but felt no compulsion to demonstrate the metaphysical and religious foundations of that political understanding. Politics, for him, was relatively autonomous from religion.

Thus, it is clear that each leader views the relationship of religion to politics differently. Jackson's political understanding was made sacred by the way in which he related the realities of the American situation to his theological understanding. King's political understanding makes the basic American ideals congruent with his theological views, but the institutional practices of racism must be cleansed by the moral forces of the gospel and the nation's ideals. The political understandings of Powell have a status of relative autonomy from his theological position. But his understanding of the realities of the American nation was such that he believed it capable of constructive change, and therefore, he preached a gospel and advocated political action that favored participation within the American societal system. Malcolm X, however, had a radical view of the American nation. He condemned it as incurably racist, and during his sojourn in the Nation of Islam his radical politics were inseparable from his radical theology. Later his political thinking maintained much of its radical nature, while he was unclear about its relationship to any actual religious views. A radical goal of a Black separate nation (whether within or without America) necessitated radical means, which were provided by his philosophy of Black nationalism.

No attempt has been made in the foregoing discussion to explain why these individuals held their respective theological and political understandings; my goal has been merely to describe the nature of those understandings and how they might be related to one another. It has been demonstrated that the understandings are quite diverse, and, although there are elements of commonality among them, the differences predominate. I have focused on the latter, because the dissimilarities pervade the leaders' respective writings and speeches and because the purpose of this study is to examine those things that hindered cooperative activity among them.

This analysis has not led to a resolution of our primary problem—how cooperative action among these selected personalities might have been possible. Insofar as Jackson and King relied on their respective understandings of the Christian faith as the sole ground of justification for political action, it is clear that each must reject the moral value of the political action advocated by the other. Since Powell did not attempt to justify his political action by an appeal to theology, his politics were replete with expediency and compromise. That fact presented immeasurable problems to King and Jackson, who felt constrained always to act on the basis of fixed and eternal principles. But because of Powell's basic commitment to American democracy and its constitution and because he had no interest in either philosophical or theological debate, it is not surprising that Jackson and King had been able to cooperate with him actively from time to time even though they could not cooperate with each other. Malcolm X presented the most difficult problems to King and Jackson, because his religious principles and his political principles were radically different from theirs. In short, he presented them with a seemingly insurmountable religious and political dilemma. But, in relation to Powell, Malcolm's thinking presented only a political problem to be resolved in a political way. It is not surprising to discover, therefore, that Powell and Malcolm were able to experience varying forms of association with each other.

At this point we are able to draw certain conclusions concerning the leadership characteristics of each of the four. On the basis of the foregoing it is possible to determine the principal dynamic that defines their respective leadership styles. Jackson and King strove diligently to demonstrate that their political thought was derived from their theological propositions. In other words, although both advocated a religious politic, the nature of their advocations differed. Jackson's societal function was priestly, while King's was prophetic. As priest, Jackson was a servant of the sacred, and insofar as the structure and ethos of the nation is harmonious with the truths of the Christian gospel, he served nation and church with loyalty and reverence. In his thought, there is no great cleavage between the American nation and the Christian gospel. Rather, the basic tenets of the latter are embodied in the Constitution and are generally manifested in the nation's social and cultural life. In other words, his thought implies that all the necessary and sufficient conditions are present for the citizens to actualize their potentialities via self-development. Further, when certain dimensions of the national life require amelioration, the latter should be effected in a reverent and peaceful manner in order to avoid the risk of disrespecting the sacred quality of the nation itself. When politics and religion are in basic harmony, there is never any justification for societal conflict. And so, the priestly character of Jackson's leadership aimed at celebrating and reaffirming the historical heritage of the nation, the race, the church, and those other institutions that share this common quality.

King, as prophet, was principally dynamic in the role of societal critic. As a religious person, he, too, was a priest of the sacred. In his judgment, the sacred was manifested formally in the nation's constitution, while it was contradicted in the nation's general customs and practices. Accordingly, he felt compelled to demonstrate the nature of that contradiction to the body politic and to seek its alleviation lest it destroy the nation. But, being dedicated to a politics that derived from his religious understandings, it was necessary for him to construct a view of political thought and action that manifested at every point its religious quality. Eventually, he discovered that the principle of nonviolence was capable of bridging the practical cleavage between religion and social reform. He contended that its philosophy was theologically sound and that its practice revealed a religiously redemptive goal for the actors and for those acted upon. Since the nation's constitutional ideals were consonant with his vision of the religious end of humankind, he called upon all those who loved his religious vision and the American dream to engage in redemptive action for their mutual realization. Thus, the action he advocated aimed at self-fulfillment for the individual actor, for those who desired social justice, and for the nation that permitted and encouraged its practice.

Jackson's thought disallowed societal conflict, because there was no basic tension between his understandings of religion and the nation's ideals and practices. But King encouraged societal conflict, because he concluded that there was a basic contradiction between the nation's ideals and its social and cultural practices. In other words, he believed that the sacred ideals were threatened by the nation's own practices. That contradiction was considered a moral problem, and those who embodied moral sensibilities were called upon to wage battle against those immoral practices. But the battle had to be a redemptive one for all concerned. The similarity between Jackson and King can be seen in the way both placed an accent of religious significance on politics. But they did so differently. The former viewed the state as fully religious and compelled thereby, from time to time, to wage a battle of conquest against those bent on the nation's destruction. King viewed his protest organizational strategy as fully religious and taught that it must wage a battle of redemption with the nation in order to save it from internal forces of destruction.

Powell was unlike either Jackson or King, in that he made no attempt to demonstrate that his political understandings were derived from his religious understandings. Indeed, he posited a seemingly unbridgeable gulf between religion and politics. That is to say, he claimed that though religion is extremely important, its substance is never unambiguously manifested in history. That did not imply, however, that the sacred is radically disconnected from history. On the contrary, it appears in history, but its opaqueness prohibits any full and complete understanding. Although Powell was able to function as priest and as prophet from time to time, neither characterized the principal dynamic underlying his thought and action. Rather, his function was that of political reformer. Theoretical thought was not his forte. Practical thought was—for example, the deliberative process of calculating means to ends. In his thought, the political end desired and sought was subject to the norm of the kingdom of God. Under normal circumstances, he believed, one knew intuitively whether human actions were immoral and unjust. Similarly, one recognized their opposites. It was his opinion that whenever or wherever one discovers injustice he or she is morally obligated to plan deliberate courses of action designed to eradicate it. After he had made his decision to work primarily through the elective governmental processes, many things pertaining to goals and loyalties were implied or taken for granted. Powell, like most politicians, spent

little time philosophizing or theologizing. Rather, he
dealt with concrete issues and sought effective means
to desired goals. He learned the art of working constructively with many diverse persons whose thoughts
and desires and actions were quite different from his
own. Such knowledge was invaluable in developing the
capacity to function in coalitional politics within and
without the government. Also, such experiences were
indispensable in helping him to develop the attitude of
tolerance for different viewpoints. In short, Powell
mastered the art of becoming an effective political
reformer.

In order to function as a political reformer one must
gain access to some political arena and must secure
one's position therein. The starting point for political
action is clear—self-initiative. That was the basic principle underlying Powell's thought and action. He
viewed Blacks as a group that had been denied the
right for self-initiative and, therefore, were destined to
enter the political game late. Whether the issue be social, economic, or political, Powell believed that
Blacks and others had to initiate their own action, and
in that process they would, with careful organization
and good practical judgment, win some victories while
losing others. A skillful politician knows the importance of rhetoric and how to use it effectively for one's
own desired ends. But that politico also knows, as did
Powell, that political rhetoric is a form of political action although not identical in all respects with its
substance.

Because Powell established no easy connection between his religious thought and his political thought,
he had to exert no energy in justifying the latter by
appeals to the former. Indeed, for the most part, Powell viewed politics as autonomously designed by
humans, informed by religious ideals and visions, and
ultimately subject to religion's norm but not presently
in need of demonstration. Consequently, Powell felt
free to do and to say whatever practical judgment re-

quired so long as it was lawful and did not contradict his oath of office.

Finally, Malcolm X functioned as a political nationalist desirous of founding a nation that would be controlled by Black Americans. He did not advocate the revolutionary overthrow of the American government. There is no evidence that he conspired with any foreign government to commit treason. Rather, he sought the establishment of a nation within a nation. Although he did not give a clear portrayal of how the new nation would be related to the larger one, it appears that he envisioned the former as being constructed by the latter, that is, via an act of Congress. As a political nationalist, his primary aim was that of teaching his people the truth about themselves, their history, and their contemporary situation. His ideological commitments were unshakable, and he believed in the social and political implications of that ideology throughout his life. When he could no longer continue to be loyal to Elijah Muhammad and his religious beliefs, that cleavage caused no changes in his social and political thought. That fact demonstrated at least one thing: that political nationalism may or may not be grounded in religion. Like Powell, Malcolm was a practical person who knew the ends he desired and concentrated on the means for their realization. Like King and Jackson, he was often disposed to considerable speculative thought. By and large, he concentrated on mastering the skills of good rhetoric in order to be more effective in teaching his ideology to Blacks. That ideology was in basic conflict with America's dealings with Blacks. Malcolm called for a nonracist state, and he was convinced that such could only be realized in a state that was ruled and shaped by Blacks themselves. Accordingly, all action that had the interests of Blacks at heart must be controlled by Blacks. Self-determination, therefore, was the basic ethical and political principle underlying all his thought. It is a principle appropriate to national sovereignty, and, in his perspective, the realization of a Black sovereign nation was a necessary condition for racial justice.

Like Powell, Malcolm's thought was characterized by his politics, but unlike Powell, his politics was rooted in an ideology that was intolerant of others and abhorrent of compromise.

It is now clear these four religious leaders had different styles of leadership that did not easily lend themselves to cooperative action. Indeed, it appears that we have not yet discovered adequate grounds on which they might have united for cooperative action. Clearly, our findings thus far could lead us to construct some ontological argument in support of reconciliation among them, but that would be so far removed from action that it could never become the basis for any concrete coalitional activity. Consequently, the basis for the type of cooperative action we seek must be found only in some concrete moral issue the eradication of which was desired by all four leaders. And the issue itself must have sufficient breadth so as to preserve and to promote their diverse thought and action. It remains for the following chapter to explore that issue from another vantage point.

7

Diversity in Unity: Pluralistic Conceptions of Racism

A careful analysis of the theological and the political thought of the personalities selected for this study reveals that the problem of racism forms the contextual framework for the development of their respective understandings. That is to say, racism and its eradication is, in large part, the subject matter of their political and theological reflections. In this chapter I will argue (a) that each of the figures has a different view of racism; (b) that those respective views of racism are complementary; (c) that their respective understandings of social change emerge out of their respective understandings of racism and are also complementary; and (d) that the complementarity of their pluralistic understandings of the problem of racism requires pluralistic forms of action and cooperative activity for its eradication.

It is a fact that racism is described variously and that those diverse descriptions imply their own respective policies. This fact is evidenced by the several ways in which the specialized human sciences have defined racism. Further, it has been understood differently even by its most prominent Black opponents. Those latter understandings constitute the starting point of this chapter's argument, an argument that aims at discovering the grounds for cooperative action while af-

firming diversity of thought and action. Let us
illustrate the salient characteristics of their respective
understandings of the problem, beginning with Jackson's conception.

Jackson contended that racism was a prejudicial attitude based solely on racial differences. He argued
that those who exercise racial prejudice were themselves victimized along with those on whom the injustice is perpetrated.[1] He was adamant in his claim that
racism was not inherent in the basic values and ideals
promulgated and institutionalized by the nation's originators. Rather, he insisted that it had always been
perpetrated by a minority of self-interested persons
who, unfortunately, succeed occasionally in gaining
sufficient power to make their prejudicial claims
overtly visible in acts of discrimination and segregation. In addition, he avowed that those persons did an
injustice not only to the victims of their prejudices and
to themselves but also to those sacred principles on
which the nation has been established. In short, he
considered them to be outlaws who presently had
gained a measure of power but, in due time, would be
defeated by those same values and institutions that
they had discredited. Thus, he admonished all good
citizens to remain loyal to the nation's basic values
and institutions in order to restore the social order to
its original virtue.

A closer analysis of Jackson's conception of racism
reveals that he regarded one of its main causes to be
the low valuation Blacks bestow upon themselves.
Time and again he taught that racial prejudice was
based on the notion that Blacks dislike and disrespect
themselves and prefer whites to members of their own
race. An obvious implication of such teaching is that
racial prejudice is a defense mechanism devised by
whites in abhorrence of those who are lacking in self-
respect. This type of analysis led Jackson to develop
his own philosophy of racial preference, which he contrasted with racial prejudice. Accordingly, he urged
Blacks to give priority in action to those policies and

programs that engender racial pride and self-respect. Frequently, he tried to persuade them that all efforts toward racial self-development and every achievement along that line contribute to the restoration of racial pride and self-respect. Thus, he encouraged Blacks to cease focusing on the evils perpetrated upon them by whites and in its stead to aim at actualizing those creative possibilities that they can achieve through various imaginative means of self-development. He was convinced that Blacks must solve the problem of racial self-disrespect before any other victories could be won. Since racism is an attitudinal response on the part of whites to the negative views Blacks have toward themselves, they (Blacks) are admonished to expend all their efforts toward altering their self-image. The achievement of such an objective requires the embodiment of the basic values and ideals of the nation— patriotism, democracy, Christianity, moral virtue, self-development. By removing those conditions that foster racial prejudice they would succeed in liberating themselves and white America from their mutual victimization.

Let us now turn to Powell's conception of racism. Although he agreed that racism is, in part, an attitudinal problem of prejudice, he contended that it pertains primarily to the exclusion of Blacks from positions of power. Hence, he viewed it as basically a political problem rather than a psychological one. Fundamentally, he considered it to be a problem of imposed powerlessness that incapacitated Blacks in terms of initiating action and controlling their own destiny. But he did not look upon it as a problem for Blacks alone. Rather, he viewed whites as victims of hypocrisy who professed belief in nonracist doctrines and creeds while practicing the contrary. In general, he saw the problem as a paramount threat to the social order that violated not only the law of God but also the fundamental precepts of our democratic government and the sensibilities of the nonwhite peoples of the world.

Powell's experience had taught him that most instances of powerlessness among Black people were caused by racial injustice. Throughout his public career he focused his attention on actual situations of powerlessness. He fought vigorously for the consistent application of federal law in all states. He waged many battles to ensure that federal funds would not go to those states that openly violated federal civil rights laws. This was a most effective way to engage the federal government in the process of enforcing its laws within the states. Powell's conception of powerlessness implied forms of action that would effect some actual change in the condition of Blacks by enhancing their capacity for free, independent action. Contrary to Jackson's idea, his notion did not suggest that the state of powerlessness was caused by Blacks themselves but, rather, by the hypocritical and undemocratic acts of white racists. To alter that condition would necessitate the employment of effective means. Successful social change would be evidenced by the measure of actual power that would accrue to Blacks economically, politically, socially, et cetera. Clearly, Powell's understanding of the problem did not indicate any rejection of the nation's basic values and ideals. While he affirmed them at all times, he remained skeptical about their actual practice. He perceived racism as America's primary social problem, designed and maintained by human decisions. Hence, he believed that action in relation to it would either save or destroy the nation. He was frequently unhappy, however, concerning his estimation of America's moral capacity to do the right in that regard. In a baccalaureate address delivered at Howard University in 1966, he expressed a measure of uncertainty about the matter.[2]

In principle, he affirmed the basic economic, political, and social institutions that constitute the social order. There was no doubt in his mind, however, that the most basic social problem was the arbitrary exclusion of Blacks from participatory access to the arenas of power in that social order. He questioned the basic rules governing societal participation only when they were used to exclude Blacks or other minorities. In short, he believed that the problem of racism could be solved, but not without struggle and conflict. He considered legislative action the formal means of its solution and the enforcement of that legislation the substantive means.

King's thought represents another understanding of racism. Throughout his public life Martin Luther King viewed racial segregation and discrimination as the social problem he was bent on resolving. In his writings he sometimes appears to have equated racial prejudice with segregation and discrimination, but his mature understanding was more complex than that. He judged racial prejudice to be an attitude shaped by misunderstanding, falsity, and fear. He knew that the task of effecting substantial attitudinal change was not a goal that could be attained easily or quickly. He felt it extremely important that schools, churches, and other social and civic organizations employ every available means to reshape the mistaken ideas and attitudes concerning Blacks. He also knew that racial prejudice was an attitude that was reinforced by certain institutional practices of segregation and discrimination. Indeed, he viewed those practices as overt acts that expressed covert racial prejudice. He asserted that such acts could be arrested by calling upon the nation to acknowledge their illegality. As a result, he spent his public career struggling to persuade various legislative bodies and the law courts to outlaw racist customs. He knew that legislative and judicial justice would not in themselves change the attitudes of people, but he hoped that they could alter the kind of overt behavior that is set in motion by such attitudes, behavior that has such a dehumanizing effect on Black people.

During the Montgomery bus boycott, King gradually concluded that racism in the form of segregation and discrimination seriously dominated the character of the nation, that it would not be cured simply by ethical and moral suasion, and that its opponents would need to engage in a moral struggle of nonviolent direct resistance in order to gain a just victory. It was also characteristic of King to condemn racial discrimination and segregation on theological and moral grounds.

King was convinced, however, that as long as racism was widespread throughout the land, it contradicted the nation's basic values and fundamental ideals. In fact, he publicly repudiated its practice by some of the nation's most sovereign and sacred institutions—law courts, legislatures, churches, schools—viewing its persistence as inimical to the nation's moral integrity. Thus, he agreed with those who called the problem the American Dilemma. While his speeches are replete with vivid descriptions of how Blacks are victimized sociologically, economically, politically, and psychologically by racism, they also portray the perpetrators of racism as being victimized by their obsession with racial hatred and fear. He taught that oppressor and oppressed alike suffer the effects of evil and that both stand in need of liberation. But since the oppressor never gives up power freely, the agents of liberation must be the oppressed. King's insistence that the goal of the struggle must be the restoration of interracial harmony (community) intimated that the means to that goal should be commensurate with it. In other words, both the means and the goal must be redemptive.

Even though King did not oppose those who advocated the use of moral suasion and various forms of education for the elimination of racial prejudice, and although he did not oppose those who seriously attempted to help Blacks gain access to arenas of power, he contended that racism would never be dealt with successfully by those means alone. Rather, he believed that priority must be given to the structural reform of public institutions. Accordingly, his thought and action were aimed at the realization of more justice in the institutional structures of the social order. He viewed the legislative and the judicial systems as the primary agencies for such change.

Finally, Malcolm X perceived racism to be endemic

to the American culture, to pervade its fundamental values, and to inhere in all its institutions. He concluded that white America was incurably and inevitably racist.* Further, he regarded the problem of racism to be integrally connected with the international problem of colonialism. He argued that racism in America and international colonialism aimed at the political and the economic exploitation and subjugation of the darker peoples of the world. His judgment that the problem was international in scope implied that an international agency would be needed to effect its solution. Hence, he declared that the focus on civil rights was erroneous, because the dilemma was not merely domestic but worldwide. By limiting the nature of the problem to civil rights, one precluded the possible engagement of others from beyond America's leadership. However, when the problem was judged to be an international one, it became, in his view, a problem of human rights, because it threatened the humanity of the world's oppressed peoples.

> I say in conclusion that the Negro problem has ceased to be a Negro problem. It has ceased to be an American problem and has become a world problem, a problem for all humanity. Negroes waste their time confining their struggle to civil rights. In that context the problem remains only within the jurisdiction of the United States. No allies can help Negroes without violating United States protocol. But today the Black man in America has seen his mistake and is correcting it by lifting his struggle from the level of civil rights to the level of human rights.[3]

---

*Prior to his break with Elijah Muhammad, Malcolm felt that racism was a natural problem, in that whites were, by nature, racists who had been created as devils. Later, however, he renounced that doctrine and viewed the problem as a political one designed and maintained by most whites but not necessarily by all. In those early days he believed in the cosmic battle of Armageddon that would reestablish Black freedom from white oppression. At the time of his death he had come to view that battle as more political than eschatological in nature.

Since he considered America incapable of changing its basic racist values and its concomitant institutional practices, the only reasonable direction for Black liberation must lie in violent revolution or in peaceful separation. Very few Blacks in this country have ever advocated violent revolution in the sense of overthrowing the government and reconstituting the nation. But there have been many who have advocated peaceful separation on the basis of a nationalist principle such as colonization or racial autonomy in terms of development and control. Malcolm's conception of the problem is a radical one in the sense that it makes no appeals to the consciences of white people. Rather, it offers racial separation as the only solution, the realization of which is heavily dependent on its ability to win the support and loyalty of Blacks. That latter goal—persuading the masses to accept this particular way of conceptualizing the problem—had to be the first priority or else the enterprise would fail. Thus, Malcolm spent his public life trying to change the so-called slave mentality of Black people in order to convert them to his analysis and its implications.

It must be pointed out that Malcolm believed that those who composed the Black revolution were not fighting for integration or for separation but rather for basic human rights, that is, the right to be respected as human beings. He felt it absurd to think that white people desired or would permit racial integration. Further, he was convinced that the Black masses themselves did not want racial integration. More important, he insisted that voluntary racial separation did not imply a reverse kind of racism. Rather, it embraced a type of pluralism that did not exclude the possibility of kinship among racially and culturally diverse peoples.

Thus, in Malcolm's thinking, the problem of racism was fundamentally one of powerlessness on the part of oppressed people to affirm and to protect their humanity, to define and crush the enemy, to determine their own destiny in spite of the costs. The realization of those goals necessitated the empowerment of the oppressed, which could only be gained by force. The fruits of Malcolm's revolution would be the actualization of freedom, justice, and equality.

Thus, I have now described the four different conceptions of the problem of racism as held respectively by each of the four leaders. Those ideas may be typified accordingly: (a) racism is the problem of racial prejudice caused by Black self-disrespect; (b) racism is the problem of Black powerlessness caused by coercive forces of exclusion; (c) racism is the problem of institutional practices of discrimination and segregation caused by misunderstandings and irrational fears; (d) racism is a form of the international problem of colonialism whereby the darker peoples of the world are exploited and subjugated by whites.

A more detailed analysis of those views of racism as held by the four individuals being studied reveals some common facts. First and foremost, each of the selected figures has publicly advocated some form of resistance to the objectifying process of racism. Although they understood racism in differing ways, each viewed it as a major threat to the personhood of Blacks and to the moral character of whites. Each perceived the intensity of that danger differently, and each advocated forms of resistance in accordance with their respective perceptions. That fact is extremely significant, because it indicates that any interpretations of the thought of these personalities must clearly demonstrate that each resisted racism in accordance with his own understanding of the problem. Hence, explanatory terms, such as conservative, moderate, accommodative, that do not explicitly denote some form of resistance are misleading and erroneous. Not only do they distort the thought of these persons, but they misunderstand the nature of human response to external control. Persons who do not resist their own objectification evidence the destruction of their own personhood and are necessarily reduced to some pathological state of being, capable of being servants (use objects) but incapable in thought or action of leading any op-

position against that status. Further, I contend that
whether legitimate or moderate, militant or radical,
the resistance of our leaders (in thought or in action)
was extremely significant, because it manifested some
measure of transcendence over racism's victimizing
aim. Another important implication is that it gives us
a significant formal basis of commonality among our
leaders: namely, they all resisted racism.

Second, I maintain that their respective views of the
nation were based fundamentally on their perceptions
of racism's impact. That is to say, each viewed the
character of whites in particular and the nation in general as having been morally scarred by the practice of
racism. Although they arrived at different conclusions
about the nature of that problem and its suggestions
for action, each viewed racism from his understanding
of its moral consequences for white racists and for a
nation that legitimates racist practices, not merely
from the perspective of its effects on Blacks. Jackson
was especially discerning in insisting that persistent
acts of bitterness, hatred, violence, and so on caused
people to assume a character that corresponded with
such acts. His belief in the moral virtue of the founders of the nation and of those citizens who demonstrate the spirit of goodwill gave him hope that one
day America would manifest fully in thought and deed
the kinship of all its citizens. Thus, his commitment to
a firm patriotism was for the sake of that hope. It was
rooted in his understanding that America was basically good, although it had been rendered deficient in
morality by the self-serving and un-American acts of a
minority bent on the destruction of the type of community espoused by the nation's founders. His opposition to racism was, therefore, not merely for the
liberation of Blacks but also for the liberation of the
nation from the threat of those who sought its demise.

Martin Luther King, Jr., believed strongly in the
ideals on which America was founded, ideals immortalized in the nation's laudable constitution. But the practices of the nation violated those constitutional ideals

and, like a cancer, threatened the well-being of the whole corpus. Like Jackson, King agreed that by upholding the practices of racism the nation was embarked upon a self-destructive enterprise. Similarly, his opposition was motivated by the consequences of racism suffered by Blacks and by the moral threat its continuance had for the republic. He viewed his movement of resistance as the agency for the nation's salvation.

Adam Clayton Powell, Jr., frequently reflected upon the oath of office he took when he first went to Congress. That oath was a pledge to uphold the Constitution, which embodies the nation's ideals. He believed that those Americans who upheld the Constitution on the one hand and who practiced racism on the other made themselves into hypocrites, because their actions contradicted America's ideals. Similarly, he asserted that the practice of racism made Americans hypocritical in their religious life, since they affirmed their belief in the Christian God who, in turn, blesses no superordinate-subordinate relations based on race as a principle. Therefore, Powell viewed his opposition to racism as a means of setting America free from its own hypocrisy, thus enabling a nation to emerge based on human respect and honesty instead of pretension and contradiction.

As stated above, Malcolm X believed for a time that white people were racist by nature. Later he altered that belief by contending that most white people were inevitably racist. In the latter view, he had rejected the tenet that racism was caused by natural necessity while maintaining the confidence that it was widespread among white people. In his judgment, racism was an evil practiced by evil people, and hence, he considered it necessary for Blacks to separate themselves from the evil ones by building their own independent nation. In short, Malcolm had no faith that the character of white America could be changed significantly. His understanding of national community presupposed separate racial development. He affirmed that white America would treat a sovereign Black nation with as much respect and honor as it treated any other sovereign entity. But as long as Blacks lived in a dependent relationship with white America, the latter would never respect them as persons or enable them to receive justice. Blacks must gain their own freedom and should cease petitioning whites for that freedom. Blacks must rid themselves of all forms of dependency on whites and must become a self-determining people. Malcolm believed that interracial community between Blacks and whites could result only after both races had attained national status.

Thus, from this perspective the thought of Jackson, King, Powell, and Malcolm can be characterized as basically resistant to the forces of racism and intrinsically concerned about the possibility of community. But their thought varied as to the form that resistance should take and the shape community should have. In any case, their judgments were determined largely by their respective understandings of the nature of racism and by the way it inhered in the nation's character.

Obviously, their respective conceptions of racism are different, but it is also clear that they shared a commonly desired goal—the eradication of racism. Although they disagreed on the nature of the resistance necessary to attain such a goal, a careful analysis of their views reveals that the four understandings fall along a continuum ranging from minimal threat to the social order to maximal threat. In other words, if a continuum be thought to represent the movement of resistance from low to high intensity or from right-wing to left-wing politics, then our various conceptions can be arranged accordingly:

Conceptions

Maximal Threat			*Minimal Threat*
(Left-wing)			(Right-wing)

Malcolm X	*King*	*Powell*	*Jackson*

In the diagram the conceptions of Jackson and of Malcolm X represent the two extreme positions of the continuum, while Powell and King occupy places right and left of the center respectively. Jackson's conception can be viewed as the one that places a higher valuation on the nation's ideals and basic institutions than any of the others. Further, he perceives the problem as primarily rooted in Black self-disrespect. But in Malcolm X's thought we discover that the nation's ideals and institutions are of very little value. In fact, he placed the cause of racism solely in the evil decisions and designs of most white Americans, including the nation's founders. His chief priority was purging the minds of Blacks of the brainwashing substance that had been effectively implanted by the coercive and subtle techniques of white racism. I have placed King to the left of center, because his analysis focuses on the nation's institutional practices, the effective reform of which must imply considerable resistance. Powell's conception is placed to the right of center, because it is calculative and pragmatic. Its aim is the design of ways and means of using the rules, procedures, and forms of action of the nation's governmental institutions to achieve the goals Blacks desire. In this regard, I assume that, procedurally, Powell's style of thought and action was reflective of traditional ethnic group politics in America.

On the one hand, Jackson and Powell affirmed the American societal system—that is, its basic values and institutions. They simply differed in their views of how Blacks should relate to them. Jackson favored a racial self-development process within the framework of a vigorous patriotism, while Powell diligently worked for the establishment of conditions that would guarantee Blacks fair access to the various arenas of power. But, on the other hand, King and Malcolm X believed that the American system could not work well apart from significant social change. King desired to bring the American institutional practice into harmony with its values and ideals. He boldly and persistently attacked the institution of Jim Crow, which was destined to fall under the impact of his movement. Malcolm X challenged the basic values and ideals on which the republic had been built, charging that Blacks were never intended (not even by the nation's founders) to be free citizens. Thus, Jackson and Powell have their rightful place to the right of center, while King and Malcolm merit their places on the left. If we have been successful in arranging the four conceptions of racism along a continuum, it follows that at least in certain respects they together compose a wholistic perspective. That is to say, none constitutes a complete perspective in itself. Rather, each is limited and, therefore, inadequate. It may be that the inadequacy of each is compensated for by the others. If that should prove true, then we will have demonstrated the complementary nature of the four conceptions. Consequently, we would be able to state that all of them would be required for a comprehensive understanding of the problem.

The notion that the four conceptions together constitute a wholistic perspective is strengthened by the fact that racism has been viewed as a Black problem by Jackson, as an American problem by Powell and by King, as a world problem by Malcolm X. Hence, the locus of the problem is given varying degrees of breadth by the various perspectives. But the primary locus for each perspective is not exclusive of the others. Assuredly, Malcolm X viewed white people in this country and abroad as the inevitable (although not necessary) cause of the problem. Since Blacks have been brainwashed by a slave mentality, he considered their mental illumination the first step in the order of analysis and prescription. Similarly, Jackson focused analytically on the problem of Black self-disrespect but hastened to demonstrate how the solution to the problem in America could be a model for the resolution of similar types of discord elsewhere in the world. King and Powell saw each local expression of racism as being symptomatic of the national problem, which, in turn, has political ramifications that resound throughout the world.

Further, the notion that the four conceptions constitute a wholistic perspective is strengthened by the fact that each is capable of eliciting considerable affirmation from any Black American audience as long as its spokesperson be someone in whom the audience has not developed a high degree of distrust. In other words, the experience of racism for Blacks has been multidimensional, and most can identify with the basic elements of each perspective. In this regard it is significant that the four leaders rarely, if ever, made public attacks on the logic of any of the alternative conceptions without grossly misconstruing that logic by way of caricature or some other form of mockery.

The thesis that the four conceptions constitute a wholistic perspective and that they are related to one another as parts are related to wholes has not yet been fully established. Clearly, the parts of a whole are complementary. Accordingly, an adequate argument for the complementarity of the four conceptions of racism will determine the way in which they together constitute a whole. Such an argument requires a demonstration that each of the conceptions is inadequate in relation to specific facts of experience and that the inadequacy of each is compensated by the others.

I will proceed by showing, first of all, how Jackson's conception fails to take into account certain important facts of experience. His definition of racism as a problem of racial prejudice caused by Black self-disrespect is only partially adequate. He erred by oversimplifying a phenomenon that pervades all dimensions of our social life. Although racial prejudice is indeed a reality, his attempt to explain racism solely in terms of psychology is inadequate. In fact, such an understanding fails to grasp the nature of a problem that is an integral part of the nation's institutions and mores. Further, while Black self-disrespect is regrettable, there is little evidence to support his claim that it is the cause of white racism. On the contrary, most studies have viewed it as one of the pathological effects of racism. Also, Jackson's understanding of racism is limited by his idealization of the American democratic process, and hence, he was apparently incapable of seeing that that process itself can become perverted and racist. Neither King, Powell, nor Malcolm X was ignorant of these facts. While affirming the measure of truth implied by Jackson's understanding, their conceptions are adequate in relation to all the limitations stated above.

Second, King's conception of racism as the public practice of racial segregation and discrimination caused by misunderstandings and irrational fears is also inadequate when considered in relation to certain facts. While his understanding accurately described the situation of Black people in the South, it was incapable of embracing the subtle forms of racism that confronted Blacks in northern urban areas.[4] Further, his commitment to racial unity under the conditions of constitutional democracy caused him to ignore the fact of cultural pluralism and its positive implications for Black Americans. Consequently, he was not able to perceive the fact that cultural plurality is a basic condition for making American democracy effective. Thus, King had little to say about the importance of racial self-development, because at each and every point in the struggle his emphasis was on the principle of racial integration. In differing ways, the conceptions of Jackson, Powell, and Malcolm X avoid the inadequacies implied by King's thought. Each had a view of racism that transcended regional experiences; each had an appreciation for action that was motivated by the principle of racial self-help. Finally, each had his own vision of community and interracial harmony built on the preservation of racial solidarity within both races.

Third, Powell's conception of racism as the exclusion of Blacks from participation in the various arenas of power is insufficient, because it does not include all the salient facts of experience. Blacks have long known that even when they do manage to gain some important measure of economic, social, or political power, they are not liberated thereby from the constraints of racism. No amount of achieved power seems to release them from its control. Neither education, money, social status, nor political office ensures freedom. Hence, Powell's conception that the plight of Blacks is analogous to that of European ethnic groups in their struggles to gain power fails to grasp the way in which racism functions as an independent variable. The latter is a fact that neither King, Jackson, nor Malcolm X ever failed to recognize. Unlike the other three, Powell's consistent pragmatism led him to assume an attitude of operational relativism, which he applied to everything, including his religion, his politics, and his morality. Consequently, his cynicism regarding theology, philosophy, and ethics prevented him from developing an independent theory of racial justice. Again, none of the others was deficient in that respect.

Fourth, Malcolm X's conception of racism as a domestic form of international colonialism, whereby the darker peoples of the world are exploited and subjugated by the whites, assumes a worldwide racial conspiracy that implies a necessary mistrust of all white people. That implication was contradicted by his own actions. Malcolm utilized the resources of white institutions—the press, publishing houses, television networks, university lecture circuits—to promulgate his message. It was a message aimed at reeducating Blacks, to be sure, but he also put forth a great effort to persuade white Americans, else why address them with such eloquent rhetoric and from such esteemed platforms. Those actions were not suggested by his conception of what was needed by way of corrective action. A similar contradiction is seen in the way his commitment to Black nationalism within the borders of the United States tended to blind him to the fact that his position presupposed the willing participation of the American nation in establishing the desired goal of Black sovereign autonomy. Neither Jackson, King,

nor Powell ever thought that the struggle against racism could be won by Blacks alone. Hence, they were
not confused about the importance of addressing
whites in persuasive speech and with legal action. Malcolm denounced such activities but failed to see that
his own actions were similar. While he accused them
of begging America for their desired goal, they could
have accused him likewise.

Thus, it has been demonstrated how the various conceptions of racism as held by the selected figures are
deficient in their adequacy to address the empirical
facts of experience. It has also been shown how the various deficiencies point to the need each had of the others, thus proving that they were complementary rather
than irreconcilably conflictual. It must be noted, however, that my argument has not attempted to destroy or
to diminish their differences. Neither have I attempted
to devise a definition of racism that would include all
their understandings. Although that could be a fruitful
enterprise, it would not contribute to my purpose in
this study, which is to find some important grounds for
cooperative action without requiring the four leaders to
forsake their own understandings. Up to this point I
have simply clarified their understandings, determined
their limits, and cleared the way for improved understanding, power, and action.

If the four conceptions of racism together compose
one comprehensive, wholistic analysis of the problem,
it should follow that the implied recommendations for
the problem's resolution also form a comprehensive
pattern of action. Let us view briefly those implied
policies. Jackson's conception indicates policies of racial development in all dimensions of life—educationally, economically, politically, morally, and so on.
Powell's conception suggests policies leading to actual
racial empowerment by virtue of full access to and
participation in those public arenas of power. King's
conception embraces policies of nonviolent resistance
to ensure the death of Jim Crowism in all public institutions of our social order. And finally, Malcolm X's

conception denotes policies that will enable Blacks to discard white definitions of themselves and to determine their destiny in their own way.

Now, let us look more closely at those policies in order to discern their implications for social change. Throughout Jackson's thought the principle of racial self-development emerges prominently as the norm for social change. He considered that principle the best guideline for voluntary civic action apart from the arena of legislative change. In his understanding, the latter functioned on the basis of its own rules and procedures for the maintenance of the social order and not for purposes of social change. The principle of racial self-development intimates that citizens should seek to improve their social condition by employing their own resources, however meager they might be. Jackson regarded that method to be the most effective one for dealing with economic, social, political, and psychological problems. It signifies that the citizens basically affirm the predominant values and institutions of the society and that they neither threaten nor abuse them by irresponsible criticism or militant action. Jackson consistently viewed societal harmony as a matter of paramount importance and, therefore, preferable to any public conflict that might be initiated by a minority group. It does not appear that he was insensitive to the agony and the suffering of Blacks. Yet, in spite of their sufferings, he believed that it was better for them to engage in racial self-development than to challenge the whole society in open conflict and run the risk of substituting chaos and anarchy for unity and order. In his view, racial self-development can only be fostered under the conditions of law and order. Further, he deemed the principle an appropriate one, because he assumed that Blacks had not yet done all that they could to improve their lot. Rather, he felt that they must expend even greater effort in the development of racial self-respect through hard work, much perseverance, and meaningful achievements. He assumed that the burden of responsibility for effecting change in their own social condition rested primarily on Blacks. Jackson's own paternalism toward the masses was hidden by his insistence that they should break out of the paternalism of others and cease thinking as if the present relationship of superordination-subordination would always characterize the relation between the races. He asserted that that state of affairs could be corrected only by Blacks engaging in self-development. Significant achievement in the latter is the only adequate measure of social change.

It is important to note that during his presidency all the programs of the National Baptist Convention, U.S.A., Inc., were guided by the principle of racial self-development—for example, the purchase of a farm in Fayette, Tennessee; the acquisition of a bathhouse in Arkansas; the establishment of scholarship funds, voter education projects, the J. H. Jackson Library. All of these projects evidenced Black Baptists autonomously designing and implementing programs for the economic and educational development of the race. In brief, Jackson's programs aimed at racial self-development from within the race rather than from without. In that respect he was similar to Malcolm X.

Thus, another reason may be discerned for his intense opposition to civil disobedience. Racial self-development is, in his view, a positive program only if its agents respect the law. In other words, racial self-development is meaningfully undertaken only when it contributes to the welfare of the greater whole, the nation itself. His insistence that Blacks give their unqualified assent to the basic values and institutions of the American society is accounted for in part by his organic social theory. If a minority should withdraw from the national consensus, its achievements would not contribute anything to the whole organism. Rather, its relationship to the latter would necessarily be deviant and dysfunctional. Hence, he viewed Black Power as unequivocally wrong insofar as it advocated separation from the whole or aimed at a new form of domination over the majority. But he had no argument with it insofar as it called Blacks to racial self-development within the framework of the law. Racial self-development, in his understanding, is a sufficient principle when it aims at full participation in the larger society rather than at separation from it. Jackson's view of self-development as a principle of social change necessitated his commitment to civil rights legislation. Yet after the 1954 Supreme Court decision he did not consider the struggle for civil rights to be a major priority for Blacks, because he believed that the Constitution and its amendments established all the legal rights for Blacks to enjoy full and equal citizenship.

Clearly, Martin Luther King, Jr., had considerable appreciation for the philosophy of racial self-development. The spirit and influence of Booker T. Washington is unmistakable in King's early writings and speeches. Yet racial self-development was not his preferred principle for social change. Rather, the principle of racial self-fulfillment was basic to his thought and action. He easily affirmed the basic values and ideals of the American nation, which were immortalized in the Constitution and celebrated by the citizenry. He abhorred the cleavage between those lofty principles and the practice of racism. His commitment to the nation's basic values was as firm as Jackson's, but his criticism of the American practice was much more rigorous. Jackson's thought was characterized by his consistent praise for the goodness of America and by his fervent desire for the preservation of national unity. King's thought was characterized by his criticism that America's practice of racism contradicted its most fundamental beliefs. While Jackson called on Blacks to engage in self-development for the sake of themselves and the nation, King called upon Blacks and whites to demonstrate the hypocritical nature of America's racism by nonviolent resistance to those structures that prohibit participatory justice for Blacks. While Jackson's principle of social change was aimed at Blacks themselves, King's principle was aimed at the transformation of all public institutions that exclude Blacks because of their race. Both leaders assumed that the American system of law was good, but the thought of King illumined those areas of conflict that existed between the law and the day-to-day experience of Black people. While Jackson's thought easily leads one to view him as a religiocultural priest who affirmed and maintained the basic structures of the society, King's thinking was pregnant with prophetic criticism, and he seriously challenged the nation by demonstrating against its hypocritical practices.

King considered racism to be a moral problem. Further, he believed that Blacks had a moral obligation to refuse to participate in the institutional practice of racism. Consequently, he admonished his followers to resist that injustice nonviolently. Insofar as the law served to perpetuate such immorality, King advocated its resistance by strategies of nonviolent direct confrontation. To the degree that nonviolent resistance guided action, it functioned as a strategic principle. But as it became a way of life, it represented the principle of self-fulfillment, which was the desired end of Blacks and of whites. King's prophetic leadership was rooted in the principle of racial self-fulfillment and in its strategic corollary of nonviolent direct action as a major weapon against racism. He viewed it as a moral code of conduct empowered by what he called soulforce. He understood such a doctrine to imply that the actors were moral persons seeking a moral end via moral means. That is to say, all who strive for the eradication of racism affirm not only their own humanity but also that of their opponents.

It is now possible to see clearly King's moral reasoning for choosing to engage in civil disobedience. Immoral laws must be resisted by moral persons lest the latter contribute to immorality via compliance. Similarly, one can discern reasons for justifying school boycotts. One can also see how King's fears of Black Power became so overwhelming; he was not able to divorce it from notions of violence, domination, and a new form of racism, all of which he believed to be antithetical to the moral principle of self-fulfillment. In addition, his commitment to the basic values and ideals of America caused him to view the Black Power movement as one that implied a new value system which he could not entertain.

In the thought of Adam Clayton Powell, Jr., the basic principle governing social change is racial self-initiation. It is also one of the basic principles underlying the American form of democratic government. Powell felt, as did others before him, that politics is a matter of self-interest and that the body politic consists of a multiplicity of competing interests. Since each interest group is bent on the domination of society, its drive for autonomy can only be controlled by similar actions of alternative groups. Solutions for such conflicts must depend on various forms of compromise. In the Federalist Papers, James Madison advocated that the promotion of factionalism, coupled with a commitment to compromise, would protect the nation against the potential dangers of centralized authority. The promotion of factionalism can only be justified in a society wherein the freedom of speech, of expression, of assembly, and of association are taken for granted. Self-initiation is a principle that governs the process of policy formation. It suggests that any and every interest has a right to compete in the public arena and through discussion and debate to increase its support and eventually to win a solution through compromise. It is a method well grounded in the governmental experience of this country. It indicates that each citizen and each group of citizens have equal opportunity to organize and to engage in debate with others about strongly desired interests and goals. Whenever that opportunity is denied, it is a serious matter for the body politic per se, since it threatens the freedom of all. The principle of racial self-initiation is violated whenever part of the citizenry demonstrates that it has been prevented from initiating action in accord with its own interests. The ability to initiate action is power, and maximum power is the ability to actualize all of one's desires. For Powell, public action was guided primarily by that principle. Bloc voting in his congressional district enabled him to be elected repeatedly to represent the needs and interests of Blacks in Harlem and throughout the United States. He was able to encourage differing groups in their struggles against racism, but when they would choose to compete with him, he would use every possible method to deter them from their goal. He had no difficulty in joining forces temporarily with certain groups for specific goals. He had no political vision of a complete society of peace and harmony and hence promulgated no ideology that would ensure the loyalty of his followers. He never assumed that political alliances with other groups meant an endorsement of the beliefs of those groups. He was not a Black nationalist in terms of philosophy, but on numerous occasions he was able to ally himself with Black nationalists. His term for Black Power was *audacious power,* and this, in his opinion, represented the heart of the American form of government—the possibility for all citizens to gain power by inserting themselves into the public arena and by vigorously advocating their own self-interests. All who engage in that process must be content with compromise solutions, since they could never gain everything they might desire immediately.

In short, one might say that Powell viewed the American governmental process as a game that is praiseworthy when it works well for all its citizens. He judged the problem of racism as the attempt to prevent Blacks from participating in the public arena by disallowing them the legal and the economic resources with which to initiate public action. In his view, significant social change will accrue to Blacks when they will have been granted the necessary conditions for racial self-initiation. Little by little he worked away at the political system and tried to use its own instruments as effective means for the kind of criticism and change he believed America needed so desperately.

The basic principle governing Malcolm X's understanding of social change was racial self-determination. In his thought, racial self-determination is the first principle of any nationalism, and since it is sought by Blacks, it must entail radical change in the American societal system. He considered it a revolutionary principle. Malcolm did not perceive himself to be a citizen but, rather, a victim of white America's racism. Because he believed that the nation would never voluntarily change its racist practices, he taught that the only viable alternative for Blacks was racial separation in order to develop a new nation that would be shaped and determined by themselves. The logic of his position is similar to the following: Victimization results from other-determination. Others (non-Blacks) have determined the situation of Black Americans. Black Americans must separate themselves from external control in order to avoid victimization. Self-determination is freedom to determine one's own destiny. It is the mark of nationhood. It implies that alternative principles are self-destructive of Black people. Since Blacks have not been self-determining, they must be educated and converted to a belief in its virtue. Its usefulness in nation-building is determined, in large part, by the way it inheres in the being of the people. A people must feel itself to be a self-determining people or else the principle becomes a mere abstraction and thus meaningless. Therefore, Malcolm saw such events as school boycotts, Black Power, and civil disobedience as signs of the emerging spirit of racial self-determination.

In summary, it can be stated that Jackson's principle, racial self-development, is based on the value that Blacks should develop a high measure of racial self-respect by various self-help programs in order to earn the respect of white America. Powell's doctrine, racial self-initiation, is rooted in the value that, as citizens, Blacks should be assertive in gaining access to the arenas of power in the social order in much the same way as other ethnic groups have done in the past. King's precept, racial self-fulfillment, is based on the value that the fundamental dilemma in the social order is self-destructive. And finally, Malcolm X's principle, racial self-determination, implies the value that every person and every race should have the freedom of self-definition and control of its own destiny.

I contend that these four principles, designating four different understandings of social change, are not mutually exclusive but, rather, complement one another. First, their complementary relationship may be seen by looking again at the values underlying the principles. Racial self-development suggests the importance of Blacks preparing themselves for full participation in the social group. Racial self-initiation intimates that Blacks must assert themselves in order to gain participatory power. Racial self-fulfillment proposes that the social order itself must be free of contradictions in order to preserve its own health. Racial self-determination implies that all free persons must be moved by internal principles of motion rather than by external ones. A close analysis of these values reveals that they are all necessary conditions for the actualization of full citizenship rights in a democratic state. Indeed, citizens who are denied the opportunity to act under any one of those principles are thereby denied freedom.

Second, their complementarity may be viewed in a more complex way. Each of the principles implies all the others but organizes them under its own perspective. In other words, each assumes the functions of the others ambiguously, because those functions are altered when they are organized under the authority of any one of them. For example, racial self-development assumes racial self-initiation in setting various self-help programs in motion; it assumes racial self-fulfillment in the sense of having a vision of a healthy race free of internal conflict and contradiction and harmoniously related to the larger society; it assumes racial self-determination in the sense that self-help programs are shaped and controlled by the actors themselves. It is not necessary to demonstrate further how each of the other principles implies the functions of the others. It is clear, however, that whenever one principle becomes the principle for organizing the others, it gains a transcendent status over the elements it organizes. The danger of that transcendent position is that it tends to subordinate the others and to view itself as comprehensive and preeminent.

Third, their complementarity may be evidenced by an analysis of the respective understandings of power that are indicated by the above understandings of social change. In Jackson's view, power is the capacity of individual Blacks to achieve specific, tangible goals. Those goals tend to be viewed as educational and/or economic, and the individuals who attain them are thought to be an inspiration to others. That understanding of power focuses on the lack of individual achievement in the Black community, which is considered a serious internal constraint that hampers the community's self-being and development.

Malcolm discerned power as the capacity of Blacks to give up their slave mentality and to adopt a specific ideology that reveals the truth about themselves, their situation, and their enemy. Commitment to that ideology, together with the resultant group solidarity, was regarded as a necessary condition for the development of a new nation. Like Jackson's, Malcolm's view of power focused on a deficiency within the Black community (psychological and/or cultural) that was thought to be a serious internal constraint. Unlike Jackson, he did not see it as the lack of individual achievement but, rather, as false self-understanding.

Powell understood power to be the capacity of groups to organize themselves on the basis of self-interest in order to exert the necessary pressure to actualize their interests. He acknowledged power as the organized effort to calculate effective means to desired ends. He assumed that things desired by one group were controlled by others and that that control could be weakened by various forms of legitimate pressure. Unlike Jackson or Malcolm X, he did not focus on

Black deficiency in terms of achievement or ideology but on the most effective way of wresting power from those who had it.

King called power *soul-force,* which referred to the moral capacity of a people to resist evil nonviolently. He considered the principle of nonviolence to be reflexive, in that one became nonviolent by acting nonviolently. The moral capacity to use moral means in pursuing moral ends implied that the actor affirmed the enemy's humanity while resisting the enemy's evil actions. King believed that the application of that moral force would change any nation that was potentially moral and that had the capacity to respond appropriately to moral action.

Thus, in summary, four different understandings of power can be identified: the capacity for individual achievement; the capacity for true self-understanding; the capacity to organize on the basis of self-interest; the capacity to resist evil in a moral way. None of those understandings of power necessarily contradicts any of the others. Indeed, one would expect all human beings to affirm each of them, since they all appear to be necessary human capacities. In that case, the lack of any one of them would be an important reduction in human power.

If the four principles designating four understandings of social change constitute a whole, then a serious problem arises when one or another of them assumes predominance. Whenever the part assumes the status of the whole, one is confronted with the danger of tyrannical rule. Ideological and dogmatic domination always imply perspectival and practical tyranny. Such positions fail to see their real limitations and have no capacity for respecting different perspectives and practices. Black opposition to racism has been weakened greatly by such factionalism, that is, the kind of factionalism whereby each part makes absolute claims about itself while disparaging all others.

This chapter has demonstrated that four different conceptions of the problem of racism and their implied policies can be viewed as complementary to one another rather than as mutually exclusive. The argument has shown that the four perspectives on the dilemma can be observed as constituting a whole and that the four principles of action indicated by those perspectives and the four understandings of power assumed by those actions can be judged as mutually compatible. Certain implications follow from this argument: (a) each conception of the problem of racism and its implications for action is a true but limited perspective; (b) a denial of that limitation prevents a comprehensive analysis of the problem and severely limits the possible forms of opposition.

Since each of the understandings of racism is limited by its perspective, it is clear that the problem of racism is not adequately defined by any one conception, and therefore, no one form of action adequately resolves it. Each conception represents a certain degree of knowledge concerning the problem. The knowledge that is discovered and revealed through each of them must be affirmed and promoted. Similarly, each conception implies a certain form of action for the resolution of the problem. Each form of action must be affirmed and promoted. A major problem emerges when advocates of one conception war with advocates of another and view one another as necessarily contradictory and undesirable. Such a problem is a practical one that has hindered effective opposition to racism.

Since the various conceptions and their implied actions complement one another, and since the problem is much larger than any one conception can possibly describe, it would follow that cooperative activity among them is desirable. This fact does not imply that the differences among them are unimportant, accidental, or reducible to some kind of superficial unity. On the contrary, the differences are real and important and must be preserved as long as the problem remains. Like the parts of a living organism, each conception has its own unique and discrete contribution to make to an understanding of racism and to a plan as to how it might be eradicated. But, also, like the living organism, its specific function is altered when it cooperates with the others in contributing to the formation of a functional whole. In unity with the others its particularity is not lost; neither is its function merely particular. Biologically, the parts of the body obey the principle of wholeness, and the resulting harmony is often taken for granted. In the realm of human affairs, however, diverse understandings among people often lead to tension and conflict. Hence, the realization of cooperation among such diversity constitutes a political problem that requires considerable practical wisdom for its resolution. That cooperation may take many forms. First, on the basis of our present analysis, it would appear that if the four conceptions of racism and their implied policies constitute a functional whole, then all are necessary for the total eradication of racism. This fact should be made abundantly clear to the promoters of each of them so that they might cease fighting one another and begin respecting and supporting one another. It is hoped that when each comes to see its perspective on the problem as important yet limited, the desire for domination over others and the claim that its perspective alone is comprehensive and final will end. Like the diverse parts of a living organism, these several conceptions and their implied actions can function as a harmonious whole.

It is important to note that the category of the whole constitutes a fifth position. Its status is quite different from that of the others. It includes all the others while transcending each one. Its perspective is that of the four in relationship. Its function is a delicate one, because it is subject to the ambiguous possibility of running roughshod over one or the other of the particular perspectives in the interest of the whole. But such a danger is offset by the fact that the exclusion of any valid perspective from the whole necessarily weakens the latter and is virtually self-defeating.

The wholistic reality about which I speak is in one sense a matter of thought. In another sense it is practical and can be concretized in coalitions. In that sense it is a political reality. In short, the whole can be embodied in those political associations that are sufficiently pluralistic in their composition. Up to now the way the nature of that whole has been described suggests that its appropriate associational form is that of a federation,* wherein each of the parts would maintain its autonomy while working together on things that are held in common. Moreover, acting as one on those commonalities would strengthen the spirit of unity and would enhance the ongoing activity of each of the parts. Further, since the federation would be composed of diverse parts, it is important that each of them justify its participation according to its own understandings. In other words, the notion of a federation or any kind of cooperative activity must be justified in many different ways and not in one alone. That is a matter of practical wisdom. A federation may be a loosely constituted association that advises its constituent parts without legislating, or it may be a duly representative body that legislates on matters pertaining to the whole, excluding from its jurisdiction those matters that pertain to the internal life of the parts. Our present analysis implies the importance and desirability of some sort of federated association that would include all the diversity already described.

------

*This notion of federation is not a new idea in the history of Black opposition to racism. Rather, at many crucial periods in history Blacks have come together in federations comprising much of the relevant diversity present at the time. The purposes of those federated assemblies were primarily those of conceptualizing the nature of the problem they confronted, planning new strategies, and encouraging one another in the struggle. The Negro Convention Movement began in 1830 and held annual meetings for many years (see John Hope Franklin, *From Slavery to Freedom* [New York: Knopf, 1969], pp. 236–37). In recent times the Black Power conferences held in Washington, D.C.; Newark, New Jersey; and Philadelphia during the years 1966, 1967, and 1968, respectively, are immediate forebears of the African Congress that met in Atlanta, Georgia, in 1970. See Imamu Amiri Baraka (LeRoi Jones), ed., *African Congress: A Documentary of the First Modern Pan-African Congress* (New York: William Morrow & Co., 1972).

Although the logic of this inquiry leads us to describe the appropriate associational form for cooperative activity in terms of a federation, that logic does not exclude other forms of cooperation. Alternatives may be centered on a particular project, issue, or strategy. In no case can that sort of cooperative activity or any other kind be taken for granted. Rather, they are always political in the sense that their coming to be, their maintenance, and even their passing away are public matters that require deliberation and choice. Their permanence is conditioned in that they can endure only as long as their form is adequate to the desired end and only as long as there exists mutual respect among the entities forming the coalition. Since these entities composing the coalition are diverse, the desired goal of cooperation must be subjected to rigorous deliberative processes. This process is delicate and time-consuming.[5] Coalitions of this sort are never finally settled for all time and all places. In some particular time and place it might be decided that all parties should pool their resources in order to give political strength to one particular conception of racism and to one particular form of action. That is likely to occur rarely because of the level of suspicion and the various types of jealousy that inevitably characterize the relationships between diverse leaders and their groups. Yet such an alliance can happen in those situations in which the various leaders and groups have had the opportunity of working cooperatively and in which a degree of mutual respect has been established. Coalitions may also be formed around some particular program or issue on which none of the groups is generating action and on which all are in agreement about its importance. But that agreement may not and should not appeal to any one reason. Rather, each of the diverse groups should be able to justify the action from within the framework of its own basic thought. Accordingly, it must be understood that coalitions are always tenuous and fragile. They serve to maximize power in order to effect agreed-upon goals.

Conclusion

This analysis has been an inquiry into the thought of four prominent Black religious leaders. More specifically, it has focused on their respective understandings of how racism should be opposed. Since there was considerable conflict among them, and since their theological and political thought was quite diverse, this inquiry has sought to determine whether or not cooperative action among them would necessarily be hindered by their respective understandings. That is to say, does irreconcilable conflict necessarily result from their thought, and if not, how might their diversity be affirmed and promoted while advocating cooperative action among their followers?

An internal analysis of their respective theological and political understandings has revealed that racism was the focus for most of their political and theological reflections. This examination has discovered that any attempt to grasp their general theological and political understandings apart from a focus on the problem of racism heightens the risk of distorting their thought considerably. At all the crucial points of the study, it is found that racism was implicitly or explicitly the subject matter of their reflections. Consequently, the relationship of the state and of God to the problem of racism was of paramount importance to each of them.

Further, if one fails to make racism the significant subject matter for this kind of inquiry, one will discover
no grounds for cooperative activity. Rather, one will
be hard put to advance beyond a description of their
diverse understandings with no means, relative to the
concerns of each, for bringing those understandings
into a unified relationship.

Therefore, this investigation is methodologically significant, because it has demonstrated that a careful
analysis of diverse understandings of racism reveals
that they are complementary rather than conflictual,
that they imply specific understandings of social
change that are also complementary, that those theo-
ries of social change can be analyzed as diverse views
of power that are complementary, that the various
conceptions and their implications for policy are necessary for a comprehensive understanding of the problem and for its eradication. Further, I have shown that
their complementarity requires institutionalization in
the form of a federation as a prerequisite for whatever
other coalitions might be considered desirable and
possible from time to time.

In addition, it is shown in chapter 6 that there is a
correlation between the four leaders' respective understandings of politics and theology. Chapter 7 reveals
that there is a correlation between their political understandings and their conceptions of racism. Therefore, I conclude that there is also a correlation between
their conceptions of racism and their political understandings and theological understandings respectively.

This analysis began with a practical problem,
namely, how to make an argument for cooperative action among the followers of four prominent leaders
whose relationship was characterized by considerable
conflict. It was discovered that a breakdown of their
various conceptions of racism implies various political
actions. The end of relating those political actions to
one another was sought via the principle of a federation and possibly other subsequent forms of coalition.
The capacities and powers of the leaders and of their

cooperative possibilities have been described. Individually and cooperatively, their conceptions of racism are valid and, insofar as their followers continue to hold these conceptions, cooperative relationships among them are not only possible but desirable and even imperative. This study calls for processes of deliberation to begin in order to form a federation comprising all those who hold various understandings of the problem of racism. Such a federation will strengthen their mutual relationships and will prevent their respective work from being weakened by internal conflicts among racism's opponents. Further, it will hasten achievement of the goal when all of racism's opponents might affirm the relevant understandings of the problem and their respective policy implications, thus making pluralism in unity a primary condition for the eradication of racism. Subsequent to the formation of a federation, other forms of coalition might become desirable and might be set in motion.

Appendixes

Appendix A

An Appraisal of "A Black Theology of Liberation"
in the Light of the Basic Theological Position
of the National Baptist Convention, U.S.A., Inc.*
By Dr. J. H. Jackson, President

PART I: The Basic Theological Position
of the National Baptist Convention, U.S.A., Inc.

We begin with this statement of faith: "God is a spirit and they that worship Him must worship Him in spirit and in truth." (At John 4:24.) We do not know all the qualities of things spiritual, and we cannot analyze the spirit into component parts. However, we know that spirit cannot be weighed in scales made by human hands or measured in terms of inches or feet. Neither can spirit be defined in terms of any material substances, and the most gifted artist cannot put on canvas a true picture of what spirit is. Whatever is spirit must be approached by the power of spirit or the soul forces in man. Our concept of God is spirit, and our approach to Him must be in spirit and in truth.

---

*From the Record of the 91st Annual Session of the National Baptist Convention, U.S.A., Inc., held with the Baptist Churches of Cleveland, Ohio, September 7–12, 1971.

Jesus revealed God as spirit and as creative force, and as life-giving and life-sustaining power; and because of His all inclusive nature, God to us is Father.

Our acceptance of Jesus Christ as our personal Savior is based on His message from the Sermon on the Mount. His personality and life force that He sheds in the gospel writings and through the revelation of truth that comes to us in all of the epistles of the New Testament.

We are drawn to Him by His divine character and by His redemptive love and mercy, and the goodness and justice through which and by which His kingdom is built—and by His sacrificial life, death, and resurrection, all sinners are invited and made welcome into His eternal kingdom.

In the light of these facts the invitation that He extends for salvation is to all men. That is why we preach "Whosoever will let him come."

The Need for the Universality of the Gospel

The need for the universality of the gospel grows out of the universality of the sins of all mankind.

> But now the righteousness of God without the law is manifested, being witnessed by the law and the prophet; Even the righteousness of God which is by faith in Jesus Christ unto all and upon all them that believe for there is no difference; For all have sinned and come short of the glory of God; Being justified freely by His grace through the redemption that is in Christ Jesus; Whom God hath set forth to be propitiation through faith in his blood, to declare his righteousness for the remission of sins that are passed through the forbearance of God. To declare, I say, at this time his righteousness: that he might be just and the justifier of him which believeth in Jesus.
>
> —Romans 3:21–28.

In the light of the truth revealed above, there are no pure races and no superior nations in the sight of God. There are no individuals who can by their wisdom, their knowledge, their rank, and their possessions win for themselves salvation or liberation from the sins that do so easily beset all the children of men.

The Universality of God's Plan of Redemption

God's knowledge of this universal imperfection of man, and God's concern for all are some of the reasons why He included all men in the plan of salvation and in the scheme of redemption. The writer of the Fourth Gospel gives to us the divine motivation for human redemption:

> For God so loved the world, that he gave his only begotten son, that whosoever believeth in him should not perish, but have everlasting life.
>
> —St. John 3:16.

The mission of Jesus Christ into the world was not to condemn the world or to set one race over against another, or to liberate one race by leaving another in chains:

> For God sent not his son into the world to condemn the world; but that the world through him might be saved.
>
> —St. John 3:17.

Only those who refuse him, only those who reject him, fall under the shadow of condemnation by their own choice and by their own acts.

The Theology that We Reject

Any theology that denies or negates the above principles falls outside of the theological tradition of the National Baptist Convention, U.S.A., Inc. Any theologian, be he black or white, that limits the redemptive effort of Jesus Christ to any race, to any color, to any nationality or any rank or group in society denies and negates the positive principles of redemption as discussed above.

Racial discrimination and any form of racial segregation cannot be supported in the light of the principles of redemption as stated above. There is no revealed truth that teaches us that God is white or black. God is a spirit. National Baptists was founded and organized by Negro Christian leaders and they themselves refused to restrict their message to their own race and their own nationality. They have not written a creed of exclusiveness against other races or nationalities. What we say against white segregationists by the gospel of Christ we must also say against members of our own race who insist on interpreting the gospel of Christ on a strictly anti-white and pro-black foundation.

National Baptists' Theological Position and Civil Rights

Our idea of God inspires us to work for the establishment of social justice for all the citizens of the nation. We participate in the struggle for first class citizenship under the guidance of the supreme law of the land. From the teachings of the eighth century prophets and the message of Jesus, we believe God is on the side of the right, the just and the good. Our faith encourages us and our theological position allows us to feel a sense of obligation to help break the chains of all those who are oppressed.

PART II: An Appraisal of "A Black Theology of Liberation," by Professor James H. Cone, Associate Professor of Theology, Union Theological Seminary, New York, N.Y.

Professor Cone has dedicated two hundred and forty-nine pages to his thesis that he seeks to prove, and to his conviction that he most positively and clearly shares. The author displays a wide range of acquaintance and a profound knowledge of theological thought. He has not willfully sought to leave out the great themes of Christian theology. He has included them. He has not embraced naturalism or theistic naturalism or humanism.

In the very first chapter he begins with the content of theology and speaks the truth when he says:

"Christian theology is a theology of liberation" (p. 1.)

He embraces the sources and norms of theology and deals with revelation with clarity.

He makes no attempt to bypass the subject of God or to render man less than a creature who needs salvation.

Christ is also a conspicuous part of his moving discussion, and the Christ of his theology recognizes and gives due regard to the historical Jesus.

It is further significant that the author here relates all of the great Christian themes to a specific historic struggle.

Some Weaknesses

The outstanding weakness of this brilliant theological work on the part of Professor James H. Cone is his attempt to relate divine concern, and to reduce all of the great historic theological truths of the Christian religion to the historic conflict between blacks and whites.

The author's thesis and his purpose both circumscribe him and render all of his basic conclusions too narrow to accommodate and to properly appreciate and appraise the universality of the Christian gospel of liberation.

For him liberation means simply the liberation of blacks from the oppression of whites. One would assume from the author's argument that if the day ever comes when the blacks are totally liberated from the oppressive deeds of whites the Kingdom of God would be at hand.

The author advocates that aspect of liberation that has to do with the individual's victory over the temptation and the demonic forces within man that must be conquered before he can be considered totally liberated.

With this thesis and his commitment to the revolt of blacks against whites—or the black revolution—he reduces, and maybe he is forced to reduce, revelation, Jesus Christ and God himself to a level of blackness. Although the author admits that the only way to have Christian theology is that it must be Christ-centered. But when one reads A Black Theology of Liberation, one must conclude that the entire document is black-centered. But the author seems to avoid the pitfall by making or reducing both Jesus Christ and God to blackness. At one point he says:

"People who want to know who God is and what He is doing must know what black people are and what they are doing . . . Knowing God means being on the side of the oppressed, becoming one with them and participating in the goal of liberation. We must become black with God." (p. 124.)

The author does not at all times use black or blackness as a symbol. Sometimes he means physical blackness. He says in another place:

"Even some black people will find this view of God hard to handle. Having been enslaved by the God of white racism so long, they will have difficulty believing that God is identified with their struggle for freedom. Becoming one of his disciples means rejecting whiteness and accepting themselves as they are in all their physical blackness. This is what the Christian view of God means for black people." (p. 125.)

Some Personal Reflections

1. A Black Theology of Liberation can easily be interpreted as a gospel of hate of blacks against whites.

2. It could become required reading for those who wish to crusade in a violent manner against the so-called white establishment. The author says:

"Speaking for the black community, black theology says with Eldridge Cleaver 'we shall have our manhood. We shall have it, or the earth will be leveled by our attempt to get it.'" (p. 34.)

3. Professor Cone in his conclusion could well defeat all of the constructive efforts in better race relations in America, and could write off the past achievements in civil rights as of little or no value.

4. He not only polarizes blacks and whites in this country, but he freezes that polarization and leaves little or no latitude for future harmony to be achieved.

5. To assume that the total so-called black experience deals only with the confrontation with whites overlooks many other areas of that experience, part of which has accounted for the great institutions of the Negro church and

other achievements by Negroes without bitterness or hatred against people of other races and groups.

If the Negro church accepts the point of view and the leadership of A Black Theology of Liberation, then black people will become the outstanding proponents of racial segregation in the United States of America.

Appendix B

Reaffirmation of Our Faith in the Nation*
By J. H. Jackson, President,
National Baptist Convention, U.S.A., Inc.

1. We believe in the United States of America: land of opportunity, a country dedicated to freedom and democracy.

2. We believe in its Constitution: the supreme law of the land.

3. We believe in the right of all citizens to participate equally according to their several abilities in all the cultural privileges, in all the political and economic affairs of this great Republic.

4. We believe that all citizens should take their full share of the responsibility in building a greater, stronger, and better America for the weal of man and to the glory of God.

5. We believe that segregation and discrimination based upon race, national origins, or religion are not only sins against the fundamental laws of the land but also against the Supreme Lawgiver. We must continue to fight the sins against human freedom without apology, without compromise.

---

*From the Record of the 79th Annual Session of the National Baptist Convention, U.S.A., Inc., held with the Baptist Churches of San Francisco, California, September 9–13, 1959.

6. We are convinced that every state has far more to gain by applying the principles and the ideals of the Federal Constitution at the local level.

7. We believe that no race or group should be discouraged for seeking to improve their mental, economic, political and moral status but rather should be encouraged and guided since the development of a part contributes to the enrichment of the whole. To neglect a minority greatly weakens the nation as a whole handicapping the majority and penalizing those in places of power and influence.

8. We believe that a voluntary togetherness of the race based upon constructive and creative ventures is desired and should be encouraged in the interest of the preservation of racial values and the growth of the group as a whole within the democratic framework of the nation.

9. We believe that our leaders, our organizations, and our press should more and more recognize the presence and the positions of a vast number of white people who are dedicated to the laws of the land, who are ashamed of the sin, being committed against the soul of the nation, who are working for the growth of democracy and who are SUFFERING for the fulfillment of America's dream of freedom.

10. We also believe that the minority groups should be willing to cooperate with other people of goodwill whenever and wherever they are committed to the task of upholding the laws of the land, defending the country's cause, working for complete democracy, and a full victory for freedom.

11. We believe that the battle for freedom is not only America's battle but also the battle of all humanity supported by the moral laws of the universe and by the God who made out of one blood all races of men to dwell in peace on the face of the earth. And the struggle must move forward to victory since right is right and God is God.

12. We believe that first-class citizenship is essential for the realization of a first-class democracy and that a first-class democracy will give first-class freedom in which will be developed first-class personalities, first-class people, first-class thinkers, and first-class statesmen; all of these working together will build a first-class social order of good will, justice, understanding, and peace.

13. While we believe in the separation of Church and State, we believe in the Christian Church not only as a community of believers held together by a common loyalty to Jesus Christ but also as a redemptive influence and a vital part of the soul of the nation.

14. We believe in God, the Creator of heaven and earth; we believe in the dignity of man, in the triumph of justice, and in the victory of truth.

Appendix C

A Call for National Unity*
By J. H. Jackson, President,
National Baptist Convention, U.S.A., Inc.

The United States of America is a great democratic republic dedicated to human dignity, justice, freedom, and equality of opportunity for all. Her supreme law, the Federal Constitution, is so constructed and so structured that it allows for political, social and economic evolution and basic changes in amendments. Therefore all Americans both conservative and liberal can support and be loyal to the Federal Constitution and to the nation itself. All citizens can obey its fundamental principles and take part in its evolutionary changes through amendments when time, experience and change demand it.

Therefore in this hour of crisis we call upon all American citizens and all groups to support the fundamental principles of the nation's life. We would call upon all to support the following ideas:

I. Unqualified loyalty to, and support of the nation as a whole.

---

*From the Record of the 86th Annual Session of the National Baptist Convention, U.S.A., Inc., held with the Baptist Churches of Dallas, Texas, 1966.

II. Risk all that we have and possess, for the life, soul, and salvation of the nation and trust a just nation to protect and save us as citizens and all that we hold dear, so long as it does not include the values of religion which are above the dominion of the State.

III. Let us recognize that our common enemies are those persons and groups who by ideology and purpose are committed to the destruction of this nation and said enemies make use of all our divisions to weaken and to destroy this republic.

IV. We must recognize the fact that it is better to live in an imperfect America with the freedom to work for its improvement and fulfillment than to be a helpless slave in a perfect totalitarian state without the freedom even to question its policies or to change its evil practices.

V. Let us always recognize the right of freedom of thought, freedom of expression, and freedom of action, and the right to differ with and to be different from others. But let us never seek to defend and protect these differences by denying to others their constitutional just and God given rights as free men in a free society.

VI. Let us be as wise as the enemies of this nation, who when it is to their advantage will join with any groups in the United States and work through them for their evil purposes. If being a segregationist furthers their cause these enemies will join the ranks of segregationists. If and when they find being an integrationist serves their purpose to negate the nation's life they will become an integrationist and work through integration to achieve their negative ends. They will also play one group against another to divide and weaken the nation.

We are in a national crisis and at this moment are engaged in a bloody conflict with international communism in Vietnam, and are potentially in conflict with the same forces throughout the world as well as at home. Americans can no longer afford the luxury and the negative weights of past prejudices, hatred, envy, discrimination, disrespect for law and order and for one another, race riots and bloodshed. All of us must unite and work together as one for the nation's life and cause or eventually perish.

VII. All groups are called upon to rise above all differences of creed, color, caste, and join together as Americans and work for and live for, and if need be, die for the ideals, values and principles of justice, freedom and equality as proclaimed by this great nation.

VIII. We are called upon not only to obey federal law, but we should rise above it and make a good neighbor policy of our own by which we will build a community spirit and community organizations based on good will for the education of our children, for the security and development of our families, the advancement of culture, and the moral and spiritual growth of all who dwell therein. This can be done only by cooperation and not by contest and conflict. Such community spirit will not only enrich our several communities, but will greatly strengthen our national government both home and abroad.

IX. This call is for positive thinking and positive action. It is not enough to be anti-communist, anti-poverty, anti-segregationist, anti-integrationist, we must be pro-America, pro-freedom, pro-justice, and pro-goodwill. A commitment to build a great democratic society for the enrichment of human personality is far more elevating and far more lofty than to set ourselves to the task of destroying the enemies that disturb us.

X. To paraphrase the historic statement of the great educator Booker T. Washington (could not all Americans say) in all things strictly personal and in all matters purely private, we can be separate as the finger but one as the hand in all things tending towards the mutual progress of the individual and groups, and the fulfillment of the nation's life itself.

Notes

Notes

Introduction to the Second Edition:
A Methodological Essay

1. Malcolm X's life was abruptly ended by assassination in 1965, less than a year after his departure from the Nation of Islam and his founding of the Organization for Afro-American Unity. The work of Martin Luther King, Jr., culminated in the passage of the 1964 Civil Rights Act followed by his receipt of the Nobel Peace Prize in December of the same year and by passage of the Voting Rights Act in 1965. Joseph H. Jackson's presidency of the National Baptist Convention, U.S.A., Inc., began in 1953 and was firmly secured in 1961; in total he held the position for twenty-nine years. The greatest political accomplishments of Adam Clayton Powell, Jr., occurred after he became chair of the powerful Education and Labor Committee in 1960, in which capacity he guided the passage of over sixty major pieces of legislation within his first five years in that position.

2. See Max Weber, *The Methodology of the Social Sciences* (Chicago: The Free Press, 1949), ch. 3. See also Max Weber, "Religious Rejections of the World and Their Directions," in Hans H. Gerth and C. Wright Mills, eds., *From Max Weber: Essays in Sociology* (New York: Oxford University Press, 1958), pp. 323ff.

3. E. Franklin Frazier called this preinstitutionalized religion among the slaves the "Invisible Institution." See Fraz-

ier, *The Negro Church in America* (New York: Schocken Books, 1964), p. 16.

4. The most recent history of this society's origin and development is written by one of its founders, Charles Shelby Rooks, *Revolution in Zion: Reshaping African American Ministry, 1960–1974* (New York: Pilgrim Press, 1990).

Chapter 1:
Diversity in Conflict:
Pluralistic Proposals for Political Action

1. From Anthony Lewis, *Profile of a Decade: The Second American Revolution* (New York: Bantam Books, 1965), p. 69.

2. John Hope Franklin, *From Slavery to Freedom* (New York: Knopf, 1969), p. 651.

3. Charles V. Hamilton, *The Black Preacher in America* (New York: William Morrow & Co., 1972), p. 25.

4. Lewis, *Profile of a Decade*, p. 3.

5. Annual Address of President J. H. Jackson, delivered at the 86th Annual Session of the National Baptist Convention, U.S.A., Inc., September 8, 1966, Memorial Auditorium, Dallas, Texas (Nashville: Sunday School Publishing Board, 1966).

6. Martin Luther King, Jr., *Stride Toward Freedom* (New York: Harper & Brothers, 1958), p. 168. Copyright © 1958 by Martin Luther King, Jr. Reprinted by permission of Joan Daves Agency.

7. Louis Lomax, *The Negro Revolt* (New York: Signet Book, 1963), p. 85.

8. Excerpt from Adam Clayton Powell, Jr., *Adam by Adam*, p. 120. Copyright © 1971 by Adam Clayton Powell, Jr. Reprinted by permission of The Dial Press.

9. Archie Epps, ed., *The Speeches of Malcolm X at Harvard* (New York: William Morrow & Co., 1968), p. 130. Copyright © 1968 by Betty Shabazz. Used by permission.

10. See Joseph H. Jackson, *Unholy Shadows and Freedom's Holy Light* (Nashville: Townsend Press, 1967), p. 45.

11. The Record of the 76th Annual Session of the Na-

tional Baptist Convention, U.S.A., Inc., and the Women's Auxiliary held with the Baptist Churches of Denver, Colorado, September 1956 (Nashville: Sunday School Publishing Board, 1956), p. 65.

12. Ibid.

13. Ibid., p. 245.

14. An excellent abbreviated description of the ensuing crisis is found in Taylor Branch, *Parting the Waters: America in the King Years, 1954–63* (New York: Simon & Schuster, 1988), pp. 221–225.

15. Edward Peeks, *The Long Struggle for Black Power* (New York: Charles Scribner's Sons, 1972), pp. 311f.

16. William Robert Miller, *Martin Luther King, Jr.: His Life, Martyrdom and Meaning for the World* (New York: Avon Books, 1968), p. 137.

17. Ibid., p. 261.

18. David I. Lewis, *King: A Critical Biography* (Baltimore: Penguin Books, 1970), p. 333.

19. See Jackson, *Unholy Shadows*, p. 168.

20. Gayraud Wilmore, *Black Religion and Black Radicalism* (New York: Doubleday, 1972), p. 245.

21. Benjamin Muse, *The American Negro Revolution* (New York: Citadel Press, 1970), p. 115.

22. Ibid., p. 123.

23. The Record of the 83rd Annual Session of the National Baptist Convention, U.S.A., Inc., September 3–8, 1963, held with the Baptist Churches of Cleveland, Ohio (Nashville: Sunday School Publishing Board, 1963), p. 82.

24. Wilmore, *Black Religion and Black Radicalism*, pp. 248–249.

25. Ibid., p. 249.

26. Jackson, *Unholy Shadows,* p. 191.

27. August Meier and Elliott Rudwick, eds., *Black Protest in the Sixties* (Chicago: Quadrangle Books, 1970), p. 41.

28. Robert Penn Warren, *Who Speaks for the Negro?* (New York: Vintage Books, 1965), p. 137. Used by permission of Random House. Copyright © 1965, by Robert Penn Warren.

29. Ibid., p. 138.

30. Adam Clayton Powell, Jr., *Marching Blacks: An Interpretive History of the Rise of the Black Common Man* (New York: Dial Press, 1945), p. 39.

31. Herbert J. Storing, ed., *What Country Have I? Political Writings by Black Americans* (New York: St. Martin's Press, 1970), pp. 138–139. Used by permission.

32. The Record of the 86th Annual Session of the National Baptist Convention, U.S.A., Inc., held with the Baptist Churches of Dallas, Texas, September 6–11, 1966 (Nashville: Sunday School Publishing Board, 1963), p. 246.

33. Gunnar Myrdal, *An American Dilemma: The Negro Problem and Modern Democracy* (New York: Harper & Brothers, 1944).

34. Martin Luther King, Jr., *Why We Can't Wait* (New York: Harper & Row, 1963), p. 88. Copyright © 1963, 1964 by Martin Luther King, Jr. Reprinted by permission of Joan Daves Agency.

35. Ibid., p. 90.

36. Storing, *What Country Have I?*, p. 161.

37. Ibid., p. 149.

38. Simon Booker, "Adam Clayton Powell, Jr.," *Ebony* 22, no. 5 (March 1967), 27–28.

39. The Record of the 77th Annual Session of the National Baptist Convention, U.S.A., Inc., and the Women's Auxiliary, held with the Baptist Churches of Louisville, Kentucky, September 3–8, 1957 (Nashville: Sunday School Publishing Board, 1963), p. 48.

40. Alex Haley and Malcolm X, *The Autobiography of Malcolm X* (New York: Grove Press, 1966), p. 179. Reprinted by permission of Grove Press, Inc. Copyright © 1965 by Alex Haley and Betty Shabazz.

Chapter 2: Joseph H. Jackson

1. It must be noted that in dealing with King and Malcolm X I have chosen to merge these first two steps of the descriptive process, since it is not possible to separate their political and theological understandings. Rather, they are integrally connected at all crucial points.

2. See Joseph H. Jackson, *Many But One: The Ecumenics of Charity* (New York: Sheed & Ward, 1964), p. 77.

3. See Appendix A.

4. The Record of the 91st Annual Session of the National Baptist Convention, U.S.A., Inc., held with the Baptist Churches of Cleveland, Ohio, and Vicinity, September 7–12, 1971 (Nashville: Sunday School Publishing Board, 1971), p. 95.

5. Ibid., p. 96.

6. Ibid., pp. 96–97.

7. Ibid., p. 97.

8. The Record of the 81st Annual Session of the National Baptist Convention, U.S.A., Inc., held with the Baptist Churches of Kansas City, Missouri, September 5–10, 1961 (Nashville: Sunday School Publishing Board, 1961), p. 45.

9. Jackson, *Many But One*, pp. 62–63.

10. Ibid., p. 63.

11. Ibid., p. 82.

12. The Record of the 88th Annual Session of the National Baptist Convention, U.S.A., Inc., held with the Baptist Churches of Atlanta, Georgia, September 3–8, 1968 (Nashville: Sunday School Publishing Board, 1968), pp. 244–245.

13. See Jackson, *Unholy Shadows*, p. 30.

14. Ibid.

15. Annual Address of President J. H. Jackson, delivered at the 86th Annual Session of the National Baptist Convention, U.S.A., Inc. (Dallas, Texas, 1966), p. 4.

16. Jackson, *Unholy Shadows*, p. 5.

17. Ibid., pp. 6, 9.

18. Ibid., p. 8.

19. See Annual Address of President J. H. Jackson, delivered at the 83rd Annual Session of the National Baptist Convention, U.S.A., Inc., held with the Baptist Churches in Cleveland, Ohio, September 5–8, 1963 (Nashville: Sunday School Publishing Board, 1963), pp. 200f., where Jackson describes the oppressor of Blacks as those who have tried to reverse the Emancipation Proclamation of Abraham Lincoln and to remove from the federal Constitution those sa-

cred amendments guaranteeing citizen rights to all. Such people, as Jackson describes them, have tried to undermine the doctrine of States' Rights and have twisted their own state laws in an attempt to set up an alternative way of life in contrast to the American way of life—the former being called the Southern Way of Life. Such people are a minority in Jackson's understanding, and they seek to force their opinions and corrupt values on the majority by forming secret societies with purposes of intimidation and harassment and violence and by using state laws to hinder federal law. See also Jackson's open letter, "A Plea to the White Citizen's Councils of the South," in The Record of the 77th Annual Session of the National Baptist Convention, U.S.A., Inc., held with the Baptist Churches of Louisville, Kentucky, September 3–8, 1957 (Nashville: Sunday School Publishing Board, 1957), pp. 50–51.

20. See Jackson, *Unholy Shadows*, pp. 21–22.

21. See ibid., pp. 28f.

22. Ibid., p. 28.

23. Ibid., p. 42.

24. Ibid., p. 51.

25. Ibid., pp. 52–53.

26. Ibid., p. 60.

27. Ibid., p. 55.

28. Ibid., p. 63.

29. See The Record of the 90th Annual Session of the National Baptist Convention, U.S.A., Inc., held with the Baptist Churches of New Orleans, Louisiana, September 8–13, 1970 (Nashville: Sunday School Publishing Board, 1970), p. 75.

30. The Record of the 88th Annual Session of the National Baptist Convention, U.S.A., Inc., held with the Baptist Churches of Atlanta, Georgia, September 3–8, 1968 (Nashville: Sunday School Publishing Board, 1968), pp. 244–245.

31. See The Record of the 82nd Annual Session of the National Baptist Convention, U.S.A., Inc., held with the Baptist Churches of Chicago, Illinois, 1962 (Nashville: Sunday School Publishing Board, 1962), p. 165.

32. Ibid., p. 166. See also The Record of the 88th Annual

Session of the National Baptist Convention, U.S.A., Inc. (Nashville: Sunday School Publishing Board, 1968), pp. 241f. for summaries of those programs.

33. The Record of the 90th Annual Session of the National Baptist Convention, U.S.A., Inc., held with the Baptist Churches of New Orleans, Louisiana, September 8–13, 1970 (Nashville: Sunday School Publishing Board, 1970), pp. 285–286.

34. Ibid., p. 287.

35. See Jackson, *Unholy Shadows*, ch. 5, for a full discussion of Thoreau and Gandhi.

36. See ibid., pp. 105f.

37. The Record of the 90th Annual Session, pp. 273–274.

38. See "Busing of Students and the Business of Education," The Record of the 91st Annual Session, p. 99.

39. See Appendix A, Part II.

40. Jackson, *Unholy Shadows*, p. 165.

41. The Record of the 83rd Annual Session, p. 211.

42. The Record of the 90th Annual Session, p. 75.

43. The Record of the 82nd Annual Session, pp. 163–164.

44. See Appendix B.

45. The Record of the 85th Annual Session of the National Baptist Convention, U.S.A., Inc., held with the Baptist Churches of Jacksonville, Florida, September 7–12, 1965 (Nashville: Sunday School Publishing Board, 1965), p. 219.

46. See Appendix C.

Chapter 3: Martin Luther King, Jr.

1. Kenneth L. Smith and Ira G. Zepp, *Search for the Beloved Community: The Thinking of Martin Luther King, Jr.* (Valley Forge, Pa.: Judson Press, 1974).

2. Martin Luther King, Jr., "A Comparison of the Conception of God in the Thinking of Paul Tillich and Henry Nelson Wieman" (Ph.D. dissertation, Boston University Graduate School, 1955), pp. 313–314. Reprinted by permission of Joan Daves Agency. Copyright © 1977 by Estate of Martin Luther King, Jr.

3. From Martin Luther King, Jr., *Strength to Love* (New York: Harper and Row, 1963), p. 94. Reprinted by permis-

sion of Joan Daves Agency. Copyright © 1963 by Martin
Luther King, Jr.

4. King, "A Comparison of the Conception of God,"
p. 316.

5. King, *Strength to Love*, p. 141.

6. Ibid., p. 107.

7. Ibid., p. 94.

8. Ibid., p. 76.

9. Ibid., p. 60.

10. Ibid., p. 64.

11. Ibid., p. 89.

12. Ibid., p. 90.

13. Ibid., p. 91.

14. Ibid.

15. Ibid., p. 92.

16. Ibid., p. 133.

17. From King, *Stride Toward Freedom*, pp. 66–67.

18. Ibid., p. 86.

19. Ibid., p. 87.

20. Ibid., p. 40.

21. Ibid., p. 85.

22. Ibid., p. 156.

23. King, *Strength to Love*, p. 121.

24. Ibid., p. 105.

25. Ibid.

26. Ibid., p. 9.

27. Ibid., p. 97.

28. Ibid., p. 47.

29. For a detailed description of this event, see David J.
Garrow, *Bearing the Cross: Martin Luther King, Jr., and the
Southern Christian Leadership Conference, 1955–1968*
(New York: William Morrow & Co., 1986), p. 202ff.

30. King, *Why We Can't Wait*, p. 68.

31. Ibid., pp. 68–69.

32. Ibid.

33. Ibid., p. 84.

34. Ibid., p. 85.

35. Ibid., pp. 85–86.

36. Ibid., p. 86.

37. Ibid., p. 102.

38. Martin Luther King, Jr., *Trumpet of Conscience* (New York: Harper & Row, 1968), p. 47.

39. King, *Strength to Love*, p. 23.

40. Martin Luther King, Jr., "The Ethical Demands of Integration," *Religion and Labor*, May 1963:4.

41. Martin Luther King, Jr., *Where Do We Go from Here: Chaos or Community?* (New York: Harper & Row, 1967). Copyright © 1967 by Martin Luther King, Jr. Reprinted by permission of Joan Daves Agency.

42. Ibid.

43. Ibid., pp. 32–33.

44. Ibid., pp. 45–46.

45. Ibid., p. 37.

46. Ibid.

47. Ibid., p. 49.

48. Ibid., p. 50.

49. Ibid., pp. 63–64.

50. King, *Strength to Love*, p. 68.

51. King, *Stride Toward Freedom*, pp. 167–168.

52. Ibid., pp. 168–169.

53. King, *Why We Can't Wait*, p. 130.

54. Ibid., p. 131.

55. King, *Where Do We Go from Here*, p. 5.

56. Ibid., p. 75.

57. Ibid., p. 83.

58. Ibid., p. 84.

59. King, *Stride Toward Freedom*, p. 77.

60. Ibid., pp. 75–76.

61. King, *Strength to Love*, p. 52.

62. King, *Why We Can't Wait*, pp. 150–151.

63. Ibid., p. 156.

Chapter 4: Adam Clayton Powell, Jr.

1. Powell, *Adam by Adam*, p. 43.

2. Ibid., p. 39.

3. Ibid.

4. Ibid., p. 43.

5. Ibid., pp. 39–40.

6. Ibid., p. 40.

7. Ibid., pp. 40–41.

8. Ibid., p. 41.

9. Ibid., pp. 41–42.

10. See Adam Clayton Powell, Jr., *Keep the Faith, Baby* (New York: Trident Press, 1967), p. 200.

11. Powell, *Adam by Adam*, pp. 42–43.

12. See Powell, *Keep the Faith, Baby*, p. 147.

13. See ibid., p. 180.

14. See ibid.

15. See ibid., p. 255.

16. See ibid., pp. 256–257.

17. Powell, *Adam by Adam*, p. 52.

18. Ibid., p. 46.

19. See Powell, *Keep the Faith, Baby*, p. 157.

20. Powell, *Adam by Adam*, p. 128.

21. Ibid., p. 128.

22. Ibid.

23. At this conference, held in Bandung, Indonesia, the term "Third World" was first used as a means of distinguishing the southern continents from the Western world and Eastern Europe. Powell discussed his endeavors in overcoming the U.S. boycott of the meeting in ibid, p. 102ff.

24. Powell, *Adam by Adam*, p. 107.

25. Ibid., pp. 108f.

26. Ibid., pp. 185f.

27. See Powell, *Keep the Faith, Baby*, pp. 184–185.

28. Powell, *Adam by Adam*, p. 72.

29. See Powell, *Keep the Faith, Baby*, pp. 157–158.

30. See Powell, *Adam by Adam*, p. 42.

31. See Powell, *Keep the Faith, Baby*, p. 131.

32. Ibid., pp. 231–232, 236.

33. Ibid., p. 151.

34. Ibid., p. 89.

35. *Jet,* June 11, 1970, 14.

36. Warren, *Who Speaks for the Negro?* , p. 137.

37. See Powell, *Keep the Faith, Baby*, p. 151.

38. Powell, *Adam by Adam*, p. 249.

39. Warren, *Who Speaks for the Negro?*, p. 140.

40. Ibid.

41. Ibid.
42. Powell, *Adam by Adam*, p. 74.
43. Ibid., p. 81.
44. Ibid.
45. Ibid., p. 91.
46. Ibid., p. 203.
47. For a complete listing of Adam Clayton Powell's legislative record, see James Haskins, *Adam Clayton Powell:
Portrait of a Marching Black* (New York: Dial Press, 1974),
pp. 166–170.
48. Powell, *Adam by Adam*, p. 203.
49. Ibid., p. 241.
50. See Powell, *Keep the Faith, Baby*, p. 53.
51. See ibid., p. 135.
52. Ibid., p. 89.
53. Ibid.
54. Ibid., p. 92.
55. Powell, *Adam by Adam*, p. 71.
56. Ibid.
57. Ibid., p. 118.
58. Ibid., p. 90.
59. Ibid., p. 63.
60. See Floyd B. Barbour, ed., *The Black Power Revolt*
(Boston: Porter Sargent Publishers, 1968), pp. 257f., for a
full text of that position paper.
61. Ibid., p. 257.
62. See Powell, *Keep the Faith, Baby*, pp. 10–11.
63. Ibid., p. 16.
64. Powell, "Can There Any Good Things Come Out of
Nazareth?" in *Rhetoric of Black Revolution*, ed. Arthur L.
Smith (Boston: Allyn & Bacon, 1969), p. 157.
65. Ibid., p. 158.

Chapter 5: Malcolm X

1. Elijah Muhammad received his mantle of authority
from the founder of the Nation of Islam, Wallace D. Fard,
who named him Minister of Islam in 1934. See C. Eric Lincoln, *The Black Muslims in America* (Boston: Beacon Press,
1970), pp. 10–17.

2. Haley and Malcolm X, *The Autobiography of Malcolm X*, p. 179.

3. Benjamin Goodman, ed., *The End of White World Supremacy: Four Speeches by Malcolm X* (New York: Merlin House, Inc. 1971), pp. 44f.

4. Haley and Malcolm X, *The Autobiography of Malcolm X*, p. 163.

5. Ibid., p. 321.

6. Ibid., p. 323.

7. Ibid., pp. 340–341.

8. Ibid., p. 341.

9. Ibid., p. 289.

10. George Breitman, ed., *Malcolm X on Afro-American History* (New York: Pathfinder Press, 1972), p. 38. Used by permission.

11. Haley and Malcolm X, *The Autobiography of Malcolm X*, p. 294.

12. George Breitman, ed., *Malcolm X Speaks* (New York: Grove Press, 1965), p. 21.

13. Ibid., p. 20.

14. See Malcolm's lecture at the Leverett House Forum, March 18, 1964, in Epps, *The Speeches of Malcolm X,* pp. 140f.

15. Breitman, *Malcolm X Speaks*, p. 21.

16. Haley and Malcolm X, *The Autobiography of Malcolm X*, pp. 381–382.

17. Breitman, *Malcolm X Speaks*, p. 60.

18. Ibid.

19. Haley and Malcolm X, *The Autobiography of Malcolm X*, pp. 368–369.

20. Ibid., pp. 174–175.

21. Epps, *The Speeches of Malcolm X*, pp. 164–165.

22. Ibid., pp. 174–175.

23. Haley and Malcolm X, *The Autobiography of Malcolm X*, p. 368.

24. Kenneth B. Clark, ed., *The Negro Protest* (Boston: Beacon Press, 1963), pp. 26–27.

25. Epps, *The Speeches of Malcolm X*, p. 171.

26. Breitman, *Malcolm X Speaks*, pp. 116–117.

27. Epps, *The Speeches of Malcolm X*, p. 140.

28. Breitman, *Malcolm X Speaks*, p. 116.

29. Ibid., p. 111.

30. Ibid., p. 113.

31. John H. Clarke, ed., *Malcolm X: The Man and His Times* (New York: Macmillan, 1969), p. 117. Copyright © 1969 by John Henrik Clarke, Earl Grant, and A. Peter Bailey. Used by permission of John Henrik Clarke.

32. Ibid.

33. Breitman, *Malcolm X Speaks*, p. 119.

34. Ibid., p. 14.

35. Ibid., p. 16.

36. Epps, *The Speeches of Malcolm X*, p. 174.

37. Ibid., pp. 172–173.

38. Breitman, *Malcolm X Speaks*, p. 42.

39. Ibid., pp. 40f.

40. Ibid., p. 41.

41. Clarke, *Malcolm X: The Man and His Times*, p. 338.

42. Epps, *The Speeches of Malcolm X*, p. 70.

43. Breitman, *Malcolm X Speaks*, p. 76.

44. Ibid., p. 53.

45. Haley and Malcolm X, *The Autobiography of Malcolm X*, p. 281.

46. Breitman, *Malcolm X Speaks*, p. 150.

47. Breitman, *Malcolm X on Afro-American History*, p. 30.

48. Breitman, *Malcolm X Speaks*, p. 8.

49. Ibid., p. 40.

50. Ibid., p. 51.

51. Ibid., p. 26.

52. Ibid., pp. 30–31.

53. Ibid., p. 142.

54. Ibid., p. 214.

55. Clarke, *Malcolm X: The Man and His Times*, p. 265.

56. Breitman, *Malcolm X Speaks*, p. 122.

57. Ibid., p. 224.

58. Clarke, *Malcolm X: The Man and His Times*, p. 339.

Chapter 6: Theological and Political Understandings: Differences and Similarities

1. King, *Why We Can't Wait*, p. 143.

2. Ibid., p. 144.

3. It is important to note that Washington severely criti-

cizes King for making *agape* an instrumental principle and uses that fact to demonstrate his thesis that Black religion is outside the orthodox Christian tradition. See Joseph R. Washington, Jr., *Black Religion: The Negro and Christianity in the United States* (Boston: Beacon Press, 1964), pp. 7f.

4. Ibid., p. 15.
5. Ibid., p. 59.
6. Ibid., p. 28.
7. Ibid.
8. Powell, *Adam by Adam*, p. ix.
9. Ibid.
10. Epps, *The Speeches of Malcolm X*, p. 116.
11. Ibid., p. 119.

Chapter 7: Diversity in Unity: Pluralistic Conceptions of Racism

1. See Jackson, *Unholy Shadows*, pp. 64–65.
2. See Powell, *Keep the Faith, Baby*, pp. 13–14.
3. Epps, *The Speeches of Malcolm X*, p. 173. Copyright © 1968 by Betty Shabazz. Used by permission.
4. This is nowhere argued more convincingly than by Alan B. Anderson and George W. Pickering in their monumental case study, *Confronting the Color Line: The Broken Promise of the Civil Rights Movement in Chicago* (Athens, Ga.: University of Georgia Press, 1986). See especially chapters 1–3; 13–16.
5. Alvin Pitcher has described many of the necessary stages and inevitable problems involved in any attempt to bring diverse groups together into a coalition. He argues that effective coalitions should be established around specific programs and that those programs must be justified according to multiple reasons, for example, in accordance with the principal understandings of each of the groups involved. See Alvin Pitcher, "The Politics of Coalition" (an unpublished paper), University of Chicago Divinity School, 1975.

Bibliography

Bibliography

Anderson, Alan B. and George W. Pickering. *Confronting the Color Line: The Broken Promise of the Civil Rights Movement in Chicago.* Athens, Ga.: University of Georgia Press, 1986.

Baldwin, Lewis V. *There is a Balm in Gilead: The Cultural Roots of Martin Luther King, Jr.* Minneapolis: Fortress Press, 1991.

Baraka, Imamu A. *African Congress: A Documentary of the First Modern Pan-African Congress.* New York: William Morrow & Co., 1972.

Barbour, Floyd B., ed. *The Black Power Revolt.* Boston: Porter Sargent Pub., 1968.

Branch, Taylor. *Parting the Waters: America in the King Years 1954–63.* New York: Simon and Schuster, 1988.

Breitman, George, ed. *Malcolm X on Afro-American History.* New York: Pathfinder Press, Inc., 1972.

Cannon, Katie G. *Black Womanist Ethics.* Atlanta: Scholars Press, 1988.

Childs, John Brown. *The Political Black Minister: A Study in Afro-American Politics and Religion.* Boston: G. K. Hall & Co., 1980.

Clark, Kenneth B., ed. *The Negro Protest: James Baldwin, Malcolm X, Martin Luther King Talk with Kenneth B. Clark.* Boston: Beacon Press, 1963.

317

Clarke, John H., ed. *Malcolm X: The Man and His Times.* New York: Macmillan, 1969.

Cone, James H. *Martin and Malcolm and America: A Dream or a Nightmare.* Maryknoll, N.Y.: Orbis Books, 1991.

Dewart, Janet. *The State of Black America: 1989.* Washington, D.C.: National Urban League, 1989.

Drake, St. Clair and Horace Cayton. *Black Metropolis: A Study of Negro Life in a Northern City.* New York: Harcourt, Brace & Co., 1945.

Du Bois, W. E. B. *The Souls of Black Folk.* Chicago: A. S. McClurg & Co., 1903.

Epps, Archie, ed. *The Speeches of Malcolm X at Harvard.* New York: William Morrow & Co., 1969.

Fluker, Walter E. *They Looked for a City: A Comparative Analysis of the Ideal of Community in the Thought of Howard Thurman and Martin Luther King, Jr.* Lanham, Md.: University Press of America, 1989.

Franklin, John Hope. *From Slavery to Freedom.* New York: Knopf, 1969.

Franklin, John Hope and August Meier, eds. *Black Leaders of the Twentieth Century.* Urbana, Ill.: University of Illinois Press, 1982.

Franklin, Robert Michael. *Liberating Visions: Human Fulfillment and Social Justice in African-American Thought.* Minneapolis: Fortress Press, 1990.

Frazier, E. Franklin. *The Negro in the United States.* New York: Macmillan, 1949.

Gardiner, James J. and J. Deotis Roberts, Sr., eds. *Quest for a Black Theology.* Philadelphia: United Church Press, 1971.

Garrow, David J. *Bearing the Cross: Martin Luther King, Jr., and the Southern Christian Leadership Conference, 1955–1968.* New York: William Morrow & Co., 1986.

Goodman, Benjamin, ed. *The End of White World Supremacy: Four Speeches by Malcolm X.* New York: Merlin House, Inc., 1971.

Haley, Alex and Malcolm X. *The Autobiography of Malcolm X.* New York: Grove Press, 1966.

Hamilton, Charles V. *The Black Preacher in America.* New York: William Morrow & Co., 1972.

Harding, Vincent. *Hope and History: Why We Must Share the Story of the Movement.* Maryknoll, N.Y.: Orbis Books, 1990.

Haskins, James. *Adam Clayton Powell: Portrait of a Marching Black.* New York: Dial Press, 1974.

Hickey, Neil and Ed Edwin. *Adam Clayton Powell and the Politics of Race.* New York: Fleet Pub. Co., 1965.

Jackson, Joseph H. *Many But One: The Ecumenics of Charity.* New York: Sheed and Ward, 1964.

———. *Unholy Shadows and Freedom's Holy Light.* Nashville: Townsend Press, 1967.

Johnson, Joseph A., Jr. *The Soul of a Black Preacher.* Philadelphia: United Church Press, 1971.

King, Martin Luther, Jr. "A Comparison of the Conceptions of God in the Thinking of Paul Tillich and Henry Nelson Wieman." Ph.D. dissertation, Boston University Graduate School, 1955.

———. *The Measure of a Man.* Philadelphia: United Church Press, 1959, 1968.

———. *Strength to Love.* New York: Harper & Row, 1968.

———. *Stride Toward Freedom.* New York: Harper & Row, 1964.

———. *A Testament of Hope: The Essential Writings of Martin Luther King, Jr.* Ed. James Melvin Washington. San Francisco: Harper & Row, 1986.

———. *Trumpet of Conscience.* New York: Harper & Row, 1968.

———. *Where Do We Go from Here: Chaos or Community?* New York: Harper & Row, 1967.

———. *Why We Can't Wait.* New York: Signet Books, 1964.

Lewis, Anthony. *Profile of a Decade: The Second American Revolution.* New York: Bantam Books, 1965.

Lewis, David I. *King: A Critical Biography.* Baltimore: Penguin Books, 1970.

Lincoln, C. Eric. *The Black Church Since Frazier.* New York: Schocken Books, 1974.

———. *The Black Muslims in America.* Boston: Beacon Press, 1963.

Lincoln, C. Eric and Lawrence H. Mamiya. *The Black*

Church in the African American Experience. Durham, N.C.: Duke University Press, 1990.

Lomax, Louis. *The Negro Revolt.* New York: Signet Book, 1963.

McKeon, Richard. *The Basic Works of Aristotle.* New York: Random House, 1966.

Meier, August. *From Plantation to Ghetto: An Interpretive History of American Negroes.* New York: Hill & Wang, 1966.

Meier, August and Elliott Rudwick, eds. *Black Protest in the Sixties.* Chicago: Quadrangle Books, 1970.

————. *The Making of Black America.* New York: Atheneum, 1969.

Miller, Robert William. *Martin Luther King, Jr.: His Life, Martyrdom and Meaning for the World.* New York: Avon Books, 1968.

Muse, Benjamin. *The American Negro Revolution.* New York: Citadel Press, 1970.

Myrdal, Gunnar. *An American Dilemma: The Negro Problem and Modern Democracy*, 2 vols. New York: Harper & Bros., 1944.

Oglesby, Enoch H. *Ethics and Theology from the Other Side: Sounds of Moral Struggle.* Washington, D.C.: University Press of America, 1979.

Paris, Peter J. *The Social Teaching of Black Churches.* Philadelphia: Fortress Press, 1985.

Peeks, Edward. *The Long Struggle for Black Power.* New York: Charles Scribner's Sons, 1971.

Powell, Adam Clayton, Jr. *Adam by Adam: The Autobiography of Adam Clayton Powell, Jr.* New York: Dial Press, 1971.

————. *Keep the Faith, Baby.* New York: Trident Press, 1967.

————. *Marching Blacks: An Interpretive History of the Rise of the Black Common Man.* New York: Dial Press, 1945.

Rooks, Charles Shelby. *Revolution in Zion: Reshaping African American Ministry, 1960–1974.* New York: Pilgrim Press, 1990.

Smith, Arthur L. *Rhetoric of Black Revolution.* Boston: Allyn & Bacon, 1969.

Smith, Ervin. *The Ethics of Martin Luther King, Jr.* Lewiston, N.Y.: Edwin Mellen Press, 1981.

Smith, Kenneth L. and Ira G. Zepp. *Search for the Beloved Community: The Thinking of Martin Luther King, Jr.* Valley Forge, Pa.: Judson Press, 1974.

Storing, Herbert J., ed. *What Country Have I? Political Writings of Black Americans.* New York: St. Martin's Press, 1970.

Warren, Robert Penn. *Who Speaks for the Negro?* New York: Vintage, 1965.

Washington, Joseph R. *Black Religion: The Negro and Christianity in the United States.* Boston: Beacon Press, 1964.

Watley, William D. *Roots of Resistance: The Nonviolent Ethic of Martin Luther King, Jr.* Valley Forge, Pa.: Judson Press, 1985.

Weeks, Kent M. *Adam Clayton Powell and the Supreme Court.* New York: Dunellen, 1971.

West, Cornel. *Prophetic Fragments.* Grand Rapids, Mich.: William B. Eerdmans, 1988.

Wilmore, Gayraud. *Black Religion and Black Radicalism.* New York: Doubleday, 1972.

Wilson, James Q. *Negro Politics: The Search for Leadership.* New York: The Free Press, 1960.

Articles

Booker, Simon. "Adam Clayton Powell, Jr.," *Ebony* 22, no. 5 (March 1967): 27–28.

Fluker, Walter Earl. "They Looked for a City: A Comparison of the Ideal of Community in Howard Thurman and Martin Luther King, Jr.," *The Journal of Religious Ethics* 18, no. 2 (Fall 1990):33–56.

Franklin, Robert Michael. "In Pursuit of a Just Society: Martin Luther King, Jr., and John Rawls," *The Journal of Religious Ethics* 18, no. 2 (Fall 1990): 57–78.

King, Martin Luther, Jr. "The Ethical Demands of Integration," *Religion and Labor*, May 1963:361–368.

Mikelson, Thomas J. S. "Cosmic Companionship: The Place of God in the Moral Reasoning of Martin Luther

King, Jr.," *The Journal of Religious Ethics* 18, no. 2 (Fall 1990):1–14.

Pitcher, Alvin. "The Politics of Coalition." An unpublished paper, University of Chicago Divinity School, 1975.

Sturm, Douglas. "Martin Luther King, Jr., as Democratic Socialist," *The Journal of Religious Ethics* 18, no. 2 (Fall 1990):79–106.

Williams, Preston N. "An Analysis of the Conception of Love and Its Influence on Justice in the Thought of Martin Luther King, Jr.," *The Journal of Religious Ethics* 18, no. 2 (Fall 1990):15–32.

Published Records of the National Baptist Convention

The Record of the 73rd Annual Session of the National Baptist Convention, U.S.A., Inc., held with the Baptist Churches of Miami, Florida, September 9–13, 1953. Nashville: Sunday School Publishing Board, 1953.

The Record of the 74th Annual Session of the National Baptist Convention, U.S.A., Inc., and the Women's Auxiliary, held with the Baptist Churches of St. Louis, Missouri, September 7–12, 1954. Nashville: Sunday School Publishing Board, 1954.

The Record of the 75th Annual Session (Diamond Jubilee) of the National Baptist Convention, U.S.A., Inc., and the Women's Auxiliary, held with the Baptist Churches of Memphis, Tennessee, September 7–11, 1955. Nashville: Sunday School Publishing Board, 1955.

The Record of the 76th Annual Session of the National Baptist Convention, U.S.A., Inc., and the Women's Auxiliary, held with the Baptist Churches of Denver, Colorado, September, 1956. Nashville: Sunday School Publishing Board, 1956.

The Record of the 77th Annual Session of the National Baptist Convention, U.S.A., Inc., and the Women's Auxiliary, held with the Baptist Churches of Louisville, Kentucky, September 3–8, 1957. Nashville: Sunday School Publishing Board, 1957.

The Record of the 79th Annual Session of the National Baptist Convention, U.S.A., Inc., and the Women's Auxiliary, held with the Baptist Churches of San Francisco, California, September 9–13, 1959. Nashville: Sunday School Publishing Board, 1959.

The Record of the 80th Annual Session of the National Baptist Convention, U.S.A., Inc., and the Women's Auxiliary, held with the Baptist Churches of Philadelphia, Pennsylvania, September 6–11, 1960. Nashville: Sunday School Publishing Board, 1960.

The Record of the 81st Annual Session of the National Baptist Convention, U.S.A., Inc., held with the Baptist Churches of Kansas City, Missouri, September 5–10, 1961. Nashville: Sunday School Publishing Board, 1961.

The Record of the 82nd Annual Session of the National Baptist Convention, U.S.A., Inc., held with the Baptist Churches of Chicago, Illinois, 1962. Nashville: Sunday School Publishing Board, 1962.

The Record of the 83rd Annual Session of the National Baptist Convention, U.S.A., Inc., held with the Baptist Churches of Cleveland, Ohio, September 3–8, 1963. Nashville: Sunday School Publishing Board, 1963.

The Record of the 85th Annual Session of the National Baptist Convention, U.S.A., Inc., held with the Baptist Churches of Jacksonville, Florida, September 7–12, 1965. Nashville: Sunday School Publishing Board, 1965.

The Record of the 86th Annual Session of the National Baptist Convention, U.S.A., Inc., held with the Baptist Churches of Dallas, Texas, September 1966. Nashville: Sunday School Publishing Board, 1966.

The Record of the 87th Annual Session of the National Baptist Convention, U.S.A., Inc., held with the Baptist Churches of Denver, Colorado, September 5–10, 1967. Nashville: Sunday School Publishing Board, 1967.

The Record of the 88th Annual Session of the National Baptist Convention, U.S.A., Inc., held with the Baptist Churches of Atlanta, Georgia, September 3–8, 1968. Nashville: Sunday School Publishing Board, 1968.

The Record of the 89th Annual Session of the National Baptist Convention, U.S.A., Inc., held with the Baptist Churches of Kansas City, Missouri, September 9–14, 1969. Nashville: Sunday School Publishing Board, 1969.

The Record of the 90th Annual Session of the National Baptist Convention, U.S.A., Inc., held with the Baptist Churches of New Orleans, Louisiana, September 8–13, 1970. Nashville: Sunday School Publishing Board, 1970.

The Record of the 91st Annual Session of the National Baptist Convention, U.S.A., Inc., held with the Baptist Churches of Cleveland, Ohio, September 7–12, 1971. Nashville: Sunday School Publishing Board, 1971.

Acknowledgments

Excerpts from *Adam by Adam* by Adam Clayton Powell, Jr., are copyright 1971 by Adam Clayton Powell, Jr., and are reprinted by permission of The Dial Press.

Excerpts from *The Autobiography of Malcolm X*, by Alex Haley and Malcolm X, are copyright 1965 by Alex Haley and Betty Shabazz and are reprinted by permission of Grove Press, Inc.

Excerpts from "A Comparison of the Conception of God in the Thinking of Paul Tillich and Henry Nelson Wieman," by Martin Luther King, Jr., are copyright 1977 by Estate of Martin Luther King, Jr., and are reprinted by permission of Joan Daves Agency.

Excerpts from *Malcolm X: The Man and His Times*, edited by John H. Clarke, are copyright 1969 by John Henrik Clarke, Earl Grant, and A. Peter Bailey and are used by permission of John Henrik Clarke.

Excerpts from *The Speeches of Malcolm X at Harvard*, edited by Archie Epps, are copyright 1968 by Betty Shabazz and are used by permission.

Excerpts from *Strength to Love*, by Martin Luther King, Jr., are copyright 1963 by Martin Luther King, Jr., and are reprinted by permission of Joan Daves Agency.

Excerpts from *Stride Toward Freedom*, by Martin Luther

King, Jr., are copyright 1958 by Martin Luther King, Jr., and are reprinted by permission of Joan Daves Agency.

Excerpts from *What Country Have I? Political Writings by Black Americans*, edited by Herbert J. Storing (New York: St. Martins Press, 1970), are used by permission.

Excerpts from *Where Do We Go From Here: Chaos or Community?*, by Martin Luther King, Jr., are copyright 1967 by Martin Luther King, Jr., and are reprinted by permission of Joan Daves Agency.

Excerpts from *Who Speaks for the Negro?*, by Robert Penn Warren, are copyright 1965 by Robert Penn Warren and are used by permission of Random House.

Excerpts from *Why We Can't Wait*, by Martin Luther King, Jr., are copyright 1963, 1964 by Martin Luther King, Jr., and are reprinted by permission of Joan Daves Agency.